About the Underground Guide Series

Welcome to the underground!

Are you tired of all the fluff—books that tell you what you already know, ones that assume you're an idiot and treat you accordingly, or dwell on the trivial while completely ignoring the tough parts?

Good. You're in the right place.

Series Editor Woody Leonhard and Addison-Wesley bring you the Underground Guides—serious books that tackle the tough questions head-on but still manage to keep a sense of humor (not to mention a sense of perspective!). Every page is chock full of ideas you can put to use right away. We'll tell you what works and what doesn't—no bull, no pulled punches. We don't kowtow to the gods of the industry, we won't waste your time or your money, and we *will* treat you like the intelligent computer user we know you are.

Each Underground Guide is written by somebody who's been there—a working stiff who's suffered through the problems you're up against right now—and lived to tell about it. You're going to strike a rich vein of hard truth in these pages, and come away with a wealth of information you can put to use all day, every day.

So come along as we go spelunking where no book has gone before. Mind your head, and don't step in anything squishy. There will be lots of unexpected twists and turns . . . and maybe a laugh or two along the way.

D1449983

The Underground Guide Series

Woody Leonhard, Series Editor

The Underground Guide to Word for Windows™:
Slightly Askew Advice from a WinWord Wizard

Woody Leonhard

The Underground Guide to Excel 5.0 for Windows™:
Slightly Askew Advice from Two Excel Wizards

Lee Hudspeth and Timothy-James Lee

The Underground Guide to UNIX®:
Slightly Askew Advice from a UNIX Guru

John Montgomery

The Underground Guide to

UNIX®

Slightly
Askew
Advice
from
a
UNIX
Guru

John Montgomery

Woody Leonhard, Series Editor

 **ADDISON-WESLEY**

An imprint of Addison Wesley Longman, Inc.

Reading, Massachusetts • Harlow, England • Menlo Park, California
Berkeley, California • Don Mills, Ontario • Sydney
Bonn • Amsterdam • Tokyo • Mexico City

Many of the designations used by manufacturers and sellers to distinguish their products are claimed as trademarks. Where those designations appear in this book, and Addison-Wesley was aware of a trademark claim, the designations have been printed in initial capital letters or all capital letters.

The authors and publishers have taken care in preparation of this book, but make no expressed or implied warranty of any kind and assume no responsibility for errors or omissions. No liability is assumed for incidental or consequential damages in connection with or arising out of the use of the information or programs contained herein.

Library of Congress Cataloging-in-Publication Data

Montgomery, John (John I.), 1967–
    The underground guide to UNIX : slightly askew advice from a UNIX
guru / John Montgomery.
       p. cm.
    Includes index.
    ISBN 0-201-40653-5
    1. UNIX (Computer file)   2. Operating systems (Computers)
I. Title.
QA76.76.063M7454   1995
005.4'3--dc20   94-41787
                                             CIP

Series Hack: Woody Leonhard
Sponsoring Editor: Kathleen Tibbetts
Project Manager: Sarah Weaver
Technical Editors: Vincent Chen and Dan Watts
Cover Design: Jean Seal
Text Design: Kenneth L. Wilson, Wilson Graphics & Design
Set in 10 point Palatino by Rob Mauhar, CIP of Coronado

3 4 5 6 7 8 MA 02 01 00 99
3rd Printing April 1999

Addison-Wesley books are available for bulk purchases by corporations, institutions, and other organizations. For more information please contact the Corporate, Government, and Special Sales Department at (800) 238-9682.

Contents

Foreword

The great challenge in creating an underground guide to UNIX lies in cramming the book full of practical advice you can use, regardless of your particular version of UNIX, your predilections, or your . . . let's say . . . religious convictions. My background is in Windows (no! Wait! Put DOWN that brickbat!), and I thought I'd heard some heavy religious debates on the virtues of Windows vs. OS/2. But I gotta tell ya, the UNIX factions have the DOS weenies beat all to hell. UNIX religious wars date back centuries; an OS/2 flame looks like a love poem compared to some of the UNIX conflagrations I've seen.

Into this storming maelstrom jumps John Montgomery, UNIX hack extraordinaire, and a long-time friend at *PC Computing*. Aided by technical editors Vincent Chen (my co-author, co-developer, dim sum buddy, and personal guru) and Dan Watts, John takes on the tough topics and delivers some upside-the-head advice. John is one of the smartest guys I know—not just in the computer field, mind you—and his mastery of UNIX's nooks and crannies shows through on every page of this Underground Guide.

You're going to see the kind of no-bull, friendly advice you've come to expect from all of the Underground Guides—advice you won't find anywhere else—told by folks who have slugged it out down in the trenches, folks like you who've experienced the angst of modern computer . . . dum.

John's wide-eyed writing style will keep you on the edge of your seat. (He kept me rolling on the floor, but then I have a certifiably weird sense of humor.) And I bet you'll find more useful info per square inch in this book than in any other UNIX book on the shelves.

Enjoy!

Woody Leonhard
Series Hack

Another UNIX Book?
Not Really

Have you ever watched over the shoulder of somebody who really knows the ins and outs of UNIX* and thought, "Gee, that's neat"? Ever stayed late at the office to perfect a shell script? Or gotten mad at the man pages because they only tell you the options to commands?**

Then you're in the right place. See, you're a power user.*** Or at least a power-user wannabe, which is just as good. You know the basics—moving around the file system doesn't scare you, you can use an editor, and you're ready for more.

You're a power user

It could be daunting to know just how much more there is. Your system has well over a thousand commands, each with its command-line parameters, file types, and bugs. Yes, bugs—despite the fact that UNIX is into its thirties, it still has bugs. (Soon, it will probably have a midlife crisis, too. Watch for it to purchase a fast car and experiment with hair implants.)

Fortunately, there are books. Hundreds, maybe thousands, of them. Go ahead, read 'em all. I dare you. You've probably already sampled some of them and you know that most are alphabetical arrangements of commands. That is boring.

There's just too much to know about UNIX unless you get selective. Most of us will never need to know the system administration commands. Nor crack the bindings of a programmer's reference. Even the most powerful UNIX power users don't use more than sixty or seventy commands.

Zeroing in

But they use them wisely.

And that's what this book is about: using standard, old-fashioned commands in new (or somewhat new) ways. It assumes that you already know something about UNIX (if you don't, try Chapter 1 to see if it gives you enough information to get comfortable fast); it also assumes that you're interested in UNIX. Being interested in an operating system may seem odd, but UNIX is interesting. It has an interesting history, and it can do interesting things. But if you have your one job you need to get done and aren't interested in the rest of UNIX, you're probably not even reading this introduction.

---

*Don't call out the lawyers yet: It's UNIX®, a registered trademark of Novell. Screw with it and you're in serious doo-doo.

** If you answer yes to all of these, you're a nerd. Seek counseling.

*** Pronounced "nerd."

HOW TO READ THIS BOOK

So here's who this book *is* for: people interested in what UNIX can do. And here's what you're about to encounter: three parts of unequal size.

The first part is a leveler. Since this book is aimed at a nonbeginning user, I have no idea how much you know. So, Chapter 1 takes care of bringing you up to speed if you don't know anything about UNIX.

The second part (Chapters 2–6) deals with doing neat things with your operating environment. It includes modifications you can make to your environment, scripts you should have if you consider yourself a power user, and all the UNIX trivia you'll need in order to talk to other UNIX people. It's here that you'll uncover the real meat of the book: favorite scripts, tips, tricks, and odd things you probably didn't know you could do.

The third part (Chapter 7) goes beyond simple shell scripts. It unleashes networking, electronic mail, and other kinds of modem-based connectivity. It's my nod to the annoying overuse of the words "information" and "superhighway." It explains how to link up your info-cul-de-sac to the info-bahn with a firm electronic macadam.

The fourth part of the three deals with the Internet, that oh-so-popular place to find information. We'll talk about connecting up, what to do, and where to go.

The fifth of the three parts (and perhaps the most interesting) is the appendices. You'll find keyboard shortcuts for popular editors, a reference for common commands, and some solutions to common problems.

CONVENTIONS

Most of the conventions in this tome resemble those in other computer books. They should look familiar if you've read another computer book recently. If you haven't, fear not. Here's a quick rundown of what I use to convey the sometimes murky message herein:

`Text that looks like this is usually a command.`

The percent sign (`%`) is usually a C shell prompt.

The dollar sign (`$`) is usually a Bourne or Korn shell prompt.

When you see `Ctrl+` something, it means hold down the control key and press the something key.

`Esc` means press the Escape key.

One other note: I'm assuming that you're using a fairly recent version of either BSD or System V UNIX. If you're using one of the old ones (like System V Release 3), I can't guarantee that the examples in this book will work.

THE MOST IMPORTANT PART

This book would not have been possible without the help of *a whole lot of people.* First off, there's Woody Leonhard, who heads up the *Underground Guide* series. He's a source of inspiration and lunacy (inspired lunacy). And, of course, Kathleen Tibbetts, my editor at Addison-Wesley, had a hand in what you're about to trudge through.

Most important are the two people who checked this book for technical accuracy: Vince Chen and Dan Watts, both of whom you'll be hearing from periodically as they comment on what I'm commenting on. Why two technical editors? Well, first off, I make misteaks rather more frequently than I'd like to admit. Plus I was late in doing *everything*. So I lucked out and got two of the most knowledgeable (and patient) tech editors on Earth.

Also, thanks to the folks at SunSoft for giving me a copy of Solaris for x86 to work with, and to Handmade Software, which makes Image Alchemy, a graphics conversion tool that seems to convert anything to anything else.

And finally, there's Mom, Dad, and Amy—the first two for having me, the last for putting up with me.

1 The Basics

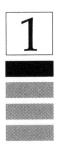

Come one, come all! this rock shall fly
From its firm base as soon as I.

Sir Walter Scott
The Lady of the Lake, 1810

Imagine you're trying to teach me how to repair my car and you start with the sentence "This is a tire." I would probably be insulted. (If I knew anything about cars, that is.) On the other hand, if you started out by saying, "Disassemble the carburetor and I'll show you some neat tuning you can do," I'd probably become frustrated. Particularly because my car has fuel injection.

So this chapter is for everyone who can't start by taking a carburetor apart. I'm assuming that you know how to log in to your system and have used it a little, but you're probably still a little uncomfortable with why some commands do what they do. In order to give you a good foundation to build on, this chapter will have a lot more "talking" and a lot less "doing" than others. Never fear: You're going to be getting bits under your fingernails soon enough.

This is the most theoretical chapter in the book—it has to be because it explains why things are the way they are. You'll learn why there are two main types of the UNIX operating system and how they came into being; you'll learn what the major shells are; and you'll learn the basic commands and tools to get you from point A to point B in UNIX.

If you know what this command does, you can probably skip to the next chapter:

Who shouldn't read this chapter?

```
% chmod -R 666 *
```

1

WHICH UNIX ARE YOU RUNNING?

Body and spirit are twins: God only knows which is which.

Algernon Swinburne
The Higher Pantheism in a Nutshell, 1880

There are two main versions of UNIX, and which one you're running can make a difference in how your commands and shell scripts wind up running. The main flavor is Novell's System V Release somethingorother—these days it's Release 4. For short, we call that SVR4 (pronounced Ess Vee Arr Four). The other kind of UNIX you could be running is the Berkeley Software Distribution (sometimes called the Berkeley Standard Derivative, but always abbreviated BSD, pronounced Bee Ess Dee). (There's also a third coming into the world, called OSF/1, from the Open Software Foundation—it's neither SVR4 nor BSD, but something quite its own.) The whole history of how we got these different UNIXes is pretty interesting (see "A Quick Diversion" on page 5), but it's not really important to getting you rocking with UNIX.

Usually, don't worry
Since most commands behave similarly no matter their parent, you usually don't have to worry about which version you have. However, there are cases where it is important—where commands will return different values and will break the examples in this book. Everything in this book, unless I note otherwise, works on SVR4. Why did I choose that? Fate. I fiddled with several different versions of UNIX, and found that SVR4 would do most of what I wanted.

That said, most of what's in this book should run no matter if you're using BSD, SVR4, or SNAFU. But, here's how to figure out which UNIX you have anyway. Remember, knowledge is power.

A: You just know
There are people out there who just know which version of UNIX they have. They're born that way, and there's nothing you can do about it. They are the people who have networks in their apartments and think electrical engineering is cute. AVOID THESE PEOPLE. They are weird and will probably alter your world view after only a short exposure.

B: Somebody told you
This is really the most common way to find out which one you're running. You're sitting at a terminal, and somebody (usually from category A) comes up behind you and says, "Say, is that SVR4 you're running? I thought I smelled a bug." They then laugh maniacally and walk away. It's okay to learn this way, but there are better ways.

C: You read it somewhere
This is nearly as bad as category B, because you have exerted no effort to figure it out for yourself. You must know the adage "Give me a fish and I eat today, teach me to fish and I eat for a lifetime." Well, if you can't wait to learn how to figure it out, Table 1.1 provides a brief list of who uses what UNIX.

Table 1.1 Some of the many UNIXes, arranged by hair color.

BSD	SVR4
Ultrix (Digital)	Irix (Silicon Graphics)
SunOS (Sun Microsystems; up to version 4.1.3)	Solaris 2 (Sun Microsystems; also called SunOS 5 and higher, but Sun becomes cantankerous when you do that)
Mt. XINU UNIX (Mt. XINU)	RISC/os (MIPS Computers)
	Dynix/PTX (Sequent)
	UnixWare (Novell)
	Consensys (Consensys)
	OpenDesktop (SCO)
	OpenServer (SCO)
	AIX (IBM)
	HP-UX (Hewlett-Packard)

As you can see, there are lots more SVR4s than BSDs. Primarily that's because over the years SVR4 has made moves to incorporate all the good stuff from BSD, while BSD has been busy inventing new good stuff that SVR4 can steal. If you ever hear anyone complain that BSD is a better UNIX flavor than SVR4, don't start an argument—you'll probably lose. Nothing except religion and databases (although sometimes I wonder if databases are a religion) will start a permanent feud faster than the BSD vs. SVR4 debate.

There are a few other *things* floating around that kind of behave like UNIX. Two of them are the Open Software Foundation's OSF/1 and NeXT's NeXTStep. Both look like UNIX, feel like UNIX, and have most of the commands of UNIX, but because they're not built on the code developed by AT&T, they're not UNIX®.

Now we're in the "teach you how to fish" segment of this section. One of the easiest ways to see which UNIX you're running is to look at the message you get when you log in. Chances are that it tells you. If it doesn't, you can fall back on running commands that extract different behaviors under each variant.

D: You followed this quick trick

The quickest of these is the `ps` command. Put simply, `ps` tells you what's running on your system. It's like the DOS `MEM/C` command or the VAX/VMS `SHOW SYSTEM` command.

Run by itself, `ps` won't look very different under BSD and SVR4. But give it a few of its options and you'll see a major difference. The biggest one is that under BSD, `ps` doesn't need a hyphen (or minus sign) before its arguments. So, to figure out which UNIX you're running, just type

```
ps aux
```

A BSD variant will return the status of every process running on your system.

```
┌─────────────────────────────────────── xterm ───────────────────────────────┐
│ # ps aux                                                                      │
│ usage: ps [ -edalfcj ] [ -r sysname ] [ -t termlist ]                         │
│          [ -u uidlist ] [ -p proclist ] [ -g grplist ] [ -s sidlist ]         │
│ #                                                                             │
└──────────────────────────────────────────────────────────────────────────────┘
```

Figure 1.1 Hmm. This isn't Kansas or BSD UNIX.

If you get an error message, you're probably running System V of some kind. (See Figure 1.1.) Just to make sure, you should then type the System V analog:

```
ps -ef
```

On a BSD system, this command returns a lot of information about every process running that's associated with your username. On a System V system, you'll see the status of every process running on the entire system, regardless of whose name is attached. (See Figure 1.2.)

```
┌─────────────────────────────────────── xterm ───────────────────────────────┐
│ # ps -ef                                                                      │
│      UID   PID  PPID  C    STIME TTY      TIME COMD                            │
│     root     0     0 80  Aug 10 ?        0:02 sched                            │
│     root     1     0 75  Aug 10 ?        1:51 /etc/init -                      │
│     root     2     0 52  Aug 10 ?        0:01 pageout                          │
│     root     3     0 80  Aug 10 ?        6:13 fsflush                          │
│     root   170     1 58  Aug 10 console  0:00 -sh                              │
│     root   169     1 80  Aug 10 ?        0:02 /usr/lib/saf/sac -t 300          │
│     root   148   140 11  Aug 10 ?        0:00 lpNet                            │
│     root    95     1 17  Aug 10 ?        0:00 /usr/sbin/rpcbind                │
│     root   110     1 80  Aug 10 ?        0:01 /usr/sbin/inetd -s               │
│     root    87     1 15  Aug 10 ?        0:00 /usr/sbin/in.routed -q           │
│     root    97     1  2  Aug 10 ?        0:00 /usr/sbin/keyserv                │
│     root   101     1 13  Aug 10 ?        0:00 /usr/sbin/kerbd                  │
│     root   113     1 17  Aug 10 ?        0:00 /usr/lib/nfs/statd               │
│     root   115     1 56  Aug 10 ?        0:01 /usr/lib/nfs/lockd               │
│     root   125     1 11  Aug 10 ?        0:00 /usr/lib/nfs/automount           │
│     root   140     1 32  Aug 10 ?        0:00 /usr/lib/lpsched                 │
│     root   132     1  0  Aug 10 ?        0:00 /usr/sbin/cron                   │
│     root   149     1 80  Aug 10 ?        0:00 /usr/lib/sendmail -bd -q1h       │
│     root   172   169 80  Aug 10 ?        0:03 /usr/lib/saf/ttymon              │
│     root   155     1 45  Aug 10 ?        0:00 /usr/sbin/syslogd                │
│     root   176   170 50  Aug 10 console  0:00 /bin/sh /usr/openwin/bin/openwin │
│     root   182   181 80  Aug 10 console 20:43 /usr/openwin/bin/xnews :0 -auth //.xnews.so│
│     root   189   181149  Aug 10 console  0:00 sh /usr/openwin/lib/Xinitrc      │
│     root   288   200 80  Aug 11 ?        0:31 /usr/openwin/bin/snapshot        │
│     root   181   176 12  Aug 10 console  0:00 /usr/openwin/bin/xinit -- /usr/openwin/bin/│
│ s:0                                                                           │
│     root   196     1 37  Aug 10 console  0:00 vkbd -nopopup                    │
│     root   201   200 24  Aug 10 console  0:00 olwmslave                        │
│     root   200   189 80  Aug 10 console  0:13 olwm -syncpid 199                │
│     root   854   215148 15:21:51 pts/2   0:00 csh                             │
│     root   206     1 66  Aug 10 ?        0:01 xterm                            │
│     root   207   206 33  Aug 10 pts/0    0:00 sh                               │
│     root   214     1 80  Aug 10 ?        0:14 xterm                            │
│     root   215   214172  Aug 10 pts/2    0:00 sh                               │
│     root   218     1 70  Aug 10 console  0:01 cmdtool -Wp 0 0 -Ws 590 77 -WP 3 701 +Wi -C│
│     root   220   218  4  Aug 10 pts/3    0:00 /sbin/sh                         │
│     root  1141  1028 16 14:30:36 pts/2   0:00 ps -ef                          │
│     root  1028   854 80 23:33:04 pts/2   0:00 sh                              │
│ #                                                                             │
└──────────────────────────────────────────────────────────────────────────────┘
```

Figure 1.2 Aha! A System V system.

There are some operating systems that will respond correctly to both of these commands. The most notable are IBM's AIX/6000 (the operating system on the RS/6000 workstations and servers) and Hewlett-Packard's HP/UX (at least versions 9 and 10—I'm too young to know any others). This is where you just gotta know: Both are SVR4 with some *serious* BSD extensions.

When both commands work

A Quick Diversion: UNIX's History

> The very ink in which history is written is merely fluid prejudice.
>
> Mark Twain
> *Pudd'nhead Wilson's New Calendar* 1897

Saying you're using UNIX is like saying you own a car. In other words, it doesn't say much. In fact, when you read trade journals and see ads for programs that "run under UNIX" or "support UNIX," call up those companies and ask if they run under Consensys and NonStop/UX (a fault-tolerant UNIX variant that runs on Tandem computers, in case you're interested). You should be able to hear over the phone the blank stare you get. In fact, these ads regularly drive my blood pressure up. But that's a different matter.

For the most part, the differences between different UNIXes don't make much difference. (And if *that* makes sense, the duck flies down from the ceiling.) However, there are certain cases where it's important to know how your version of UNIX will respond to a particular command. Mostly, though, it's just neat to know why UNIX is the way it is.

At this point, it would be fastest to say that there are two major varieties of UNIX, System V Release 4 (SVR4) and the Berkeley Software Distribution (BSD). But saying this wouldn't get you into the philosophy of UNIX, nor would it even begin to explain why users of one or the other version have such strong opinions (shall we say prejudices?) one way or the other. So, let's start down a brief historical journey.

In the beginning there was darkness. It was called MULTICS. MULTICS, short for Multiplexed Information and Computing System, was an operating system created by the folks at Bell Labs. It was much like Microsoft's Windows 3.1: great idea, but it took too much computing power to run.

How'd we get here?

Along about 1970 came a guy name of Ken Thompson. He worked at Bell Labs on the MULTICS project. He thought that part of the problem was that the hardware they were trying to run MULTICS on wasn't powerful enough, and suggested that Bell purchase one of the brand-spanking-new computers from Digital Equipment Corporation: a DEC-10. (The DEC-10, by the way, has less computing power than the Dell Dimension XPS 466V sitting on my desk. For the time, however, it was a hot computer.) Bell Labs took one look at the price tag on

UNIX comes from MULTICS

this interactive, time-sharing machine, laughed itself silly, and canceled the whole MULTICS project.

Like all good computer hackers, Thompson was undaunted by the cancellation of the MULTICS project. Okay, maybe he was a little daunted, but he had discovered a computer game that he thought was really cool: Space Travel. By today's Nintendo standards, Space Travel is a joke so bad that not even a destitute fourth-grader would want to play it. But for its time it was hot. Killer. Neat. Cool.

UNIX owes its life to a game

So Thompson teamed up with Dennis Ritchie to port Space Travel to what they termed a "little-used PDP-7 sitting in a corner." The PDP-7 was another Digital Equipment Corporation computer, but a far less expensive one than the DEC-10. It was also far less powerful. (Yikes.) But it was free (or at least paid for).

Thompson took this opportunity to probe the frontiers of Space Travel and created a file system on which it could reside. Just what every computer game needs, right? A file system. Imagine what would happen if we all went to the children of America and said, "Honey, before you can play that next game of Bloody Killer Demon Things, you have to design a file system for your Nintendo set." The response would be, "Aw, ma, do I gotta?" And when you insisted, they'd do it.

But I digress. A file system is basically a way for a computer to store information. Of course, once you've created a place for the information to go, you need to create commands to get at the information. So Thompson did just that, with some help from his friends.

To make a long story short, this game soon turned into an operating system. Brian Kernighan, one of the two creators of the C programming language, suggested the name UNICS—Uniplexed Information and Computing System, since it was basically a smaller version of MULTICS. Like all silly names, it stuck, and it was shortly shortened to UNIX.

So much for history

With a name like UNIX, it had to succeed. (The fact that it was free helped.) Thompson and Ritchie ported it to several other systems, popularized it, and sent it out into the public, where it gradually came to run on more and more systems. But it was basically unsupported. Here's where things get interesting and UNIX gets hopelessly confusing.

AT&T itself (thanks to some lawyers, twelve bananas,* and an antitrust suit) couldn't sell UNIX. Besides, it didn't want to. AT&T wasn't in the computer operating system business and didn't want to be there. (That's why it recently purchased NCR, another company that doesn't want to be in the computer business.)

Interactive and Berkeley

It wasn't until 1977 that Interactive Systems Corporation (now owned by Sun Microsystems) actually resold UNIX. Also in 1977, the University of California at

---

*Just kidding about the bananas.

Berkeley began to redistribute it with its own shell, editor, and some more drivers. And here is where the split occurred. Interactive took the version of UNIX coming out of Bell Labs—which was a division of AT&T at the time—and basically resold it.

Berkeley took the source code from Bell Labs, modified it, gave it to students to muck with, added some things, took out others, and basically created a totally different operating system that happened to support many of the same commands.

For many years, the Berkeleyites had the edge. Their operating system (BSD) had more neat things than AT&T's. And because of the liberal (get it? Berkeley? Liberal?) licensing policy, many sites (especially universities) took BSD and ran it on their computers. So, what do you get? A bunch of students graduating with experience using, programming, and hacking in BSD. Once they hit the commercial market, they were appalled that AT&T's UNIX didn't have a good editor, didn't have networking, didn't have this or that other thing. AT&T eventually responded by "borrowing" these features from BSD. (Remember: Good authors borrow, great authors steal.)

Houston, we have separation

UNIX is a perennial contender, but it never manages to make it to the top of the heap. During the 1980s, many companies started experimenting with a new microprocessor technology that was faster and less expensive to manufacture than what everybody was using. It was called a Reduced Instruction Set Computer (RISC). Some marketing person's idea, no doubt, because the actual tenets of RISC systems have very little to do with smaller instruction sets. But that's another story.

UNIX's rise

Anyway, UNIX appealed to the people developing RISC microprocessors— mostly academics like John Hennessy at Stanford and David Patterson at Berkeley. It was easy to port to the new computers, and their students already knew how to use it. Hennessy's architecture went into the MIPS microprocessor that came to be used in Silicon Graphics computers, among others. Patterson's microprocessor, called the SPARC architecture, went into Sun Microsystems computers, among others.

Taking a RISC

MIPS and Silicon Graphics both chose to use AT&T's SVR4 operating system. Sun Microsystems chose to base their operating system on BSD. The low cost of these vendors' computers drove them onto desks and into computer rooms in droves. And that is probably why you're reading this book instead of doing something fun like watching television.

Finally, in 1993, Novell purchased UNIX Systems Laboratories from AT&T, so now it's Novell's SVR4, not AT&T's anymore. Novell's brand of UNIX is called UnixWare and includes built-in NetWare networking.

Today

THE OLD SHELL GAME

Upon a mountain height, far from the sea,
I found a shell,
And to my listening ear, the lonely thing
Ever a song of the ocean seemed to sing,
Ever a tale of ocean seemed to tell.

Eugene Field
The Wanderer

Anyway, as I was saying before I so rudely interrupted myself, once you've figured out which UNIX variant you're running, you need to figure out which shell you're running. Why? Because your shell actually makes more difference in the commands you use than which UNIX you're running.

What the heck is a shell? It's a thing that crustaceans live in? Something you stuff with flavored ricotta cheese? Where you go when you die if you're *really bad??* But seriously (wipe tears from eyes), a shell is a program that lives between you and the UNIX kernel. The kernel is the part of UNIX that handles very low level grunt work, like figuring out how to allocate memory and disk space to different users and processes. Your shell is basically a command interpreter: You tell it what you want, and it figures out how to get it from the system.

At times this is no mean feat. The kernel is really complicated. It's where really important UNIX things happen—processes run, filesystems reside, memory gets swapped and paged. You and I wouldn't survive there for a second. It makes millisecond-to-millisecond decisions about how to react to what the computer is doing, what you're doing, and what various other processes on the computer are doing.

Shells put a pretty (or at least not too horribly ugly) layer between you and the kernel. It's kind of like asking a friend to ask your ogre of a boss for a raise: Your friend does the negotiating and bears the ire, and you reap the benefits. Always remember how nice your shell is to be doing all this. After all, it could be vacationing in Aruba.

Internal vs. external commands In order to protect you from the kernel efficiently, every shell has ways to deal with commands. Some commands are built into the shell itself, much the way the DOS program COMMAND.COM has commands such as DIR built in. These commands are called *internal commands*. Clever, no? The rest of the commands are external—that is, they aren't in the shell. Because of how your shell looks for commands, internal ones are generally faster to execute than external ones (but on today's really fast computers, you'd be hard-pressed to tell the difference).

When you type something at a shell prompt and hit Return, the shell looks through its archive of commands to see if it's there. If it is, it executes it. If it's not, it looks in "the usual places" for an external command matching the name you typed. For UNIX, the usual places are directories with names such as /bin (where most of the programs that come with your operating system are stored), /etc (which holds some of the auxiliary files and commands), /usr/bin (which holds programs that aren't necessarily part of UNIX, like some text editors), and a few other choice directories.

Failing that, your shell turns to the directories in your path (see the section below about directories and filenames). If it still doesn't find the command, a well-mannered shell will barf out an error message like Command not found or file not found?? and leave you to ponder what went wrong.

If you're lucky, you'll be working on a system equipped with a program called why. When something goes wrong and UNIX tells you that you've been bad, you type why and it responds with a pithy response. Many years ago, when I had no idea this program existed, I responded to a particularly stubborn error by asking why. The computer answered, "Why not?" I admit I couldn't fault the logic.

How Many Shells Are There?

> A good exterior is a silent recommendation.
>
> Publilius Syrus
> *Sententiae*, ca. 50 BC

Shells are a lot like uninvited guests and chicken pox: You look the other way and three or four more turn up. This is both good and bad. It's good because it means you can probably find a shell that fits your personality exactly. It's bad because you could search for years.

There are three common shells, and most of the others are basically offshoots of them. Table 1.2 tells you a little bit about each one.

There are a couple of others you may run into, most notably tcsh (a better C shell) and jsh and bash (better Bourne shells). Running one of these shells is great, but you risk finding that some convenience you're used to disappears when you work on a friend's system. (Vince Chen, my illustrious technical editor, points out that the consulting group he works with brings a copy of tcsh everywhere it goes and it's the first thing they install.) It's probably best to stick with the golden oldies until you're really comfortable.

I'll be flipping from shell to shell throughout this book to demonstrate my incredible prowess with . . . Hey, stop laughing. Okay, okay, I'll be flipping from shell to shell depending on which shell has the best tools for the job I'm trying to do.

Table 1.2 Tale of the three little shells.

Shell	Name	Who cares?
Bourne	sh	The original shell, it's on every UNIX system you'll find. That's probably why you'll find a lot of people who do shell programming in the Bourne shell: They know that they'll find one on their system, no matter what version of UNIX it has.
C	csh	Came from Berkeley. Need I say more? It addresses a couple of shortcomings in the Bourne shell, in particular its lack of job control and its inability to recall past commands. You aren't guaranteed to find a C Shell on every UNIX system, but damn near.
Korn	ksh	Now part of SVR4, it's Bourne plus C. It's even newer than the C Shell, and lots more powerful, but you won't find it on every system you use (although every new system you get should have it).

Which Shell Are You Running?

> No great discovery was ever made without a bold guess.
>
> Isaac Newton

If you don't know which shell you're running, you're not alone. I don't know which shell you're running either. (Ba-doom-cha. I know: Don't quit the day job). Let's figure out which shell you've got on today. There are several ways to find out. Remember that phrase. There are several ways to find out *anything* with UNIX. It's not like DOS where you get one of a command. For example, UNIX has about a dozen search commands. If you think you've found something that can only be done one way, you're probably thinking too linearly.

How to find out   There are, however, quick ways to do things and less quick ways to do them. The quickest way to find out what shell you're running is to type the command shown in Figure 1.3.

```
# echo $SHELL
/sbin/sh
#
```

Figure 1.3 Is there an echo in this shell?

You should get a simple response. Ain't it grand?

Here's how that command works. The echo command does for UNIX what it does for DOS: prints out the thing that follows. Very uninteresting. The next thing is much neater. We're telling `echo` to find out the value of the variable `SHELL` (the $ means "evaluate the thing that follows and pass that value back to whatever called it"). `SHELL` is called an environment variable, because it cleans up all sorts of trash. Just kidding again. It's because it describes how your shell will function—like where it should look for commands, what your prompt should look like, and what time zone you should be in.

There are about a billion other ways to find out what shell you're running. Each introduces a useful new command. For example, try typing the command in Figure 1.4, and wait to see what turns up.

Some other ways

```
xterm
# env | grep -i shell
SHELL=/sbin/sh
#
```

Figure 1.4 Same shell, different command.

The `env` command prints out all your environment variables—not just `SHELL`. In fact, when something is amiss with your system, `env` is a good command to remember. The vertical bar (|) is a pipe. It sends the output of one command into another. In this case, `env` is the source and `grep` is the destination. The `grep` command is UNIX's numero uno search command. In this case, we're telling `grep` to ignore the case (`-i`) of the word "shell" and to search for it.

Or you could use `grep` to take a look inside the master password file to see what your system administrator decided would be best for you. This example is slightly more complex, but it shows another way to use the `grep` command. Say your login name is `john`. Then you could execute the command in Figure 1.5.

```
xterm
# grep -i john /etc/passwd
john:x:100:1:John I. Montgomery -- csh:/usr/people/john:/usr/bin/csh
johnksh:x:101:1:John I. Montgomery -- ksh:/usr/people/johnksh:/usr/bin/ksh
johnsh:x:102:1:John I. Montgomery -- sh:/usr/people/johnsh://usr/bin/sh
#
```

Figure 1.5 Yet another way to figure it out.

Here's a quick rundown on what these commands do. The thing called `/etc/passwd` is a file. It lives in the directory called `/etc`, which is where UNIX puts a lot of its useful but "extra" commands. Hence the name "etc." The slash (a forward slash, unlike DOS, which uses a bass-ackwards slash) is just how UNIX tells one directory from another or from a filename.

Once you know that, the command in Figure 1.5 reads pretty much like it would in English: "Find the word `john` in the file `/etc/passwd`."

In any event, I'm found. The result looks something like this:

```
john:*:100:1:John I. Montgomery:/usr/people/john:/bin/csh
```

The very last thing on this line is the shell. In my case it's the C shell (`csh`), and it lives in the `/bin` directory along with a lot of other neat programs.

The rest of the stuff? Well, `john` is my username. The star (`*`) is where my password would go (but I have a shadowed password file, which you *really, really* don't want to know about—it'll make your head explode). The numbers `100` and `1` are my UNIX user ID number and group ID number. The next part is my full name, and the next thing (`/usr/people/john`) is my home directory.

The catch   There's one catch to all of these commands: They don't necessarily tell you what shell you're running *right now*. They could all respond by saying `/sbin/sh`, but you could have launched your own shell by typing `ksh`. The `SHELL` environment variable wouldn't have changed, and your entry in `/etc/passwd` would certainly stay the same. The only way out of this problem is to run through a command that will tell you what shell you logged in as, then use the command `ps` to see if you have any processes running that look suspiciously like shells (they usually have "`sh`" at their ends).

Anyway, back to the result. The C shell is one of several shells I could be running.

You can always run a different shell   No matter what your login shell is, you can invoke another one just by typing its name. So, I log in with `ksh`. If I suddenly feel the urge to run the Bourne shell, I could just type `sh`. Presto, I'm in a different shell. That's because shells are just programs like any other. They just happen to be programs that have other programs built into them and that know how to execute yet more programs.

PATHS AND FILENAMES

> Towering genius disdains a beaten path. It seeks regions
> hitherto unexplored.
>
> Abraham Lincoln
> Address at the Young Men's Lyceum, 1838

Something you've probably noticed is the peppering of forward slashes throughout what you've read (like `/bin/sh` and `/usr/home/john`). These slashes work like the backslash in DOS and the dot in VMS: They separate one directory from another. A bunch of directories strung together is called a path.

Two meanings of path   The word *path* has two meanings. When someone says that a directory is in your path, they mean that your shell will search it after exhausting its internal commands. On the other hand, when someone asks what the path to a particular file is, they mean what directory structure does it live in.

As you've already seen, UNIX directories are separated by forward slashes that read from left to right, with the leftmost directory being the "highest"—that is, the closest to the root, or top-level, directory. All UNIX directories stem from the root directory, also called slash (/). The directory structure on a UNIX computer might look something like the one in Figure 1.6.

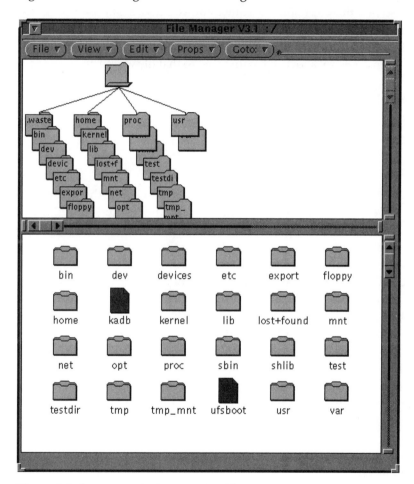

Figure 1.6 One way to look at the UNIX filesystem.

Well, *that* gets boring really quickly. Anyway, things start out at the root and work their way down through directory names to filenames. **Directories are just files**

The interesting thing is that, technically, directories are also just files—special files, but files nonetheless. A directory file contains information about where to find other files. In fact, everything you'll find on your UNIX system is a file. The reason some of them behave differently from others has to do with the properties assigned to them. This comes in handy when you want to do neat stuff.

There are a couple of things for you to notice here. The first is that UNIX's directory structure is a hierarchical tree. I realize that's old hat for most of you, but believe it or not, there are operating systems that don't have a hierarchical directory structure (I can think of one [hint: it runs on a mainframe].)

The second thing is not really something you notice, but something you know: the word *path*. When you stack directories on top of each other like this, you need a way to find files. UNIX does this by listing each file's path. If there's a file in a top-level bin directory above, the path to get to that file would be `/bin/filename`.

Theoretical Directory Stuff

> Whatever satisfies the soul is truth.
>
> Walt Whitman
> *Leaves of Grass*, 1855

Much of a discussion of UNIX can be broken into either the theoretical or the practical. People who know UNIX theory talk about interesting things. People who know its practical applications are out doing interesting things. In order to do the practical, though, you need to know a little about the theoretical. So, let's talk about inodes. Pronounce it like you have a cold and are trying to say "I knows." (Although why the heck you'd be saying "I knows" is beyond me.)

You'll probably not have much reason to have direct contact with inodes. That's because they're generally well hidden. They're data structures that describe files. Oh boy, aren't you glad I cleared *that* up?

When you create a UNIX file system, whatever tool you use to do it will create a bunch of inodes—usually a few thousand of them. Each inode holds information about a file. When you run out of inodes, you can have no more files. Usually you'll run out of disk space before you run out of inodes, but if you create enough small files (less than 1K), you may actually run out. What do you do? If you're lucky, your operating system (like AIX) will simply make more (like Doritos—use all you want, we'll make more). If you're unlucky . . . Well, let's just say you're *really* unlucky.

 What kind of information does an inode hold? First and foremost, the location of a file—where it really lives on the disk. When you try to read a file, UNIX must first figure out where that file really resides so the disk drive can figure out where to position its read/write head. In addition, inodes track who owns a file, what everybody can do to it (read it, write it, or execute it), what kind of file it is (a link, directory, or some kind of UNIX device), and when it was last modified.

If you want to know about the inodes on your computer, use the `ls -i` command or the `stat` command (if your system has it—mine doesn't). You can also see the `man` pages (type `man ls`) for more information on what these commands do.

Practical Directory Stuff

> What is a theory but an imperfect generalization caught up by
> a predisposition?
>
> J.A. Proude
> *The Lives of the Saints*, 1852

As a general rule, moving around directories is very simple. Table 1.3 lists the basic commands for doing anything with directories (if you don't already know them). There are better ways of doing most of these things (particularly the `cd` [pronounced "seedy"] command).

Table 1.3 Simple UNIX commands.

Command	What it does
mkdir	Creates a directory (one case where UNIX uses a longer command than even MS-DOS)
cd	Changes to the directory you specify
pwd	Where am I?

Here's some more stuff you need to know about directories, placed in a nice table (Table 1.4) to make it look simple (which it is).

Table 1.4 Dots and angled lines.

Symbol	What it means
.	Your current directory
..	The next directory up the tree (your parent directory)
~	Home directory tool (C and Korn shells)
/	The root directory

You can string together the double dots to move up many directories at once. For example:

```
$ cd ../../../../../bin
```

will move you up five directories, then down into the `bin` directory.

Even more useful (and underused) is the tilde (that's what the ~ is called, a tilde, pronounced TILL-duh or TILL-dee, depending on whom you ask). For C shellers and Korn shellers, it means, "take everything relative from my home directory." You can use it when you're too far afield. Click your heels together, whisper "there's no place like home," and type

```
$ cd ~
```

and you'll be home. (Just as a side note, you can type `cd` all by itself and go home just as easily. That trick works for *any* shell.) But that's boring. So why not try this instead:

```
$ ls -a ~
```

This shows you all the files in your home directory.

More interesting are the uses of the tilde to get to some file or directory in your home directory. For example, typing

```
$ cd ~/testfiles
```

takes you home and plunks you into your testfiles directory. But the tilde gets even more useful. Say you have a sudden driving urge to get to Woody's home directory, but you have no idea what it's called. You could type

```
$ cd ~woody
```

and you're there. Now you can try to access all sorts of files he doesn't want accessed, probably getting yourself into trouble in the process. Great fun. I recommend it for late at night.

Filenames

> "Yossarian? Is that his name? Yossarian? What the hell kind of name is Yossarian?"
> Lieutenant Scheisskopf had the facts at his finger tips. "It's Yossarian's name, sir," he explained.
>
>> Joseph Heller
>> *Catch-22*, 1961

Now that we've taken care of directories, you need something to put in them. How about some files? You are going to be creating files left and right in no time at all, so you should probably know a few things about naming them. Here are the golden rules:

- UNIX is case-sensitive.

- UNIX doesn't like some characters in names, especially wildcards and spaces.

- Filenames can be as long as you want (up to 256 characters) unless you're running a brain-dead kind of UNIX. (One that comes to mind is the one that runs on Motorola servers, which has a 15-character limit.)

And that's about it. Generally, if you name files with reasonable, English names, you'll be fine. Unlike DOS, which forces you into an eight-character, all-uppercase filename, you can do pretty much what you want with UNIX. There are, however, some conventions that most of us use.

The first convention concerns filename extensions—those things that follow the last period in the file's name. For the most part, the period (or dot as it's often called) is just another character, and you can use it anywhere in a filename. Sometimes, however, an application will be expecting to see a particular extension on a filename. A filename ending in `.c`, for example, should contain C programming source code. A filename ending in `.tar` is probably an archive of other files (kind of like a ZIP file in DOS). And filenames ending in `.Z` have been compressed. There are others, but you should know these at the least.

Filename extensions

After that, filenames can look however you want. Since I really love speed, I prefer fairly short names that use all lowercase letters. Rather than naming a file `Anderson_Glass_Company_Annual_Report_Version_25`, I would probably use `anderson25.rep` or `anderson.rep.25` or something like that. Notice I use the period instead of the underscore. That's a pretty standard UNIX convention, as is the avoidance of uppercase letters.

Use short names

Whatever nomenclature rules you decide to follow will probably be just fine as long as you don't try to pepper your filenames with wildcards.

Wildcards

> A point of view can be a dangerous luxury when substituted for insight and understanding.
>
> Marshall McLuhan
> *The Gutenberg Galaxy*, 1962

You can use just about any character in a filename, although I don't recommend you stray too far from the alphabet (upper- and lowercase letters—UNIX is case-sensitive), the hyphen, the underscore, and the period. Two characters you can't use when you create a filename are the question mark (?) and asterisk (*). These are wildcards—they take the place of other characters. The ? matches exactly one character, and the * matches zero or more. For example, the command

```
$ ls *.txt
```

prints a listing of all files that end with the letters ".txt," and the command,

```
$ ls file?
```

turns up all files with the name file1, file2, file3, fileS, and fileS (but *not* file), to name a few. The question mark acts as a substitute for any single letter. The asterisk, on the other hand, substitutes for any group of letters. Personally, I use the asterisk a whole lot more than the question mark. But who am I, anyway?

Note that the * works differently in UNIX than in DOS. In UNIX, you can type *file1* to find a file or files that have the phrase file1 in the middle. If you do that in DOS, you'll match *every dang file*—DOS sees the two surrounding stars and discounts what's in the middle.

How do they work?   So how does a wildcard work, you're asking? Well, the shell sees it, knows how to make a substitution for it, and returns whatever values fill that substitution. You can use wildcards with any command. (Or at least any command that comes to mind—there is probably some aberrant command out there that won't accept them, but I'm just not going to worry about it right now. Neither should you. But if you run into one, drop me a line.)

Attributes

> No great genius has ever existed without some touch of madness.
>
> Aristotle, ca. 350 BC

As long as we're on the subject of files, let's get into one of the most complicated, ornery bits of obfuscation you can possibly imagine. And it isn't some government initiative, either. It's permissions and attributes. You see, just as some files have an identifier that says, "I'm a directory," others have ones that say things like "I belong to John" or "I'm a program. Run me." These are a file's attributes. Unfortunately, they're rarely as clear as this. In fact, they're never as clear as this. Instead, you'll wind up with something that looks more like the example in Figure 1.7.

Figure 1.7 Pretty standard statistics for a file.

Okay, first—how did I get this? I used the command `ls -l test.file`. The `ls` command by itself just prints a brief listing of all the files in a directory. To that I added the parameter `-l`. (Anything that follows a hyphen is called a parameter. It's a lot quicker than calling it "that thing after the hyphen," doncha think?) Uh, when I added the parameter `-l`, I told UNIX, "print a long listing of the file—everything you know, tell me. And make it snappy." By feeding the `ls` command the name of a file, I'm saying that I only want to know about this file if it's here.

Anyway, let's do a right-to-left interpretation of the result. First, break the command down into a slightly more palatable format (see Table 1.5).

Table 1.5 We're having a breakdown—and it's very enlightening.

F	E	D	C	B	A
-rw-r--r--	1	root other	43	Aug 15 14:52	test.file

So, pretty clearly, column A is the file's name. No surprises there. Column B is the date the file was last modified (or "touched" in UNIX parlance—there's even a `touch` command that will update this date on any file). Column C is the size of the file. On my system, it's in bytes, which means that I—used to a world of kilobytes and megabytes—wind up doing a lot of math to figure out how big most files are. Depending on what version of UNIX you have, you may get a report in blocks (usually 512 bytes), kilobytes (1024 bytes), or megabytes (this is very rare—I've only heard about it and never seen it, and I've seen about fifty different variations on the UNIX theme). Column D contains the name of the user that owns that file (root) and the group that can access it (other). The system administrator creates groups so that people doing similar things and working on the same project can be granted access to facilities all at once, rather than one at a time.

Column E shows how many links there are to that file. For most files this will be 1, but directories will have more. Don't worry about it: Column F is much more interesting.

Column F shows the file's attributes or permissions (depending on whom [yes, whom] you ask). This particular file can be read or written by the owner and read by other members of his or her group, not to mention by everyone else on the system.

There are three kinds of permission you can have: read access, write access, and execute access. With read access, you can look at the contents of a file, but you can't change it. With write access, you can change it (write access almost always

Three permission types

comes with read access). And with execute access, you can run any commands that happen to be in that file (this is usually bestowed upon shell scripts and programs).

If a file's permissions look like this

```
----rwx---
```

it can be read from, written to, or executed by anyone in that user's group. And finally, if the permissions look like

```
-------rwx
```

anyone at all can read, write, or execute the file. Usually, though, permissions look something like this:

```
-rwxr-xr-x
```

Here the owner can read, write, or execute the file; members of the group and everyone else on the system can read it and execute it, but they can't change it.

I will say at this point, for the record, that the really annoying thing about permissions is that it takes a lot longer to comprehend what's going on than it should.

That leading hyphen   You're probably wondering what the heck that first hyphen does. Well, it tells you (when it's a hyphen) that this is just a file. If there's a d instead, it tells you that the thing you're looking at is a directory. And if there's an l, look out, it's a link to another file somewhere else on the system. (UNIX uses links so you don't have multiple copies of the same file all over your hard disk. Create a link and it will look like a file is stored in two places, but it's only stored in one place on the disk—there's just a little pointer at the site of the link saying, "Look for the real file at this location." Links are great for saving disk space and still making files appear in many different places.)

How to Create Permissions

> Und er kommt zu dem Ergebnis
> "Nur ein Traum war das Erlebnis
> Well," so schlisst er messerchart,
> "nitcht sein kann, was nicht sein darf."*
>
> Christian Morgenstern
> *Die unmöglich Tatsache*

---

*And so he comes to the conclusion / The whole affair was an illusion / "For look," he cries triumphantly, / "What's not permitted CANNOT be!"

Permissions mostly just happen by themselves: The operating system has some defaults that usually make sense. Unfortunately, they don't guarantee that a file will be executable. In other words, when you generate a brilliant shell script or program, UNIX won't let you run it because it won't have any x's. For that, you probably want to use the chmod (short for "change mode") command, which changes how UNIX thinks of a file's permissions (or "mode," as it calls them).

The chmod command can take various arguments, but for our purposes, the simplest thing is +x. Say you've just created a brilliant program. It won't run until you issue the command

```
$ chmod +x brilliant.program
```

Now, all of a sudden, brilliant.program will run. If you do an ls -l on it, you'll see something like this

```
-rwxr-xr-x  1 john   users  933 Aug  2 11:14 brilliant.program
```

The chmod command merely sets the execute bit on the file.

Remember that, after the first character (which can be a d, for directory; an l, for link; or a hyphen, for plain ordinary file), the remaining nine characters break down into three groups of three: The first group reflects your permissions; the second, your group's permissions; and the third, everybody else's (the others' permissions).

There are other, much more sadistic uses for chmod, involving numbers and higher math. Being a sadist, I'm about to tell you how they work. Being at heart a nice sadist, I'm going to spare you the lengthy description of octal mathematics that usually accompanies this rigamarole.

chmod and its octal math

Each of the letters in the three 3-letter rwx sequences has a value: The r is 4, the w is 2, and the x is 1. You can sum these values in various ways to determine permissions for each sequence. So, if you wanted yourself to have read, write, and execute permission on a file you created, you'd want to set the first group's value to 7, or 4+2+1. If you then wanted no one else to have any permissions, you'd set the group and world sequences to 0. The command would then look like this:

```
$ chmod 700 brilliant.program
```

Or, to give everybody read and write access only, you'd set all the sequences to 6, or 4+2+0:

```
$ chmod 666 brilliant.program
```

If you hear someone complaining about calculating octal values, don't sweat it: That's what you were just doing. They're probably doing some weird binary conversion and thinking in terms of *mode bits* or some such oddity. Now you know a shortcut.

 If you ever perform a long listing and see a directory, you'll probably see permissions for it that look something like this:

```
drwxrwxrwx
```

And if you're very observant, you probably thought, "Who the heck would execute a directory?" You'd be right—that bit shouldn't be there. But just try to take it away—you'll see fur fly. That's because UNIX decided to use that execute bit differently for directories. Now it's the search bit. In order for you (or anyone except a superuser) to do anything in a directory or any of its subdirectories, you must set the search bit on. Turning the search bit off is a great way for a superuser to block anyone from doing anything in a particular directory.

Files That Aren't Files

All that is white is not milk.

Hindu proverb

A directory is an example of something UNIX thinks is a file that most of us probably wouldn't consider a file. UNIX does that sometimes. It's a file-oriented operating system. In other words, it thinks *everything* is a file, even if it's a directory, a terminal, a printer, or (with some SVR4 releases) even a process. Nuts, huh?

Go to the /dev directory with the command cd /dev. Look around with the ls -l rmt* command. The stuff in there *looks* like files. But they ain't. No way, no how. Those are tape drives and potential tape drives.

You're probably wondering why you care—aside from winning trivia contests, that is. Because UNIX thinks of these devices as files (albeit special files), you can use the standard redirectors on them (see the section on redirectors below). That means you can stick the output of your commands, for example, into any of these devices (if you have the permission, that is). And *that* means I can run a command and have its output appear on your terminal, really messing you up in the process. So there.

Mostly, programmers will be interested in the nifty things you can do on an "everything-is-a-file" computer.

Block and character devices

So long as we're talking about devices, you should know there are two types of devices: block-oriented and character-oriented. Blocks are fixed-sized groups of characters. Block devices can only move data around in those blocks. Disk drives and tape drives are (usually) examples of block devices.

Characters . . . well, you probably know what those are. Character devices move data around one character at a time. A terminal is a character device. So are a keyboard and a printer.

Pipes and Redirection

> Don't change barrels going over Niagara.
>
> Satirically attributed to the Republican presidential race, 1932

The next basic thing you've got to know about UNIX has to do with its input/output (I/O) capabilities. In a word, it's incredibly flexible. Yes, that's two words. Sue me.* The output of any command can be directed into any other command or onto a file on disk. This trick is called redirection. Here's how it works.

Virtually every UNIX command produces some kind of output or needs some kind of input. Everyday commands such as `ls` print their output to the standard output device (that's your screen). Similarly, a command like `grep` takes its input from a standard input device (typically the keyboard). **Standard input and output**

Using the pipe we talked about above, we can string these two commands together to make a better command:

```
$ env | grep -i shell
```

Let's be amazed by technology. Ooooh. Aaaaah. Neat, huh? What's happening is that `env` is printing out all your environment variables (think of them as shell placeholders) to your screen—only before they get there, the pipe grabs them and funnels them to the `grep` command, which takes them as its input and searches them for `shell`. Like the man in the Ginsu ads, I say, "But wait, there's more."

Not only can you string commands together, you can use these commands to create files—even with commands that normally write their output to the screen. You do this with the redirector, or > (the greater-than sign). Figure 1.8 demonstrates the redirector at work.

You won't see the output of the cheerful `ls` command, but the file called `directory.listing` sure will. The `cat` command is a lot like the VAX/VMS and DOS `TYPE` commands. In UNIX, `cat` stands for concatenate, and when you just give it a filename, it prints it out on the screen. (We'll make `cat` do some other neat stuff later.) So you'll see the output of your `ls` command.

---

*Please note that the author is attempting to be humorous and is not in any way, shape, or form inviting litigation. Unless you really want to take on *my* lawyer, who sleeps two hours a night, moonlights as Ahhhhnold's personal trainer, scarfs Rocky Mountain oysters by the hundred, and breaks shnooks like your wimpy shyster just for the practice. Oh. She's also on the PTA.

```
┌─────────────────────────────────────────────────────────────────┐
│ ▽                              xterm                              │
├─────────────────────────────────────────────────────────────────┤
│ # ls -l > directory.listing                                       │
│ # cat directory.listing                                           │
│ total 32                                                          │
│ -rw-r--r--    1 root      other            0 Aug 15 15:07 directory.listing │
│ -rwxr-xr-x    1 root      other           16 Aug 14 10:50 exscript │
│ -rw-r--r--    1 root      other           43 Aug 15 09:30 file1   │
│ -rw-r--r--    1 root      other          314 Aug 11 18:45 fire.montgomery │
│ -rw-r--r--    1 root      other           43 Aug 14 10:50 jar1    │
│ -rw-r--r--    1 root      other           41 Aug 13 19:23 jar2    │
│ -rw-r--r--    1 root      other           36 Aug 13 19:32 jar3    │
│ -rw-r--r--    1 root      other           34 Aug 13 16:15 numbers │
│ -rw-r--r--    1 root      other          207 Aug 11 19:46 rolodex │
│ -rw-r--r--    1 root      other           17 Aug 13 19:29 script  │
│ -rw-r--r--    1 root      other           52 Aug 14 23:48 sedscript │
│ -rwxr-xr-x    1 root      other           43 Aug 15 14:52 test.file │
│ -rw-r--r--    1 root      other           60 Aug 13 16:44 test2   │
│ -rw-r--r--    1 root      other           26 Aug 13 16:44 test3   │
│ -rw-r--r--    1 root      other           83 Aug 13 16:38 testfile │
│ -rw-r--r--    1 root      other           52 Aug 13 10:34 trouble │
│ -rw-r--r--    1 root      other           29 Aug 11 23:11 weird.awk │
│ #                                                                 │
└─────────────────────────────────────────────────────────────────┘
```

Figure 1.8 Using a redirector.

The > redirected the `ls` command's output into the file. If you put two >s together, you can append to that file. Figure 1.9 illustrates this process.

```
┌─────────────────────────────────────────────────────────────────┐
│ ▽                              xterm                              │
├─────────────────────────────────────────────────────────────────┤
│ # ls -C >> directory.listing                                      │
│ # cat directory.listing                                           │
│ total 32                                                          │
│ -rw-r--r--    1 root      other            0 Aug 15 15:07 directory.listing │
│ -rwxr-xr-x    1 root      other           16 Aug 14 10:50 exscript │
│ -rw-r--r--    1 root      other           43 Aug 15 09:30 file1   │
│ -rw-r--r--    1 root      other          314 Aug 11 18:45 fire.montgomery │
│ -rw-r--r--    1 root      other           43 Aug 14 10:50 jar1    │
│ -rw-r--r--    1 root      other           41 Aug 13 19:23 jar2    │
│ -rw-r--r--    1 root      other           36 Aug 13 19:32 jar3    │
│ -rw-r--r--    1 root      other           34 Aug 13 16:15 numbers │
│ -rw-r--r--    1 root      other          207 Aug 11 19:46 rolodex │
│ -rw-r--r--    1 root      other           17 Aug 13 19:29 script  │
│ -rw-r--r--    1 root      other           52 Aug 14 23:48 sedscript │
│ -rwxr-xr-x    1 root      other           43 Aug 15 14:52 test.file │
│ -rw-r--r--    1 root      other           60 Aug 13 16:44 test2   │
│ -rw-r--r--    1 root      other           26 Aug 13 16:44 test3   │
│ -rw-r--r--    1 root      other           83 Aug 13 16:38 testfile │
│ -rw-r--r--    1 root      other           52 Aug 13 10:34 trouble │
│ -rw-r--r--    1 root      other           29 Aug 11 23:11 weird.awk │
│ directory.listing  jar2         sedscript          trouble        │
│ exscript           jar3         test.file          weird.awk      │
│ file1              numbers      test2                             │
│ fire.montgomery    rolodex      test3                             │
│ jar1               script       testfile                          │
│ #                                                                 │
└─────────────────────────────────────────────────────────────────┘
```

Figure 1.9 Redirecting and appending.

At the bottom of the screen, you'll see the output of your second `ls` command. As if that weren't enough, the less-than sign (<) feeds input to a command. We'll deal with that later.

MULTI-EVERYTHING

I'll take a Whopper with everything.

Anonymous

If you've ever eaten while driving, or watched television while biting your toenails, or done any two activities at once, you've done multitasking. UNIX multitasks, too, only it calls its tasks *processes*. If you run to your system and type `ps` right now, you'll see that you alone are running a variety of processes. Even if there's no one on the system, UNIX is busy running a bunch of processes— probably a print queue, some networking stuff, and who knows what else.

UNIX itself carefully orchestrates each of these processes so that all of them appear to be running by themselves. You'll hear terms like task switching, thread switching, and process switching to describe this behavior. All are slightly different, but the concept is the same: Your computer's CPU juggles the different things to be done and makes it look as though they're all getting done at the same time.

Switch hitting

One of the greatest implications of this ability to perform multiple tasks at once is that it's not a great stretch to put multiple users on one system at once. After all, if an individual user runs ten or twenty tasks at once, you can put ten or twenty users on even a lowly 486 before it becomes noticeably slower. (Well . . . sometimes.) DOS, Windows, and even Windows NT don't have this kind of power—they're single-user operating systems.

Introducing The Kernel and His Daemons

All writers are vain, selfish and lazy, and at the very bottom of their motives lies a mystery. Writing a book is a long, exhausting struggle, like a long bout of some painful illness. One would never undertake such a thing if one were not driven by some demon whom one can neither resist nor understand.

George Orwell
Why I Write, 1947

At this point, it's time to get hard-core. The master of this multitasking capability is the UNIX kernel. The kernel is the brains of UNIX—it handles the scheduling of tasks and most input and output, and it generally keeps thing running smoothly. In reality, it's not horribly large—no larger than most word processors, and usually a whole lot smaller (depending on whose UNIX variant you have).

You can probably get a glimpse of your kernel by typing the following:

```
$ cd /
$ ls -l *unix*
```

If your system is like most, you'll see some file like vmunix, or just plain old unix. On my system (SunSoft's Solaris 2.1 for x86) the file lives in /kernel and is called /kernel/unix. That's your kernel. You delete that, and your system won't boot, and will probably crash in short order. Unless you really want to spend an afternoon trying to undo your phenomenal stupidity, don't do that.

But that's just the kernel's file—its body, not its soul. You can look into the soul of this new machine (thanks, Mr. Kidder) by typing

```
$ ps -ef
```

or, on a BSD system,

```
$ ps aux
```

You'll see everything that's running on your system. Look particularly at the far right column (which will be called something like COMD). Look at all those files that live in directories like /usr/sbin or /usr/bin. They're the guts of what UNIX is. You'll see how much CPU time the kernel has sucked up to date, how much memory it's taking up, and all sorts of other arcana that really don't do you much good.

As you've probably noticed, the kernel itself is pretty small for something that does so much. That's why it has helpers, called daemons (pronounced demons). (Try going into a church and muttering to yourself about daemons. Check out the response you get. It's fascinating.) Daemons are kind of like DOS TSRs—they're processes that hang out on your system (taking very little of the CPU's attention) until they're needed, then leap into action, perform a task, and go back to hanging out. You probably have daemons for your print queues and for some tasks that get performed regularly, such as system backups.

Deep Background

> Many demons are in woods, in waters, in wildernesses, and in dark pooly places, ready to hurt and prejudice people; some are also in the thick black clouds, which cause hail, lightning and thunder, and poison the air, the pastures and grounds.
>
> Martin Luther
> *Table-Talk*, 1569

Daemons are one example of how the UNIX architecture allows you to have lots of things going on at once. You can take advantage of this capability with your own commands, too. I'm one of those people who likes to work on something, drop it for a bit, and then come back to it. I call it "personal multitasking." Most of my friends assert I have an attention-deficit disorder. Whatever. I usually have one command searching the disk for a particular file, another merging and comparing two large files, yet another transferring a file from a remote computer, and so on.

Such are the joys of background processing and multitasking. When we talked about processes, you probably had no idea why it was important to you. When we talked about certain shells having "job control" features, you probably still had no idea. *You're about to find out.*

Background processing and multitasking

Depending on which shell you're running, you may have the ability to run jobs in the background. The C shell and Korn shell both support background processing and job control really well, so we'll use the C shell for these examples.

Suppose you want to search the entire hard disk for an incredibly personal document that you've lost. Call it `embarrassing.document`. You could use the vanilla `find` command to turn it up:

```
% find / -name "embarrassing.document" -print
```

Now you'd wait for a minute or ten while `find` searched the disk. While you're drumming your fingers on your desk, your boss comes in, looks at the command you just issued, and fires you.

Fortunately, there's a better way. Try this:

Running a command in the background

```
% find / -name "embarrassing.document" -print &
% clear
```

Now your `find` command is running along just fine in the background, enabling you to issue the clear command to remove the incriminating evidence. Devious, huh? Well, not too devious—your boss can still issue a `ps` command to see what you're doing, but it's better than nothing. And besides, whose boss knows these tricks? Bosses don't read useful books like this. They generally stop at the Sunday funnies and the business section (truthfully, so do I, although some Sundays I've had trouble telling the two apart).

The ampersand tells UNIX to put this job into the background. As the command completes its dirty work, it will put its results onto your screen. That's fine, until you're tired of having it running. How do you stop it? You have several options.

First, try bringing it to the foreground and killing it:

```
% fg
find / -name "embarrassing.document" -print &
^C
```

The `fg` command means foreground, and it takes the last job you put into the background and moves it into the foreground. The shell responds by printing out the name of the command as though you typed it. Now you can type `Ctrl + C` to break out of the task, just as you would with any other command you wanted to halt. On another note, if you're using the C shell you could do this:

```
% jobs
[1] + Running   find / -name "embarrassing.document" -print
% kill %1
```

The `jobs` command lists all the jobs you have running. (Show that command to the next person who complains that UNIX commands are hard to remember.) Just feed the `kill` command the job number preceded by a percent sign to kill it. You could also run a `ps` command to see every process associated with your username, and then use the `kill` command with the process ID number. But the other ways are simpler, and simple is good.

SIMPLE SYSTEM ADMINISTRATION

> Since brevity is the soul of wit, and tediousness the limbs and outward flourishes, I shall be brief.
>
> William Shakespeare
> *Hamlet*, 1600

Speaking of simplicity, having lots of things going on at once complicates life a little bit. Mostly it means that, if you're sitting at a UNIX PC or workstation, don't just turn it off at the end of the day: You could interrupt an important process. Or someone could have logged on to your system over a network while you weren't looking. If you just flip the power switch, your system *will* turn off—those incomplete processes can leave bits and pieces of files all over your disk, or they could corrupt some part of an important file. Not to mention p.o.ing someone needlessly. Just because it doesn't look like something's happening doesn't mean it isn't. (Keep telling yourself that about our government, too.)

**Shutting down
your system**   This is probably the most important lesson in this chapter—how to turn your computer off. First, note that you can only execute the following commands if

you're the superuser, also called root. You can get to be the superuser in several ways, but they all require the secret password (or they should if your system administrator is worth his or her salary). You may need the secret handshake and the Colonel's secret recipe, too, but I doubt it.

The easiest way to begin is to log in under the username "root." When prompted for your login name, type `root`, and when prompted for the root password, enter it. But of course, I have a better way. Type

```
$ su
```

This command stands for superuser, and should make you rootlike. It'll prompt you for the root's password (provided your system administrator hasn't disabled this command or hidden it somewhere). The `su` command is very useful, because it enables you to become other people, too. You can enter `su woody` to become Woody (if you have Woody's password, which I happen to know).

There are other variations on this theme. One of my favorites is this:

```
$ rlogin localhost -l root
```

This command should have much the same effect as logging in from scratch as `root`. Sometimes you'll find that your system administrator has left a security loophole that you can drive through with this command: It may not prompt you for a password, thanks to some improper modifications to a file called `.rhosts`.

Once you're firmly rooted on your system, you'll find that there are many commands that can safely shut down your computer, and that you can use them different ways in different circumstances. On most systems, you'll use a simple command like this:

```
$ shutdown
```

Your computer will pull the plug on users, background processes, and finally the UNIX kernel itself. On some systems you have to be in the root directory (/) to issue this command; on some you have to be logged in at the console (a terminal connected to a special port at the back of the computer). When in doubt, consult the `man` page by typing `man shutdown`. Then wait for UNIX to tell you that you can flip the power switch.

Sometimes you just want to bring the system down and bring it right back up again (usually to clear some error that won't go away otherwise, or to effect some drastic change, like the installation of a new kernel). For that you use the reboot command:

```
$ reboot
```

But if you can't use these commands, try this for shutdown:

```
$ init 0
```

And try this for reboot:

```
$ init 5
```

The `init` command is pretty cool, when you get to know it. On many systems, `init` is actually a daemon (remember those?) that controls your system's running state. When you type the `init` command and follow it with a number, you're actually giving the `init` daemon a new directive for how it's supposed to run your system. The number 0 tells `init` to shut everything down. The number 2 tells `init` to bring your system into full multiuser mode, and the number 5 says, reboot the system.

The number 1 is special. In addition to being the loneliest number, it says, "Make this very powerful, multiuser UNIX computer into a single-user machine that I can boss around." Single-user mode (the single user will be root) works only from the system's console (the terminal or monitor hooked directly up to the back of the machine). You use it when you want to effect some major change to the system and don't want others logged in. You can also use it (as I do) to run benchmarks and run programs that could potentially alter the behavior of the system in a most unpleasant way (earning the everlasting ire of other users). Single-user mode is also great for digging yourself out of a hole: Say you just installed some new piece of software and now you can't mount half of the system's disk drives. On some systems, this can prevent the system from booting into multiuser mode. You should be able to boot into single-user mode, break out the administrator's troubleshooting guide, and save the day.

The moral of this story is that

```
$ init 1
```

is a good thing to know in a pinch.

SADISTICS

"What are we supposed to do." It was hard to tell who he was talking to.

Robert B. Parker
Pale Kings and Princes, 1987

Some people attach a vacuum gauge to their car so they can know exactly what the engine is doing all the time. I don't. Personally, I don't really care what my car does as long as what it's doing isn't breaking down. I do, however, have a vacuum gauge on my UNIX system. When I'm lucky, I'm working on a Silicon Graphics workstation and I can use their tool called `gr_osview`. It's a really attractive tool that tells me how much of the CPU is being used, how heavy the I/O is, and what's going on the network. Most UNIX systems don't have anything nearly as nice, and you'll be stuck with some pretty unattractive monitoring tools.

Probably the most often-used command to find out what's going on is `who`. It's a simple command to tell you who's logged on to the system. You can get more information from `who` with `who -a` (which shows all sorts of useful stuff like which `tty` they're on and how much CPU time they're eating).

Using who

If you need to look at your driver's license every time someone asks you your name, you'll appreciate `whoami` (or `who am i`, depending on what version of UNIX you have). These commands will tell you your username, which host you're logged into, and what terminal you're on (among other things). I use `who am i` all the time when I'm flipping between my own account and the root's account. There's nothing worse than running `rm -r *` and finding out that you're the root and are now blowing away everything on your computer.

After these two, C shell users will probably find the `jobs` command the next most useful. It tells you all the commands you're running in the background.

Finding jobs

A grander version of `jobs` is `ps`. Run by itself it tells you what processes you're running. You'll probably find that you've got a shell of some kind, and are running `ps`. If you're at an X terminal, you'll also see that you're running an `xterm` session. The true power of `ps` comes with its myriad command options. Check out your `man` page on `ps` (type `man ps`) to see what the options are. You can easily overwhelm yourself with its output.

Using ps

You'll probably also want to know `df` (disk free) and `du` (disk usage), the two disk information programs. The former gives you a list of the disk volumes on your computer and tells you how much free space each has left. It's really for system administrators wondering where they're going to install another program, but you can use it to see some cool stuff about what's going on with your computer. The output looks something like this:

Disk statistics

```
/    (/dev/dsk/c0t0d0s0 ): 267504 blocks  73976 files
/usr (/dev/dsk/c0t0d0s6 ): 290694 blocks 131450 files
```

Vince Chen adds: "This is my gripe about SVR4 versions of this command. Why doesn't it use kilobytes as the units, rather than 512-byte blocks? Who thinks in multiples of 512 anyways? On Solaris, you can use `df -k` or `du -k` to report in kilobytes, but this option is not universal." Hear! Hear!

Dan Watts adds even more: "BSD's `df` command tells you in-use and avail. Much nicer than the System V output." The BSD output is

```
# df -k
Filesystem      Type  kbytes      use    avail %use  Mounted on
/dev/root       efs    15522     8821     6701  57%  /
/dev/usr        efs   584803   461735   123068  79%  /usr
```

Some SVR4 systems interpret –k to mean "show in BSD format."

As a user, du will probably be more up your alley. It tells you how much space each of your files is taking up. It's very useful on systems where the system administrator has placed disk quotas.

sar (yuck)   The king of the hill here is `sar`, the system activity reporter. It's a total bear to figure out, but it can yield some interesting results. In a nutshell, your system administrator tells `sar` to watch the system, which it does. It happily dumps regular snapshots of the system into a file. You then look at that file using `sar` to see what happened.

But these are only the run-of-the-mill, must-know process monitoring commands. You want the real dirt. Try `netstat`. This command has the power to tell you everything your computer is doing with its network connection. At the very least, try `netstat -i`. This version prints out a short list that describes every network card in your computer and what network address each has.

EDITORS

> "E. E. Cummings"
>
> e. e. cummings's editor
>
> Of all my verse, like not a single line;
> But like my title, for it is not mine.
> That title from a better man I stole:
> Ah, how much better, had I stol'n the whole!
>
> Robert Louis Stevenson
> *Kidnapped,* 1886

Editors cause nearly as many fistfights as the BSD vs. SVR4 debate. I'm a big fan of one called emacs, but not every UNIX system has it. They do all have vi, though. You've probably heard about vi. Usually in phrases like, "It may be bad, but at least it isn't vi." Or, "You know how some things beat a sharp stick in the eye? Well vi doesn't."

But it's there, and it beats `ed` to heck and back. In case you're wondering, `ed` is the UNIX counterpart to DOS's `EDLIN`. It works one line at a time. Using `ed` is like trying to pick up one grain of rice with chopsticks: possible, but difficult for the uninitiated. Suddenly `vi` looks a lot better.

vi

So let's start by looking at what I know you have: `vi`. To start `vi`, type

```
$ vi test.file
```

You'll enter a world of splendor such as you have never before imagined. Not! Actually, you're about to enter a rather unpleasant place, and I urge you to avoid it if you possibly can.

You'll see a blank screen. Nice, huh? Now, say you want to add some text. Type the letter `i` and then add your brilliant words of wisdom. The `i` command places `vi` into insert mode (hence the `i`—it's not all that bad). So you can insert text. That works great until you make a mistake (and you will).

Let's say you're done typing now, and want to exit. Hit the `Esc` key once, then hit the `:` key. (That's right, type a colon.) You'll see a command line down at the bottom of your screen (if all goes well). Type the letters `wq` and hit `Return`. They stand for write and quit. You've just created a file. Easy, huh?   **Exiting `vi`**

Next, reopen that file in `vi`. You're about to learn how to navigate (move up, down, and sideways). You may think that you can use the arrow keys to do this. In fact, you probably can, but I can't guarantee it. So I'll teach you the way that works on every keyboard there is: `hjkl`. Back in the days before the modern keyboard, most computer keyboards more closely resembled typewriters than today's computer keyboards. And typewriter keyboards don't have arrow keys. But they do have the letters *h*, *j*, *k*, and *l*.

The person writing `vi` took advantage of this, and assigned these keys the motions described in Table 1.6.

Table 1.6 Moving in `vi`.

Key	Direction
h	Move one character to the left
j	Move one line down
k	Move one line up
l	Move one character to the right

One thing: These keys will move your cursor only when you're not in insert mode, so you may want to make it a practice to hit the `Esc` key before using them.

Whoever designed `vi` made use of some other keys as well. Table 1.7 shows the ones I always use.

Table 1.7 Simple `vi` editing.

Key	Effect
x	deletes the character under the cursor
a	appends a character after the one the cursor's on
A	appends a character to the end of the line (remember that UNIX is case-sensitive)

There's a lot more to `vi` than just inserting characters and moving the cursor around. There's a kind of clipboard comparable to that of most word processors, so you can cut and paste. There are also faster ways of getting around documents (in pagefuls), but I'll get into those later.

Now that you know the universal `vi` commands, try your delete key, backspace key, arrow keys, and page up and page down keys. Chances are that they work just as you'd expect. I just wanted you to get a feel for how nasty `vi` is. And no, I'm not a very nice person.

emacs

> Editor: A person employed on a newspaper, whose business it is to separate the wheat from the chaff, and to see that the chaff is printed.
>
> Elbert Hubbard
> *Roycroft Dictionary and Book of Epigrams*, 1923

Now that you know a bit about `vi`, try typing `emacs`. If you get an error message, you probably don't have it readily available on your computer. If you get a text editor, boy are *you* in luck!

The premier version of `emacs` was written by Richard Stallman and comes from the GNU (pronounce "g") project. Why is it so much better than `vi`? Because it uses control key combinations rather than a command line to do its stuff. So instead of typing

```
Esc:e filename
```

to open a new file as you do in `vi`, you type

```
Ctrl+X Ctrl+F filename
```

One thing you should know right now is that when `emacs` talks about a `Meta` key (as in `Meta+v`) it can mean either "hit `Esc`, then hit `v`" or "hold down the `Alt` key and hit `v`." You'll have to experiment to see what works on your keyboard, but hitting `Esc` first should always work.

Table 1.8 shows a quick list of `emacs` keystrokes.

Table 1.8 The emacs way.

Sequence	Effect
`Ctrl+v`	Page down
`Meta+v`	Page up
`Ctrl+x, Ctrl+c`	Exit
`Ctrl+x, Ctrl+f filename`	Open `filename`
`Ctrl+g`	Abort whatever command you just started
`Ctrl+x, u`	Undo
`Ctrl+f`	Move forward one character
`Ctrl+b`	Move back one character
`Ctrl+n`	Move down one line
`Ctrl+p`	Move up one line
`Ctrl+e`	Move to end of line
`Ctrl+a`	Move to beginning of line
`Ctrl+h`	Help

You'll probably be able to adjust to `emacs` more quickly than to `vi` simply because it comes closer to the What-You-See-Is-What-You-Get editing we're mostly used to on PC word processors.

WHERE TO GET HELP

> Something between a hindrance and a help.
>
> William Wordsworth
> *Michael,* 1800

No matter how much anyone might wish, there's far too much to know about UNIX for anyone, even a genius like *moi,* to encapsulate in one book. So here are some places you can turn to for extra help.

Dirty old man

UNIX's much-maligned `man` pages have a certain charm. They're not very well-written, they sometimes have errors, and they take up a lot of disk space, but at least there are a lot of them. Nearly one for every command. You just type `man` plus a command and UNIX pops up a nice page full of text explaining what that command does, what its command-line parameters are, any known bugs, and (frequently) a bunch of examples.

Searching through man

The problem arises when you don't know what command you need. The man pages assume you already know and just need a refresher course. Most of us don't already know. That's where you use man -k, apropos, or whatis. Each of these three commands (and you may not have all three on your computer, so try them all) searches something called the whatis database. This database contains a tremendous list of command names with one-line descriptions of what they do. These commands search every word in the database to find something that matches the word you're looking for. Say you wanted to know about bitmap files. The man pages would give you output something like what's shown in Figure 1.10.

```
xterm
# man -k bitmap
atobm           bitmap (1)      - bitmap editor and converter utilities for X
bitmap          bitmap (1)      - bitmap editor and converter utilities for X
bmtoa           bitmap (1)      - bitmap editor and converter utilities for X
magnify         magnify (6)     - screen bitmap magnifier
makeafb         makeafb (1)     - create bitmap files from scalable F3 font files
mkiconfont      mkiconfont (1)  - make an  .SM ASCII  cursor or icon font from a list o
files
postdmd         postdmd (1)     - PostScript translator for DMD bitmap files
#
```

Figure 1.10 Searching the man pages.

It's a little hard to read, but it's very useful—like flipping the pages of a dictionary just to get a feel for language.

If you get an error, get your system administrator to follow the instructions on the catman man page for making the whatis database. Usually it's a command like catman -w. Yes, it takes up disk space, but it's probably the most useful help tool to be found on every flavor of UNIX.

System-specific help

Which brings me to flavors of UNIX with their own help systems. IBM has one (info explorer) and Sun has one (Answer Book). Other vendors probably have them, too. For the most part, these systems supplement the man pages by putting extra manuals on line. For the most part, they're not worth as much as the man pages.

When confronted with a nonstandard help system, just say man.

The Good Books

> A book ought to be like a man or a woman, with some individual
> character in it, though eccentric, yet its own; with some blood in its veins
> and speculation in its eyes and a way and a will of its own.
>
> John Mitchell
> *Jail Journal*, 1854

Fortunately for all of us, there are many good sources of reference material about UNIX. For example, there's this book that you are so lovingly reading. But this is only one of a range of excellent (and not-so-excellent) books. Here are the books I keep on my shelf.

O'Reilly and Associates doesn't quite have a lock on the UNIX book market, but they do turn out consistently the best or near-best books. In particular, look for *UNIX Power Tools,* by Jerry Peek, Tim O'Reilly, Mike Loukides, and Al. You know Al, right? As in "et al." It's a must-browse.

Anything from O'Reilly and Associates

If you're hard-core, you'll want a copy of *UNIX System V: System Manuals* published by Prentice Hall. It's painful to read, but it's a pretty darn complete guide to SVR4. If you're a BSDer, try *4.3 Berkeley Software Distribution: Manual Set, Virtual VAX-11 Version*—a wonderful set of books put out by the Department of Electrical Engineering and Computer Science, University of California, Berkeley. With a title like that, it's got to be good, right?

And finally, a book that should be on everyone's shelf is *Life with UNIX: A Guide for Everyone,* by Don Libes and Sandy Ressler published by Prentice Hall. It's not a command-by-command description of UNIX, but an overview of what UNIX is, how it got to be that way, and who the movers and shakers are.

The Internet

> I bought my wife a new car. She called and said there was water in the carburetor. I said, "Where's the car?" She said, "In the lake."
>
> Henny Youngman

If you know enough to go to the Internet for help, you're hard-core already. You can use `anonymous ftp` to get into sites at AT&T and Novell, read the frequently-asked-question (FAQ) files, and copy interesting articles. You can also use Usenet's newsgroups to hear opinions and post difficult questions. Try going to some of these places for help:

- `ftp` to `ftp.novell.com`, log in as `anonymous`, and use your username (the full one, like `jmontgom@pcc.ziff.com`) as your password. Novell owns UNIX. They also post fixes to their network operating system, NetWare, here. What more to say?

- `ftp` to `ftp.microsoft.com`, again log in as `anonymous` and use your username as the password. Microsoft makes the software that makes most PCs go round. It's a good place to download fixes, patches, and problem reports.

- `ftp` to `ftp.att.com`. Or use Mosaic to retrieve the home page for AT&T. Use the URL of `http://tns-www.lcs.mit.edu/commerce.html`. It has a link to AT&T.

SCRIPTS

> If it were done when 'tis done, then 'twere well
> It were done quickly
>
> William Shakespeare
> *Macbeth,* 1606

Now you have the necessary raw materials to write some shell scripts. Put simply, a shell script is a bunch of commands strung together to do something neat. At their best, they're intricate programs.

The simplest shell script starts with you opening a file in an editor such as `vi`, like this:

```
$ vi ./scripttest.sh
```

(We're assuming that you're running the Bourne shell here.) You then add a line like this to start off with:

```
#! /bin/sh
```

On many systems, this line tells the operating system what program to use to execute it. The pound sign (#) means that this line is a comment, but your system can read it anyway.

After that, anything goes. You can insert any commands you like, string them together any old way. Well, not quite. For now, just add these lines:

```
grep `whoami` /etc/passwd | awk -F\: '{print $5}' > /tmp/td
echo "Your user name is"; cat /tmp/td
```

Note the three different types of quotation marks in these commands. You have single-back quotes (`` ` ``), which you'll find below the tilde key (~) on your keyboard. These guys tell a shell to run a command. You have single quotes (`'`), which are a kind of protection, and you have doublequotes (`"`) which are another form of protection.

Exit from your editor and save the file. You can run the script like this:

```
$ sh scripttest.sh
```

Or you can run it by doing this:

```
$ chmod +x scripttest.sh
$ scripttest.sh
```

The `sh` command tells your system to run an instance of the Bourne shell and for that instance to follow the commands in `scripttest.sh`. In a nutshell, this script searches `/etc/passwd` for who you are at this moment, and figures out what your full name is. You should already know this, but it's neat to make UNIX figure it out for you.

As a final note, see Tables 1.9 and 1.10 for my handy top-ten lists of UNIX's most useful commands and keystrokes, respectively. And now, on to the other chapters.

Table 1.9 Top Ten Most Useful Commands.

Command	What it does
10. `ls`	Prints the contents of a directory
9. `cd`	Changes to a directory
8. `rm`	Removes a file
7. `ps`	Shows the processes running
6. `which`	Locates a command
5. `chmod`	Changes a file's permissions
4. `find`	Locates a file
3. `grep`	Locates text within a file
2. `cat` (or `more` or `pg`)	Prints out a file on the screen
1. `vi`	Edits a file

Table 1.10 Top Ten Useful Keystrokes. (Start counting at 6*)

How you'll probably see it	What you'll probably type	What it does
6. `^C`	`Ctrl+c`	Kills the current command
5. `^\`	`Ctrl+\`	The same as `Ctrl+c`
4. `^U`	`Ctrl+u`	Deletes the current line back to the prompt
3. `^Z`	`Ctrl+z`	Suspends the current command (doesn't kill it)
2. `^W`	`Ctrl+w`	Deletes the previous word
1. `^H`	`Backspace`	Deletes the last character you typed

*There are lots of others, and some of them do really interesting things, but this table lists the ones you're likely to use most often. Always remember `Ctrl+c`. And know that you can probably dazzle even hard-core UNIX hackers by knowing more of these key sequences than they do.

2 | This Old Shell

Home Sweet Home

American saying

Honey, would you call a plumber?

Another American saying

I just bought a new house (honest). It's pretty nice. The roof is in good shape (brand new, in fact), the yard is well tended, the house has lots of room, and it's structurally sound. Everyone who has seen it has pronounced it "cute." (Whether I *want* a "cute" house or not is another matter . . .) All in all, it's a good house, except for the brown shag carpet ("good for hiding dirt," the real estate agent proclaimed), the sea-foam green bathroom ("classic," I believe, was her term for it), the leaky faucets ("easy to fix"), the preponderance of cement in the backyard ("a nice patio"), and the tremendous expanse of brown paint and natty brick on the exterior (stumped her on that one).

But nothing is perfect, right? And I'm pretty good with my hands. (At least, I haven't managed to hack both of them off with a radial-arm saw. Yet.) The carpet will come up with a yank and a tug to reveal lovely hardwood floors (I hope), a coat of paint will make the bathroom less reminiscent of a five-martini morning after, installing a washer takes a minute, the cement can be broken up and carted away, and I used to paint houses for gas money. *Nooooo* problem.

UNIX is a lot like my house: There are always one or two commands I really want to work a little differently (fortunately, none of them is painted brown). And some of the default keyboard mappings just don't work for me at all. And, of course, I just want my account to look like *my* account, not some generic, oatmeal-boring, straight-out-of-the-box account that some system administrator threw together when he got the e-mail that I was joining the firm.

Fortunately, adapting UNIX to your wants and needs is simple. Usually. And even if it isn't simple, at least it's possible. Heck, half the fun of UNIX is figuring out

The similarity

Dot files

how to make your account look sufficiently different from everyone else's. It's the best time-waster since somebody ported Tetris to every operating system there is.

Most shell customization (the more-or-less official term) is done in these things called dot files—files whose names start with a period, or "dot" (hence the name). You'll probably find a bunch of them in your home directory. Try typing `ls -a ~` (or `ls -a $HOME`, if you're in the Bourne or Korn shell).

These files have a Rasputinlike effect on your shell. Just tell the dot file what you want and your shell obeys mindlessly. In this chapter, we'll deal with the commands and customizations you can put into your shell's dot files so that your account opens, acts, and closes exactly the way you want it to.

One word of warning. As the czar found out, Rasputin's power can become injurious. With him at your side, you may forget what it's like to deal with ordinary shells. When you work at a different computer or on a different person's account . . . well, let's just say that without Raspy at your side, if you don't know how your shell behaves *sans* personal adjustments, you'll feel like you're in a new world.

That said, let's fire up our drill presses and table saws, break out our hammers, chisels, and screwdrivers, buy up a heap of plywood, and start fixing all those dangling problems with our UNIX home.

CHOOSE YOUR TOOLS

Every tool carries with it the spirit by which it has been created.

Werner Karl Heisenberg
Physics and Philosophy, 1958

Okay, maybe not yet. Before I tell you to start editing files, it's probably a good idea to give you a hint about what the heck's going on. Here's the quick overview: you log in, UNIX starts a shell for you, the shell reads your customizations from some files whose names start with periods (dot files), and then you're in business.

Which shell?

Think you're ready to start editing? Not quite. That's because somebody decided that each and every shell should behave differently—like children. Only less noisy. So, the first thing you gotta do is figure out which shell you're running and which shell you want to be running.

Perhaps the most annoying thing about shells is that someone else usually decides which one you're going to run long before you fire up your account for the first time. I take it back—not "perhaps." No, it's definitely the most annoying thing. The person responsible for forcing you to work their way is called the system administrator. He or she has a great deal of power. You'll probably be dealing with your system administrator at least once when you read this chapter, so it pays to be nice to him or her. (In case you're wondering, you can always tell system administrators from other people because they tend to have nervous tics and are always rushing someplace.)

Anyway, step one in customizing your shell is figuring out which one you have. For the quickest results, try typing this at your prompt (which in my case is a $):

```
$ echo $SHELL
```

The echo command says "tell me what I just said." You can use it to get your shell to say things to you. More importantly, you can use it to get your shell to evaluate **environment variables** (that's what the thing after the second dollar sign is). The dollar sign says to the echo command, "what comes after me is a variable, so don't just repeat $SHELL, go out and figure out what this variable really means, and tell me that instead." You should get a response like /sbin/sh or /bin/sh or /bin/csh, or something similar. That's your default, login shell.

A quick note on environment variables. They're kind of hard to explain, but imagine being able to wake up in the morning and say something like, "Weather: Cloudy. Breakfast: Eggs. Clothes: Blue suit." And when you get out of bed, your mandates will have taken effect. The words to the left of the colon would be environment variables, and the things to the right would be what you define them as. Your shell looks at a bunch of environment variables before you ever see a prompt, and it determines what it's going to look like. We're going to be modifying a lot of them in this chapter, so if you don't have the picture now, you will soon.

There are times when $SHELL won't be set or it won't be set correctly. That's because this environment variable holds the value it was set to when you logged in—it'll hold the correct value of your login shell, but if you've started another shell, it won't be correct anymore. For example, say my login shell is /sbin/sh, but I ran the command csh. Now, when I type echo $SHELL, it'll come back and say that my shell is /sbin/sh, but I know and you know that I'm really in the C shell. That's why figuring out what shell you're running is a two-step process. Step one is the echo command. Step two is the ps command. (See Figure 2.1.)

Which shell? step 2

```
% echo $SHELL
/sbin/sh
% ps
   PID TTY      TIME COMD
   207 pts/0    0:00 sh
   465 pts/0    0:00 csh
   472 pts/0    0:00 ps
%
```

Figure 2.1 Get the shell out of here!

After running the echo command, just type ps. If you see anything in the far-right column that looks suspiciously like a shell (hint: look for unpronounceable names with an "sh" somewhere in them) and it isn't the value returned by the echo command, then you're currently "shelled out" to this shell. If you are shelled out, you can type exit to return to the shell you shelled out from.

Being shelled out is one of the joys of UNIX: If a particular shell doesn't do what you want, just use another. The most important thing is that you shouldn't have to shell out very often; so, if the shell you log in under isn't the one you want, you should change it.

Which Shell Do You Want?

> What is the perfect way to happiness?
> To stay at home.
>
> Bhartrihari
> *The Niti Sataka,* ca. 625 AD

Now you know what shell your system administrator thought you should be running. It's probably okay to stick with whatever shell that is for now, but you're probably going to want to switch to a different one soon. At the very least, you're probably going to want to play around with different login shells. If you're *really* nice to the system administrator, you should be able to switch to a different default shell relatively easily. I recommend flowers and chocolates.

Choose a shell   I can't pick your shell for you. I have a favorite shell for working (the C shell) and a favorite shell for learning (the Korn shell) and a favorite shell for making horrendous syntax errors (the Bourne shell). To help you choose, here's a very (very, very) brief rundown of what each shell's good at.

- The Bourne Shell. Creator: Steve Bourne. The mother of all shells. Every UNIX system has a Bourne shell. In fact, UNIX needs it in order to boot. It's a little primitive (maybe *Paleolithic* is a better term), lacking sophisticated line editing or command recall features. I'd recommend against making this your default login shell. In fact, I'd suggest that you should probably seek professional help if you like it. For interactive use, both the C shell and the Korn shell are better, and Korn is at least as good as Bourne for shell scripts. The Bourne shell's trump card is that it's on every system: if you learn it on one, it'll be there on every other.

- The C Shell. Creator: University of California at Berkeley (probably Bill Joy). It's very usable (for example, it was the first shell to keep a record, called a history, of commands typed), but it isn't on every system (try that Motorola's

UNIX for a truly unfun time). The C shell's main problem is that it's pretty temperamental about interpreting special characters like ! on the command line: It thinks it knows what they mean, even if you're expecting it to think differently.

- The Korn Shell. Creator: David Korn. Combines the best of the Bourne shell (excellent shell script capabilities) with great features from the C shell (command history, command-line editing). It's fully Bourne-shell compatible (and uses that slightly awkward syntax), so your Bourne shell scripts should run without a problem. You're a little less likely to have a Korn shell on your system than a C shell because it's a little younger. It does, however, ship with every new copy of SVR4, so it's gaining force. If you can, you probably want to use it for just about everything you do.

Most every other shell is built on either a Bourne shell-like or C shell-like interface. Basically, once you understand Bourne shell and C shell syntax, you've got it made. Here are some of the others:

- The tsch shell. A version of the C shell with improved command-line editing.

- The jsh shell. The Bourne shell with job control. Don't bother unless you have to.

- The bash shell. Bourne-again shell—similar to the Korn shell.

Try them all to see which you like best. I love to play with the Korn shell, but **I'm Korny** I know the C shell a whole lot better. So when the going gets tough, I run for the good old, familiar, friendly % prompt of the C shell.

Once you've decided that you prefer one shell over the others, just drop a note to your system administrator asking him/her to change it. I recommend using something friendly and subtle like this:

Dear Bonehead, **Don't do this**
    I'm glad to see that your lobotomy was effective. Why else would you make me use the [insert your default shell here] shell? I want you to change it to [insert your preferred shell here] or [insert threat of physical violence here].
Love,
[insert your name here]

You should find your shell changed. You may also find all your files deleted, but that's life.

> Some of the more advanced UNIX systems have a command called chpass that enables you to change your default settings. Run the command man chpass for more information (and to see if it's installed on your system).

If you can't get your system administrator to change your login shell (usually for security reasons), never fear: You can run the shell of your choice with the greatest of ease. Shells are just programs, and, like any other program, you can run them by typing their name. You want Bourne shell? Type `sh`. Feel like C shell? Type `csh`. Korn shell for dinner? It's `ksh` for that one (don't forget the butter). There are a couple of drawbacks to running a second shell. One is that it's an extra step you've got to make. Another is that it's one more process your computer has to keep track of (most UNIX systems limit the total number of processes you can run—but the number is pretty darn high, so don't sweat it). Finally, there are times when you'll be running a shell script or program that will make reference to your login shell and not the overlaid shell you prefer.

Basically, if you don't like your shell, get it changed.

Shells and Their Dot Files

> It was said of old Sarah, Duchess of Marlborough, that she never puts dots over her *i*'s, to save ink.
>
> Horace Walpole, 1785

Now that you have a favorite shell, it's time to change it. (See, UNIX *is* just like a home: You pick the one you like best and change it.) The way your shell treats you is handled by one or two files. They're some of those dot files I was talking about earlier. They're called dot files because you read their names aloud (and to yourself) like this: dot-profile, dot-login, and so on. Table 2.1 contains the quick-and-dotty list.

Table 2.1 Dotting the shells.

Shell	Dot files
Bourne shell	`.profile`
C shell	`.login` and `.cshrc`
Korn shell	`.profile` and `.kshrc`

Other shells mostly follow along with either the Korn shell or the C shell. Take `tcsh`, for example. It uses `.login` (yes, the same `.login` that `csh` uses) and `.tcshrc`.

Home is ~   Okay, now plunk yourself down at your terminal and look for these files. Change to your home directory (`cd ~` or `cd $HOME`). Now type `ls`. You don't see them. Type `ls` again. You still don't see them. Now for the magic third time: type `ls`. Guess what? They aren't there. Why? Because they're hidden. Files whose names start with a dot are invisible to the normal `ls` command. It's a handy way to hide configuration files that you probably don't muck with very much.

> **You can create not only files, but whole directory trees that are hidden like this. It's a kind of poor man's or woman's security device, to keep prying eyes from finding any obviously incriminating files (like `resume.doc` or `loveletter.txt`). Just start any directory or file name with a dot and it's hidden.**

If you want to see what all your dot files are, try typing `ls -a`. The -a tells `ls` to show all the files that are there.

```
                                        xterm

solaris:/usr/people/john - 12 - Sat Jul  9 14:02:29 PDT 1994 - biff is n
% ls
testscript.sh

solaris:/usr/people/john - 13 - Sat Jul  9 14:02:29 PDT 1994 - biff is n
% ls -a
.                    .cshrc             .openwin-init        .sh_history
..                   .desksetdefaults   .openwin-init.BAK    .xnews.solaris:0
.Xauthority          .login             .profile             testscript.sh

solaris:/usr/people/john - 14 - Sat Jul  9 14:02:29 PDT 1994 - biff is n
%
```

Figure 2.2 Playing hide and seek.

As you can see in Figure 2.2, I have a lot of dot files. Most of them are specific to the version of UNIX I'm running (Solaris for x86). If you look among them, you'll see the dot files I was talking about above (configuration files).

For now, let's take a closer look at the C and Korn shells. What's so special about them that they get two startup files? Do they think they're *better* than the Bourne shell or something? Probably not (although some inveterate C shell users might argue that point), but their Creators realized that there are two different times you want customizations to occur: When you launch a brand-spanking-new shell—that is, when you log in—and when you're just running a new shell from an old one (like lighting a cigarette from another one).

Here's what I mean. The C shell will read `.cshrc` any time you start a C shell. That means not only when you log in, but also when you run shell scripts and when you escape to the C shell from a program. No matter what, when you start a C shell, whether you're running a script that calls the C shell or shelling out from a program or logging in, you run whatever is in your `.cshrc`. It's the best place to put stuff you want executed every time you do something C shell-oriented.

The C shell has two initialization files

The /bin/csh program will read .login when you log in (hence the name—clever, no?), but also when you start any new login shell (for example, if you log in again). For commands that you want to be executed only when you're performing an actual, human, interactive login, use .login. For example, if you run a window system such as the X Window System, clearly you don't want all your shell scripts to start a new copy of X every time you run them. You only want X to start up when you're really logging in. Other commands that go well here are terminal customization commands (**keyboard mappings**, which make your keys do new and interesting things) and your environment variables.

The Korn shell does pretty much the same thing with .kshrc (every time) and .profile (only when you log in).

A NOTE ON SHOP SAFETY

> "And always remember to wear *these* . . . safety glasses."
>
> Norm Abram
> *New Yankee Workshop*

Norm Abram may have predictable taste in clothes (plaid shirts and jeans *again*?) but he's right about many things. Like safety: Covering your patootie is the most important thing you can do. (One thing he *isn't* right about is how easy it is to build that pencil-post bed.)

Norm wears safety glasses (which look suspiciously like regular glasses to me, but who am I to say?); I make backups. Religiously. Nothing is worse than changing a critical file, screwing up, and having nothing to revert to. So I'll paraphrase Norm: "Always remember to make *these* [gesture toward the disk drive] . . . backup copies." It's an intelligent practice for any file. A good editor such as emacs will keep a backup file for you. Most don't. You'll probably need to develop some backup habits. Here's one I have:

```
$ cp .cshrc .good.cshrc
$ vi .cshrc
```

The first command, the cp command, copies .cshrc into .good.cshrc. The second command, vi, opens .cshrc into a text editor named (guess . . .) vi. So if something goes wrong, you can just cp .good.cshrc back into .cshrc and you're up and running again. Here's another way that works really well:

```
$ mkdir backup
$ cp .* backup
$ vi .cshrc
```

To recover from an ill-conceived edit with this second scheme, enter `cp backup/` `.cshrc ./.cshrc`.

Another tip regards testing your changes. After you change one of these files, **Test your** test it out with the `rlogin` or `su -` command. For example, say you've just **changes** finished editing your `.cshrc` file and you want to see if it works. Don't log out and then log back in again. Use this command:

```
$ rlogin localhost
```

This command will log you in to your computer again and execute your startup files. Alternately, you can substitute `telnet` for `rlogin` with similar results. If you get an error, you should be able to log out or cancel the `rlogin` session and restore the backup file. Another way to accomplish the same thing is with the `su`, or superuser, command:

```
$ su - username
```

Here *username* is your login name (if you don't supply that, the system will try to log you in as root, which won't test what we want). The dash after `su` tells `su` to execute all your login scripts.

In either case, you'll not find yourself locked out of your account.

VARIABLE SPEED

> We seek the truth, and will endure the consequences.
>
> Charles Seymour

Enough introductions! Time to edit some files. Time to tune your UNIX hot rod. Time to . . . Time to . . . uh, do really neat stuff. Finally what you've been waiting for! Thought I'd never get around to it, didn't you?

Type `env`. Go ahead. You'll see a list of your environment variables. (If you don't, try typing `printenv`—different command, same effect, typical UNIX.) Actually looking at them is a lot faster than trying to explain each one—there are hundreds of the little buggers. They control how UNIX reacts when you type commands, what your prompt looks like, where your shell searches for commands, what kind of coffee is in the office coffee machine (yuck—vanilla-mocha-java-peanutbrittle crunch), and how most of your programs function.

You control most of your environment variables with commands like `setenv` (C shell) and `export` (Bourne shell). The `setenv` command is the C shell's way of setting environment variables. That, at least, makes sense. For the Bourne shell, you've got to set a variable, then `export` it to the shell so that the shell can see it. Otherwise, you've defined a variable in vain.

Anything I discuss below you can stick into one of your dot files, usually `.profile` (Bourne shell) or `.cshrc` (C shell) or `.kshrc` (Korn shell). If something needs to go into a different file, I'll say so specifically.

Now let's change those environment variables, starting with the really important ones: PATH and PROMPT.

Path to Enlightenment

> In this world, aspirants may find enlightenment by two different paths. For the contemplative is the path of knowledge; for the active is the path of selfless action.
>
> *Bhagavad Gita*, ca. 500 BC

Most important   The PATH environment variable is the king, the ruler, and, most important of all, the variable you can change (some variables, like SHELL, get set when you log in and you probably don't want to screw with them, although you can). It controls where the shell looks for commands. Because it's so important, we're going to deal with it first. Type this:

```
$ echo $PATH
```

You'll see all the directories your shell will search when looking for commands. Figure 2.3 shows mine.

```
# echo $PATH
/usr:/usr/bin:/usr/ucb:/etc:/bin::/usr/openwin/bin
#
```

Figure 2.3 Seek and ye shall find.

You can change the PATH variable easily enough with this command:

(Bourne and Korn shells)
```
$ PATH=/usr/sbin
$ export PATH
```

(C shell)
```
% setenv PATH /usr/sbin
```

However, you'll find that, rather than *adding* /usr/sbin to your path, this command redefines PATH to search *only* /usr/sbin. Not useful, McGee. So, let's try adding /usr to your path. How, oh how, might we do this? Is it documented? I don't *THINK* so. Does the guy down the hall know? Bzzzz, thanks for playing. But *I* know. Will you worship at my feet? I don't *THINK* so. Anyway, here's how I do it:

The wrong way to set a path

```
$ PATH=$PATH:/usr/sbin
$ export PATH
```

C shell users have a slightly different thing to do. That's because their path is defined in two places. I'm still not sure why, but I'm sure that, like fishing, as I grow older it will make sense. The first (the PATH variable) sets the second (the path variable). Upper- and lowercase. (There seems to be no earthly difference, except syntax. Uppercase PATH uses colons to separate entries; lowercase path uses spaces.) So when you enter setenv PATH /usr/sbin, you're also doing this:

```
% set path=( /usr/sbin )
```

If you want to add a directory to either your path or your PATH, do this:

```
% set path=( $PATH /usr/sbin )
```

or

```
% setenv PATH ${PATH}:/usr/sbin
```

The C shell's set command used like this uses spaces instead of colons (as setenv does) to separate the different paths.

Of course, once you start messing around with your PATH, you'll pretty soon find that you've munged it beyond recognition. This is to be expected. I did it about a dozen times while writing this section. Fortunately, it's not very hard to make things work again. C shell users, try this:

Fixing path problems: Square one

```
% source ~/.login
```

The C shell's source command reexecutes a dot file. If your path is in .cshrc, you could just as easily use source ~/.cshrc. (Remember that the tilde (~) means "take the one in my home directory.") You can now use printenv to find out what your path is:

```
% printenv PATH
/bin:/usr/local:/usr/local/bin:/usr/people/john/bin:/etc::
```

Bourne and Korn shell users have a slightly different alternative. They use the dot as a command:

```
$ . $HOME/.profile
```

Make sure there's a space between the dot and the beginning of the filename. I don't know why, but I thought that the space had no right to be there for a day after I learned about using the dot like this, and consequently couldn't get it to work.

 Security and your path are intrinsically tied to each other.* This is trebly true when you're the root. Here's the golden rule: Never put your current working directory (. or : or $cwd) as the first element in your path—and it's probably best not to put it in your path *at all*. That's how Trojan horses spread: A cracker puts a rewritten command like ls in some commonly accessed, security-free directory (like his or her home directory), then root changes to that directory to try something, and executes the ls command. Well, root's not running /bin/ ls. Root's running the cracker's version (most shells search for the closest file first—it doesn't matter in what order the directories come in your path). That version could execute rm -r /—a command to blow away the entire hard disk. That would be bad.

So don't put your current directory in your path.

Prompt Attention #1: Hosts and Hostesses

> If you are a host to your guest, be a host to his dog also.
>
> Russian proverb

Sure UNIX is powerful. Sure it's robust. But it's also a heck of a lot of fun, and at least half of the fun of running UNIX is customizing your prompt to do weird things. This is also a useful ability, since you can make your prompt tell you useful information like the name of the machine you're running on, your current working directory, the current time, and your username (which may not seem too useful until you're a system administrator yourself and need to be reminded when you're the root).

It's also easy. This is perhaps its nicest feature.

The PROMPT variable Your prompt is stored in a variable called PROMPT. In the Bourne and Korn shells, you get variables called PS1, PS2, and FS, too—they are the prompts that appear when you continue a command line. Setting them works just the same as setting PROMPT, so I won't go into them.

---

*Hmmm. Bondage.

By default, your C shell prompt is a percent sign, and for the Bourne/Korn shells, it's a dollar sign. But not for long. Try this:

```
% set prompt="_____?"
```

You'll get a prompt that's really stupid:

```
_____?
```

You just set your prompt from one constant (%) to another (_____?). Who cares? The really neat prompt work comes because you can set your prompt to make use of the values in other variables. If I wanted, for example, my computer's name in the prompt, I'd do this:

```
% set prompt="`hostname` %"
```

The magic here is that you're setting a variable to run a command called `hostname`.

> **Single back quotes (below the ~) are a powerful tool. When you're setting a variable, you can place a command into single back quotes and the command will run and then pass its result back to the variable as a string. We're going to be doing a lot of this, so make a note on a Post-It and stick it on the upper right side of your monitor. At the behest of Dan Watts, technical editor, friend, Guru, I make the following exhortation: Post-It notes are great. Only insecure people don't like them. Use them often.**

Your prompt would look like this (on a machine named solaris):

```
solaris %
```

But there's even more you can do (and it's more interesting). For example, if I want my prompt to tell me my hostname and my current path, I would enter

```
% set prompt="`hostname`:${cwd}% "
```

This is the prompt I would get:

```
solaris:/usr/people/john%
```

Note the single trailing space after the % in the command. Without this, I'd have the % butting up against my commands in a most ugly way. Also note the familiar hostname getting evaluated (`` `hostname` ``) and the tag that's evaluating my current directory (`${cwd}`).

Okay, now that you know about single back quotes, it's time to learn about curly brackets (or braces, as I call them). Coupled with the dollar sign, braces evaluate variables kind of like single quotes run commands and pass their values back to variables. Write this on another Post-It and stick it on the upper left side of your monitor. And don't let anyone laugh at you for keeping notes stuck to your monitor.

In the previous example, I could have just as easily used `` `pwd` ``—a command that evaluates the current directory. The reason I chose `${cwd}` is speed. In the C shell `$cwd` is a built-in variable, so it will take a fraction less time to figure it out than would evaluating `` `pwd` ``. And yes, this is true esoterica.

Make your prompt react to new directories

Now your prompt is wonderfully helpful, telling you what directory you're in. Until you `cd` to another, that is. See, set the prompt once like this, and it won't be set again until you manually reset it. These variables aren't dynamic. In fact, they're quite lazy.

That's why you need to put this into your `.cshrc`:

```
alias setprompt 'set prompt="${cwd}% "'
alias cd 'chdir \!* && set cwd=`/usr/bin/pwd` && setprompt'
alias pushd 'pushd \!* && cd .'
alias popd 'popd \!* && cd .'
```

Thanks, Denis

Denis Haskin introduced me to this particular trick. For a full discourse on what the `alias` command does, skip to the Spy vs. Spy section of this chapter. (Just kidding. Try the "When Is a Screwdriver a Chisel?" section.) Here's the dime-novel version: `alias` makes new commands by stringing together old ones. The shell will check for aliases before looking for internal or external commands, so if you define an alias that happens to be an existing command, you won't see that command again until you unset your alias.

Watch to make sure you're using your quotes right. We have here single regular quotes ('), single back quotes (`), and double quotes ("). Make sure you use them right or your commands won't run.

Here's a quickie description of the rest. First you set up a `setprompt` command. (There isn't one already, so you're being creative.) Now you tell `setprompt` that it's supposed to set the prompt to whatever value is in `${cwd}`—that built-in variable we were just talking about.

Next up, you redefine the `cd` command. The `chdir` command does pretty much exactly the same thing—it's just built into the C shell. The string `!*` is a C shell-ism, too. It tells `chdir` to take whatever the last thing on the previous line was as an argument.

Without the backslash (\) right before the `!*`, this line will cause the C shell to barf most unpleasantly. This is as good a place as any to explain a hard fact about shells. They are monsters that eat certain characters. Among these characters are the `!` (in the C shell), the `%`, the `$`, and a couple of others. These characters need protection from the monster. That protection comes in the form of either a quotation mark (single or double), or the backslash. If ever you run a command that looks picture-perfect and you get a shell error, make sure you've protected anything important.

The double ampersand on line two is Mr. Ginsu again, saying, "But wait, there's more." Now we set the value of the variable `cwd` to the current working directory using the `pwd` command (on my system it's in `/usr/bin/pwd`—on most others it's in `/bin/pwd`). Finally, this command runs the `setprompt` command we set up on the previous line.

Now we get to `pushd` and `popd`. These guys are brothers, and their sole goal in life is to make your directory navigation easier. You see, the C shell can keep a stack of the directories you've visited. The `pushd` command pushes directories onto that stack. So, in addition to moving you to a new directory, `pushd` drops bread crumbs to tell you where you've been. You can pick up the bread crumbs with the `popd` command, which pops directories off the stack one by one. If you're forever moving among just a few directories, `pushd` and `popd` will save you hours.

Two better `cd` commands

With these aliases, we just tell `pushd` and `popd` to execute themselves and the `cd` command we just aliased, but to change to the current directory—that's what the dot is. So, rather than changing your directory, this `cd` is just setting the prompt.

Prompt Attention #2: A Bold Step

Only the bold go to the top.

Publilius Syrus
Sententiae, ca. 50 BC

Pretty clever, no? Wanna know what else you can do with your prompt? How about making it really pop off the page by adding some formatting. This is a bit more complicated than the tricks we were just pulling because it depends on what kind of terminal you're sitting at. Most terminals respond favorably to being treated like VT100s from Digital Equipment Corporation, so we'll pretend you're using one of those. If you aren't, the specifics here won't work, but we'll take care of that.

Boldface prompts

It's time to tell a boldfaced prompt. You do that by using escape sequences that tell your terminal to put text into boldface. (This trick never worked particularly well for me because I didn't know how to generate the escape sequences and nobody would tell me. Rather than being sullen and not sharing, I'm going to tell.) An escape sequence is a special bunch of characters you (or a program) can send to your terminal (or workstation or PC or whatever) to make it do weird things. For example, those arrow keys on your keyboard? When you're at a normal shell prompt, hit one and you'll probably get a beep and some odd characters on your screen. That's an escape sequence. Well, there are escape sequences to do all sorts of things to your terminal—make it go black, white, boldfaced, reverse video, or move the cursor just about anywhere. At least there should be—some terminals don't support escape sequences as well as they should.

Anyway, creating an escape sequence means creating an escape character. There are three ways I know to generate an escape character: Hit the `Esc` key (if you have one), type `Ctrl+[` (hold the control key (probably labeled `Ctrl`) and hit the left bracket), or use the ASCII value `033`.

The American Society for Cruel and Inhuman Institutions (ASCII) decided that every key on your keyboard, rather than being just a letter, should be a number. Better yet, it should be an octal number (whatever the heck that is). So the chief torturers got together and pretty much randomly assigned keys to numbers, leading to a booming business in playbooks that list the correspondences. It just so happens that the `Esc` key gets lucky number `033`.

For now, let's assume you have a Digital Equipment Corporate VT100 or are using some kind of terminal that's at least kinda sorta compatible with it. Why the VT100? There are a heck of a lot of them out there and even more that are compatible with it. Plus, I have the table of escape sequences for it handy.

The first thing you need to do is put your escape character in a safe place. A variable will do nicely. So, type this:

```
% setenv ESCAPE="`echo X | tr X '\033'`"
```

Creating an escape variable

What's going on here? An odd thing, actually. You probably get the variable assignment part, up to the =. After that, we get serious magic. We `echo` the character X (an uppercase *x*) into a program called `tr`, for "translate." Translate looks at its input for the letter X and substitutes an escape character. (By surrounding the `033` with single quotes and preceding it with a backslash, `tr` knows that it's supposed to treat the 033 as a single, octal character.) Notice that the whole line has double quotes around it (to protect the spaces) and single back quotes (to cause what's inside to be executed as a command, but to only pass the value back to whatever called it). Incredibly confusing, but you can use it in any shell script without worries.

Now you'll find that an escape character is trapped in the variable ESCAPE. (You could just have easily called this variable E or ESC or anything shorter, by the way. Actually, you probably should, unless you're really into typing.) Why did I choose to generate my escape character like this? Because it's nearly foolproof: I never know if the keyboard I'm going to be working on will have an Esc key or even a Ctrl key, so it's useful to know this little tip.

Now where were we? Ah, yes, generating interesting prompts. I like my prompt to be in boldface, while the rest of the command line isn't. To do that, I'd follow the last line of code with one like this:

```
% set prompt="${ESCAPE}[1m`hostname`:${cwd}%${ESCAPE}[0m "
```

Now I'm humming.

Here's what happened. You know `set prompt` by now. Since I'm creating a compound expression for the value of the prompt, I enclose the whole thing in double quotes. Next, I tell my shell to evaluate the variable ESCAPE (that's what the ${} does), and I tag the VT100 combination for boldface ([1m) onto it. Now I tell it to evaluate `hostname` (that's what the back quotes are for) and then evaluate the variable cwd ({} causes variable evaluation). Finally, I turn boldface off by evaluating ESCAPE again and feeding it [0m. My prompt will now look like this:

solaris:/usr/people/john%

And I look like a pro. Table 2.2 shows some of the other escape sequences you should know:

Table 2.2 There's no escape for *this* VT100.

Sequence	What it'll do
[1m	Boldface
[4m	Underscore
[5m	Blink
[7m	Reverse video
[0m	Go back to being a normal terminal

There are a whole lot more stored in `/etc/termcap` (or in the files in `/usr/lib/terminfo/*` if you're on a System V system), but these files are nearly indecipherable. If you don't have a VT100, you'll need the manual for your terminal in order to figure out what escape sequences make it do interesting and entertaining things.

Prompt Attention #3: Lining Up

> I have a new method of poetry. All you got to do is look over your notebooks . . . or lay down on a couch, and think of anything that comes into your head, especially the miseries. . . . Then arrange in lines of two, three or four words each, don't bother about sentences, in sections of two, three or four lines each.
>
> Allen Ginsberg, 1952

In the meantime, there are neat prompts you can create that don't involve complex anythings. For example, if you use the Korn or C shells, you can create a prompt that spans multiple lines.

Multiline prompt Now you're probably asking yourself why the heck you'd want to do that. Well, let's take a look at our previous prompt. What happens when you get a really, really long directory name? Simple: You don't have any room to type commands. *That's* why you might want a multiline prompt. Creating it is simple, and it doesn't involve any escape sequences. Remember using the alias command up above to create a new **setprompt** command? Well, we're going to do it again, C shell style:

```
alias setprompt 'set prompt="\\
`hostname`:${cwd}\\
% "'
alias cd 'chdir \!* && setprompt'
```

Now what? Well, type **setprompt** and watch your prompt change to something like this:

```
solaris:/usr/people/john
%
```

You just type at the %, and whenever you **cd** to a different directory, the line above your prompt will change. So what's going on? Well, the double backslash forces your prompt to contain a regular-old carriage return. You can, in theory, anyway, have a prompt that's as long as your imagination.

There's one catch to the way I did this, which I soon discovered. The top line of the prompt runs the `hostname` program each time you `cd`. Unfortunately, `hostname` takes about a half second to a second to run, so it takes about that long for your prompt to come up. Never fear, there's a better way: store `hostname`'s value in a variable, then just suck the variable's value out:

Put hostname in a variable

```
set host=`hostname`
alias setprompt 'set prompt="\\
${host}:${cwd}\\
% "'
alias cd 'chdir \!* && setprompt'
```

Now everything should be fine.

> **Vince Chen, my technical editor and a hard-core `tcsh` user, introduced me to a `tcsh` shortcut for getting at the hostname: the string `%m`. And one for getting the history: `%h`. So his prompt setting looks more like this:**
>
> ```
> set prompt="(vince@%m:%h} "
> ```
>
> **So he works at a prompt that looks like this:**
>
> ```
> vince@rti:32
> ```
>
> **Neat, huh?**

There are a million things you can put on this top line of your prompt. Here are my suggestions:

- C shell users, take advantage of the history facility and include a `\!` somewhere in there, like just after the `${cwd}`.
- Include the current time on the top line every time you `cd` to a different directory, by adding `` `date` `` to the line just after `${cwd}`.

If you do everything I suggest, you should have an alias line that looks like this:

```
alias setprompt 'set prompt="\\
${host}:${cwd} - \! - `date` \\
% "'
alias cd 'chdir \!* && setprompt'
```

And you'll have a prompt like this:

```
solaris:/usr/people/john - Wed Jun 29 22:12:46 PDT 1994
%
```

And you'll be the envy of every hacker in the galaxy. Of course, your prompt will also take a minute to calculate each time you hit `Return` (slight exaggeration), but it'll be worth it. If you want to make all that stick every time you log in, go to your home directory (type `cd ~`) and add all those lines to your `.cshrc`.

Automatic Typing

> Think much, speak little, and write less.
>
> Giovanni Torriano
> *Italian Proverbs,* 1666

Filename completion

Everybody knows how to modify `PATH` and `PROMPT`. You need something different. Something to set you apart from the masses. That's what some of this next batch of variables is for—impressing your friends. At least I hope that's what they're for, because I've never thought about them in any other light.

Microsoft Word for Windows has a really neat feature. It's called AutoText. You type a character, Word looks at it, decides that it really means something else (something you've told it to mean), and performs an automatic translation right then and there. This feature got the attention of just about everybody, and it was hailed as a brilliant stroke of genius. Well, folks, Microsoft is behind the times: The C shell has been able to do this for you for *years.* (Even the Korn shell can do it, but you have to enter into one of its editing modes. See the next chapter.)

Hit Esc

It's called file completion. Basically, you type the first few, unique letters of a filename, then hit the `Esc` key and the shell completes the name for you. If you're as speed-conscious as me, you're drooling at this point, thinking, "No longer must I type `accounting.section1.beancounting`." Just enter this command either on a command line or in your `.cshrc`:

```
set filec
```

And BINGO, you're ready for business. Now when you want to open `accounting.section1.beancounting`, you can just type:

```
% ls
accounting.section1.beancounting aptitude.training.money
test.file
% vi acEsc
```

The moment you hit that beautiful `Esc` key, you'll see the name of `accounting.section1.beancounting` expanded fully and probably hear a beep from your terminal. (There are some terminal types on which this doesn't work, most notably Sun's `cmdtool` window.) This only works with unique names. If you had two files that began `accounting.section1`, file completion would complete as much as it could (up to the period after `section1`) then make your terminal beep, warning you that you had a nonunique filename. You've saved yourself some typing, though.

I'm told that not all C shells support filename completion. I haven't met one that doesn't, but if it doesn't work for you, you probably have.

Unfortunately, there are times when you have a lot of files in a directory that have slightly different endings. In these cases, you wind up typing the whole gosh-darn name, even though you never edit some of the files. That's what `fignore` is for. If you're a programmer, you'll be particularly happy with `fignore` (usually pronounced FIG-nore). It enables you to cause file completion to ignore some file name extensions.

Yes, I know that UNIX doesn't require file extensions, nor does it make as much use of them as some other operating systems. But certain applications (like compilers) need them to get their work done. The `fignore` command enables you to arrange for your shell to ignore certain file extensions.

Filename extensions

Let's say you have a directory with one file in it: a source code file called `sourcecode.c`. When you compile it, you get two more files: `sourcecode.o` and `sourcecode`. The file with the `.o` extension is an object file—an intermediate file that many compilers generate and then leave lying around in case it's needed later (which it usually isn't unless you're a serious programmer). In any event, you know you don't ever want to edit `sourcecode.o`. But you *do* want to edit `sourcecode.c`.

If you turn file completion on and type `vi sEsc`, it will start completing your command line, then beep after it flushes it out to `sourcecode`—leaving you to type those last two characters. Horrors! Two characters!!

So, type this:

```
% set fignore ( .o )
```

Now when you hit `Esc`, it will still complete down to `sourcecode` but instead of typing the `.c` yourself, your shell will ignore any file whose name ends `.o` and it will fill in the c for you.

This probably doesn't sound like it's very efficient. It's not. Unless you have a directory full of `.c` and `.o` files with different names (it's very common to see

Don't bother with fignore

this—most programmers create many different files to put source code into and, during the compile, these files are turned into object files that get linked together). Now you can just type a partial file name, hit `Esc`, and you'll see the full filename, including the `.c`. Probably.

You Korn shell users have a slightly different way to get at filename expansion. In a nutshell, you just type `Esc` the same way you hit `Esc` for the C shell. But instead of saying `set filec` as you do with the C shell, you type `set -o vi` (or `set -o emacs`). In addition to giving you command completion, the `set -o` command turns on command-line editing (which we'll get to in the next chapter). For now, be content with using the `Esc` technique to expand directory names and filenames.

Timeliness

> Time is a file that wears and makes no noise.
>
> H.G. Bohn
> *Handbook of Proverbs*, 1855

Fall back, spring forward. Or is it fall forward and spring back? Darn, I forgot again? Well, `TZ` (short for time zone) takes care of that. This variable controls what time your system will report to you when you type `time` or `date`. You set it like any other variable:

```
$ TZ=US/Pacific
$ export TZ
```

But how do you know what the time zone is called? Weeellllll, you look at the files in `/usr/lib/zoneinfo` (on my system, it's in `/usr/share/lib/zoneinfo`). There should be directories with names like US and Canada. They, for their part, should have subdirectories for time zones in those countries. Like US/Mountain, US/Pacific, US/Samoa (yes, Samoa), and so on. You'll probably only use this command when you want to find out what time it is someplace else in the world, but UNIX makes a great universal clock.

The date command On another time-related note, I hate it when I don't have a date. UNIX does, too. That's why there's the wonderful `date` command. We've already used it once (in our prompt), but there's a whole lot more you can do with it than just type `date` to find out what time and day it is. Mostly, you can change the way it presents its output with a couple of single quotes and a plus sign. See, the date command gives you "field descriptors" (letters) that you can precede with a percent sign. Each field descriptor stands for one of the fields in `date`'s output. This is them:

- a abbreviated weekday name
- A full weekday name

- b abbreviated month name
- B full month name
- c locale's appropriate date and time representation
- C default date and time format
- d day of month (1-31)
- h abbreviated month name
- H hour (00-23)
- I hour (1-12)
- j day of year
- m month of year
- M minute
- p insert PM or AM

There are a bunch more, but they're pretty boring to deal with. In essence, though, **Using this info** you can make `date` give you the output you want to see, rather than that nasty, over-complicated, too-terse version it's prone to. For example (Korn shell):

```
# alias datum="date '+It is %A, %B %d at %I:%M %p'"
# datum
It is Thursday, June 30 at 07:57 AM
#
```

Experiment—it'll make you feel better.

Speak! Shut Up!

> Silence is still a noise.
>
> H.W. Shaw
> *Josh Billings' Encyclopedia of Wit and Wisdom*, 1874

When you want to debug a shell script, you want to see what the shell is doing to what you wrote. Most every shell has some capability to print on the screen what it's doing to your commands. In the C shell, the two variables `echo` and `verbose` handle it. So, if you want to see what the shell is doing before it evaluates your shell variables, use this command:

```
% set verbose
```

To see what's happening after it evaluates the variables, use this:

```
% set echo
```

To turn them off, use `unset verbose` and `unset echo`, respectively.

Debugging Bourne and Korn shell scripts   Bourne and Korn shell users have equivalents, but they invoke them differently. The `set -v` and `set -x` commands substitute for `verbose` and `echo`, respectively. If you can, the best way to invoke either of these two friendly commands is from within a shell script, by making the first line read `#! /bin/sh -xv`. Although the pound sign usually means "what comes next is a comment," most shells are clever enough to know that a pound followed by an exclamation point means "read this and make it your shell." When you do that, you get wonderfully verbose debugging output, as shown in Figure 2.4.

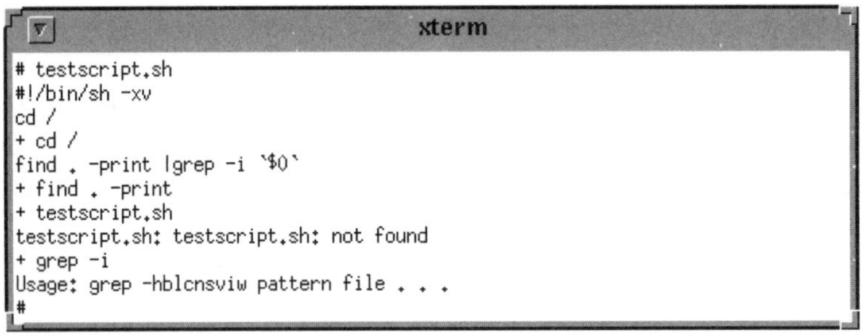

```
# testscript.sh
#!/bin/sh -xv
cd /
+ cd /
find . -print |grep -i `$0`
+ find . -print
+ testscript.sh
testscript.sh: testscript.sh: not found
+ grep -i
Usage: grep -hblcnsviw pattern file . . .
#
```

Figure 2.4 A perfect setup.

WHEN IS A SCREWDRIVER A CHISEL?

> There are moments when everything goes well; don't be frightened,
> it won't last.
>
> Jules Renard

Anyone who has ever used a pair of pliers for a hammer knows what an alias is: It's when you make one thing behave like another. (Actually, UNIX aliases are a lot more elegant than pounding in that eighteen-penny spike with your best set of Vise Grips.)

The alias command   The `alias` command is a tool for making tools. You use the single-quote, double-quote, and piping power of the C or Korn shell to string together many commands to perform one action, then `alias` that string of commands into one nice, brief command name.

Aliasing is one of those things that make the Bourne shell fall down flat on its face. Splat. Ouch. You can get around the problem, but you'll never have true aliases in the Bourne shell. You can get them in the Korn shell, however, so if you're really hooked on Bourne shell syntax and want aliases, try the Korn shell instead.

You can use aliases either on the command line or in one of your dot files. In the examples I'll be using, I'm putting them on the command line. Big deal. Feel free to stick them into your `.cshrc` (or `.kshrc`) file or even your `.login` or `.profile` files. Experiment with the difference—some aliases go better in one place or the other.

The basic syntax of an alias is pretty much what you'd expect:

```
% alias what-you-want-it-called all-the-commands-you-want
```

For example, a standard C shell alias is:

```
% alias cp 'cp -r'
```

This alias not a good one, because you're redefining the behavior of an existing command. But it's damnably common. Notice the single quotes around the command you're redefining. These protect the space that comes between the `cp` and the `-r`.

Don't redefine existing commands

In general, don't alias an existing command to itself. True, your alias will be read first, but if someone else sits down at your terminal (or you sit at someone else's), they'll be expecting behavior that they won't get. It's best to know when you're using an alias and when you aren't.

The exception to the rule is `rm`. You *should* alias `rm` to `rm -i` so that you're prompted before any files are removed. Too often somebody (namely me) types `rm *` without thinking. That `-i` will really save your buns. Do it like this: `alias rm 'rm -i'`.

Syntax Note: C shell aliases don't have an equals sign; Korn shell aliases do. Aside from that (and the standard syntax differences between the two shells), they work pretty much the same.

There are some aliases that are so standard that you should probably just type them into your `.cshrc` right now. These are described in Table 2.3.

Table 2.3 What did you say your name was?

Good alias	What it does
`alias cpr 'cp -r'`	Recursive copy command
`alias la 'ls -a'`	Lists all files
`alias lf 'ls -F'`	Lists directories with / after the name, executables with *
`alias ll 'ls -l'`	Long listing
`alias lr 'ls -R'`	Lists files and keeps going into all subdirectories
`alias mi 'mv -i'`	Renames, but confirm if you're writing over an existing file
`alias ri 'rm -i'`	Deletes, but ask for confirmation
`alias rr 'rm -i -r'`	Deletes down into subdirectories, but ask for confirmation

By the way, although all these aliases are in C shell syntax, you can add an equals sign after each occurrence of the word `alias` and put them into your `.kshrc` file just as easily.

Why put these in your `.cshrc` or `.kshrc` file? Why not your `.login` or `.profile` file? Since the C shell only reads `.login` when you're really logging in and *aliases aren't inherited by subshells*, you should put aliases you want to run everywhere in your `.cshrc` file. What the heck does that mean, you ask? Say you're at a C shell prompt and you execute a script you've written. It spawns a new subshell. In other words, it goes off into its own world. If the script sets an environment variable, when the script finishes running, it will unset it. Similarly, when the script goes off to do its merry work, it doesn't inherit the environment variables set in `.login` (because it's not really logging in). It does, however, read the setup information from `.cshrc`, because `.cshrc` does get executed every time you spawn any kind of subshell (whether you know it or not).

A Brief History

> History has the great virtue of soothing.
>
> Victor Duruy
> *Instruction ministerielle*, 1863

Using C shell history   I'm about to use a couple of examples of aliases that make use of the C shell's history function. Before I do, you should probably know a bit about how they work. See, history repeats itself. Hannibal. Napoleon. Eisenhower. `ps -ef | grep -i jsmith`. Basically, when you've done something once, you'll probably need to do it again sometime soon. (Speaking of which, will you excuse me for a second—I need another cup of coffee.)

Fortunately, the C and Korn shells provide powerful mechanisms for making sure that you aren't a victim of history. (But they won't fetch you another cup of coffee.) (Yet.) Let's take the C shell's history first (because it falls alphabetically first, I guess).

If you type the command `history`, you'll see a list of your previous commands (probably about twenty of them). The list will have the lowest number at the top (that is, the command you executed earliest) and the highest at the bottom (the last command you typed). You can type `history -r` to reverse the order. You can also type `history 20` to see the last twenty commands, or `history 10` to see the last ten, or whatever you want.

You can recall and use any of the historied commands by preceding their command number with an exclamation point (called a bang). So let's run a history command to see what it does (see Figure 2.5).

```
% history
```

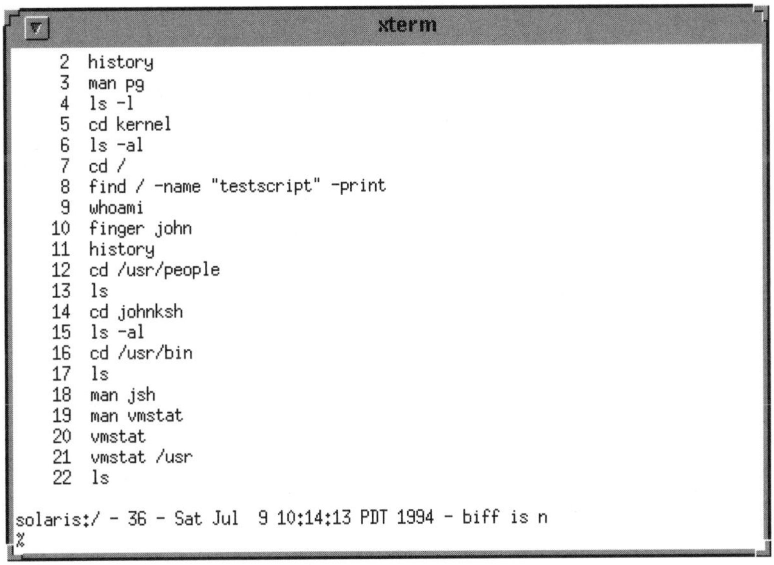

```
                                    xterm
    2  history
    3  man pg
    4  ls -l
    5  cd kernel
    6  ls -al
    7  cd /
    8  find / -name "testscript" -print
    9  whoami
   10  finger john
   11  history
   12  cd /usr/people
   13  ls
   14  cd johnksh
   15  ls -al
   16  cd /usr/bin
   17  ls
   18  man jsh
   19  man vmstat
   20  vmstat
   21  vmstat /usr
   22  ls
solaris:/ - 36 - Sat Jul  9 10:14:13 PDT 1994 - biff is n
%
```

Figure 2.5 Once upon a time, there lived a command . . .

Now let's run a recall command like this:

```
% !5
```

Read this line to yourself (and others) as "bang five." You'll get output similar to that in Figure 2.6.

```
 ┌─────────────────────────────────────────────────────────┐
 │ ▽                           xterm                       ▽│
 ├─────────────────────────────────────────────────────────┤
 │      6  ls -al                                           │
 │      7  cd /                                             │
 │      8  find / -name "testscript" -print                │
 │      9  whoami                                           │
 │     10  finger john                                      │
 │     11  history                                          │
 │     12  cd /usr/people                                   │
 │     13  ls                                               │
 │     14  cd johnksh                                       │
 │     15  ls -al                                           │
 │     16  cd /usr/bin                                      │
 │     17  ls                                               │
 │     18  man jsh                                          │
 │     19  man vmstat                                       │
 │     20  vmstat                                           │
 │     21  vmstat /usr                                      │
 │     22  ls                                               │
 │                                                          │
 │ solaris:/ - 36 - Sat Jul  9 10:14:13 PDT 1994 - biff is n│
 │ % !5                                                     │
 │ cd kernel                                                │
 │                                                          │
 │ solaris:/kernel - 37 - Sat Jul  9 10:14:58 PDT 1994 - biff is n│
 │ %                                                        │
 └─────────────────────────────────────────────────────────┘
```

Figure 2.6 . . . And then it lived again.

If twenty commands aren't enough, edit your `.cshrc` file and add the line `set history=100` (or `1000` or `10000` or whatever you want).

But what if you don't want the whole command? You can use the C shell's built-in line editing power to edit it. For example, if you just wanted to take the last word of the line, but precede it with a different command, you could type:

```
% ls !$
```

The C shell sees the dollar sign and interprets it as "take the string following the last space." Combined with the bang, you get "take the string following the last space in the previous command."

The Korn shell's history works a little differently. It's great when you're editing a command line, but less great when you're trying to make clever substitutions. Usually this isn't a problem, but I'm about to show a case where it is with the `find` command. It's fairly easy to write a shell script to get around the limitation, but a C shell alias is a bit more elegant.

Back to Aliases

> When fate writ my name it made a blot.
>
> Henry Fielding
> *Amelia*, 1752

I have many aliases. Some of my friends call me Jon, some call me Johnny; those who know me best call me nincompoop. I also have many computer aliases (and that's probably what you thought I was talking about in the first place). Here's the first one—it's a good example of the syntax:

```
% alias locate 'find / -name \!$ -print &'
```

Now when I type `locate lost.file`, I execute a lengthy `find` command in the background. This alias also has an interesting twist: It takes a command-line argument (that's what the `\!$` does). The `!$` syntax is colloquial C shell for "take the last word typed on the line and use it here." It's part of `/bin/csh`'s history capabilities. You can also use `!*` to mean to say "take *everything* on the line and use it here."

The backslash protects the next character from interpretation by the shell. In other words, the `!` means something to the C shell. (It means, "what follows will have something to do with what's stored in the shell history." More or less, anyway.) If you don't put in the backslash, the C shell will see `!$` and interpret it as "when you define the alias" as opposed to "when you run the alias." Get it? The backslash is just another kind of quotation mark. So why don't we use a real quotation mark? Because a real quotation mark wouldn't protect the `!`—it would still be evaluated. (Quotation marks in shell scripts are something computer science students write senior theses on in college. Like, "What did Dickens mean by 'It was the best of times'?" and "What did Berkeley mean by '\'?" At some point it gets philosophical.)

An alias can also store multiple commands. Here's an alias for `rm` that will copy files to a holding directory—a safe way to prevent accidental deletion of files:

```
% alias saferm 'cp \!$ ~/holding; rm \!$'
```

Any file you "delete" with `saferm` will be stored in a directory called `holding` in your home directory. Then, at the end of every day, you can execute the command

```
% rm -f ~/holding/*
```

which deletes everything in your `holding` directory, without asking you if it's okay. You could even put this command in your `.logout` file. Of course, if you put it in `.logout`, every time you log out you'll clean this directory: So the `saferm` alias is only good in one session, but it's better than nothing.

This `alias` beats `rm -i` because it's automatic—if you're like me, you get so annoyed with confirming the deletion of every file that you pretty soon just start typing "y" every time, deleting innocent files along with the guilty.

A Bourne Alias

You Bourne shell users aren't completely left out in the cold. You can create something like an alias by using small shell scripts. Put them into a directory like `~/Bourne.alias`, and add that directory to your path. Although you lose some of the neat things you can do with C shell aliases, at least you have something.

BUILDING A DISPLAY CASE

> A man said to the universe:
> "Sir, I exist!"
> "However," replied the universe,
> "The fact has not created in me
> A sense of obligation."
>
> Stephen Crane
> *War Is Kind,* 1899

Devices generate the most annoying problems with UNIX, and terminals are the worst kind of device. There are too many darn types of terminals, and they all act differently. In one corner you got your IBM 3270s, in another DEC has the VT100, VT220, VT320, VT420, and about a billion others. Then there are the Hewlett-Packard terminals, the Data General terminals, and the terminals from Joe Bob's Terminalle Shoppe.

Heaven forbid someone might just come along and say, "Read my lips: No New Terminals."

And the worst of it is that each terminal behaves *totally differently*. What works great for a VT100 will lock up an HP terminal and cause a Data General terminal to rush to the kitchen and consume the contents of your freezer.

Fortunately for you and me, a long time ago someone else (Bill Joy, in case you're wondering) realized that this was a problem and figured out how to handle it. Rather than writing different versions of each program for each terminal (can you imagine running one version of `vi` for a VT100 and another for a 3270?), he wrote a database that described how each terminal behaved. Then he created a mechanism for programs to check to see which terminal type they're running on.

Thus was born `termcap` (short for terminal capabilities). Most BSD systems still use `termcap`, which is basically a HUGE text file that describes nearly every terminal in creation. Of course, it's slow to read a huge text file. So AT&T created `terminfo`, which is a faster version—basically an index to terminal types stored in separate files.

By reading an environment variable called `TERM` then looking in `termcap` or `terminfo`, your shell determines what kind of terminal you're sitting at and how to treat it.

When Everything Works Right

> Come, follow me, and leave the world to its gabble.
>
> Dante
> *Purgatorio,* 1320

If you're running the C shell, you probably have a line like this in your `.login`:

```
setenv TERM vt100
```

If you're a Bourne or Korn shell person, it probably looks like this:

```
TERM=vt100
export TERM
```

These lines tell your shell what kind of terminal you're sitting at. Very simple, very easy, very nice. But guess who has to put them there? What if you don't know your terminal type?

Well, you can guess. Try looking in the lower right and lower left corners of your terminal. See a name? Try it in place of `vt100` above. Use lowercase letters (the VT100 actually has capital letters in Digital's catalog). **Look for a name**

Still doesn't work? Well, you may be out of luck. The UNIX manual will tell you to use `tset` or `tput`, but I'd recommend against it.

The Myth about `tset`

> A good dog deserves a good bone.
>
> Ben Jonson
> *A Tale of a Tub,* 1633

Woof. In fact, `tset` is a double-woof. It's so nasty, this is what the `man` page has to say about it:

```
The tset command is one of the first commands a user must
master when getting started on a UNIX system. Unfortunately,
it is one of the most complex...Something needs to be done...
```

In other words, this is a command so ugly, not even its mother loves it. And I for one disagree that it's one of the first commands you've got to learn. In fact, I had never even heard of it until about two months before I sat down to write this chapter. I won't argue about its being one of the most complex, though. Nope, definitely not.

Heck, just for yucks, I sat down at my terminal to see what `tset` would do for me. I typed:

```
$ tset -
```

to find out what kind of terminal I was on. It said back,

```
xterm
```

Now *there's* a surprise. Gosh, if I hadn't set that variable myself just a minute before, I'd *never have known*. So then, my ire rising, I tried this:

```
$ TERM=
$ TERMCAP=
$ export TERM
$ export TERMCAP
$ tset -
```

What's `tset` good for? The first four lines cleared my terminal type from my environment variables. So did `tset` figure out my terminal type? Was it at all helpful?? This one gets a big, fat, hairy NO. That's right folks, this terminal-setting program can't figure out what kind of terminal I'm on. So what good is it, you ask? For you and me, I say none.

Okay, maybe I'm being a little hard on the little guy. After all, he's just a four-letter command. There is a time when I can envision you wanting to use `tset`—two times, actually. The first is when, for some reason, your **TERM** and **TERMCAP** entries get blown away and all your keyboard mappings cease to work. This doesn't happen very often, but it does happen—I just did it here. You'll still have to know what kind of terminal you have. You'll just have to set your **TERM** type and then run `tset`, which will read the values out of the **TERM** variable and make its best effort at restoring your settings.

The second time I envision you needing `tset` is if you suddenly decide to change your **TERM** variable. There are times when you'll be logging in from a different kind of terminal—maybe one that's not defined correctly by the **TERM** variable in your `.login` or `.profile` or `.cshrc` file, or whatever. That's when you can set **TERM** manually and then run `tset`.

Another Case When `tset` Isn't So Bad

There is another time when `tset` can help out—when you use it for exactly what it was written to do. See, `tset` isn't really a terminal fixer at all. It's supposed to be able to decide what kind of terminal you're using based on the line speed at which you're attached.

When you sit down at a terminal, dial in through a modem, or even open an X window, there are programs that figure out what line you're connected through. UNIX, thanks to its somewhat ancient roots, thinks that everybody who connects in has to be directly connected to some kind of port on the back of the computer. These ports are called ttys (sometimes pronounced to rhyme with "kitties," but more usually you just spell it out to avoid embarrassment), which stands for "teletypes." It's not important what a teletype is (imagine a cross between a typewriter and a VT100 and you'd be close). It is important that UNIX never really shook off the teletype aura. In fact, you could say that UNIX revels in it.

Anyway, a program called `getty` listens to every port (even to ports that aren't really connected to your computer—like network connections) and, when it hears something, it figures out how fast that connection is going and gets you logged in.

And `tset`, for its part, takes the line speed from `getty` and uses it to make a choice about what kind of terminal you're attached to. It makes a choice based on information you provide it in advance. But it still can't actually do something useful, like figure it out on its own.

Say you almost always connect to a computer from the same type of terminal—like a VT100. Sometimes, however, you don't—like when you dial in. Then you're on a Wyse 50. Well, you know that the VT100 is connected to the host with a 9,600 bps serial line, but that you dial in with your Wyse 50 on a 2,400 bps modem. You could have three lines like these in your `.login` program:

Here's what `tset`'s good for

```
set noglob
eval `tset -s -m 'switch>2400:?vt100' -m 'switch<=2400:wy50'`
unset noglob
```

(The two `noglob` lines suppress wildcard expansion.) If you're a Bourne shell user, you'd edit your `.profile` file and use something like this:

```
TERM=`tset -s -m 'switch>2400:?vt100' -m 'switch<=2400:wy50'`
export TERM
```

The best advice I can give is that, if you're still connecting using a Wyse 50, throw it out, buy a V.32bis or V.42 modem and a terminal emulator for your PC, and enter the modern age. The `tset` command is an anachronism.

How to Make Your Keyboard Work

> Life is rather like a can of sardines —
> we're all of us looking for the key.
>
> Alan Bennet
> *Beyond the Fringe*

Learn stty instead of tset

The UNIX man page says tset is one of the first commands you should learn. I say that stty (usually pronounced "settie," although you may hear it spelled out as "ess-tee-tee-why"), not tset, is. Type this:

```
$ stty
```

Watch the output. You'll probably see a speed in baud (misidentified, by the way—stty really means bits per second), the values for your special keys, and lots of words that aren't quite words, like echoe and echok.

Here's what stty's good for. After your TERM variable is set and tset has reinitialized everything, you may find you still have problems. For example, your backspace key is mismapped, or you want a particular keyboard mapping.

Never fear, stty is here.

Proper key mappings

One of the biggest problems I have is when I log in to a Sun workstation from another vendor's terminal across a dial-up line or a network. The Sun keyboard has some weird keys, and for some reason, it refuses to treat my VT100 emulator like a VT100, with the backspace key actually deleting the last character I typed. Instead, I get ^H on my screen. My keyboard sends the right signal, but the Sun workstation expects something else.

So I use this command:

```
$ stty erase ^H
```

I don't actually type a caret (^) and a capital H. I hit the Backspace key, then hit Return. Now when I hit Backspace, it erases the last thing I typed.

What else can you do with stty? Lots of stuff. Table 2.4 contains a quick list. Read this table from right to left to see UNIX's neat built-in keyboard shortcuts.

Add stty to .profile or .login

The trick is getting stty to figure out your keyboard mappings when you log in. You should do that by editing either .profile (if you're running the Bourne or Korn shell) or .login and adding a line like this:

```
stty erase ^h
```

That is, just type stty erase, then a caret (above the number 6) and the lower-case letter h. According to all the manuals, this should work great. I did exactly this and the next time I logged in, I got the message, "h: not found." I was logging in as root, which has as its default shell the Bourne shell. After spending several hours scratching my head and trying to insert various types of control characters into my .profile file, I finally threw up my hands.

Table 2.4 `stty`'s friends.

Option	What it does	Default
`erase` character	The character will remove the last thing you typed.	`^H` (`Backspace`)
`kill` character	The character will delete the whole line you're on.	`^U`
`eof` character	The character will become the "end of file." Also used to end free-input commands like `cat` and to log out of some shells.	`^D`
`intr` character	The character will interrupt the current process.	`^C`
`quit` character	The character will interrupt the current process and generate a core dump.	`^\`
`stop` character	The character will stop output to your screen and freeze your process.	`^S`
`start` character	The character will start output to your screen.	`^Q`
`flush` character	The character will turn off output to your screen but keep your process alive and well. This is useful when you're running a command that generates a lot of useless output.	`^O`
`susp` character	The character will suspend your current process so you can move it to the background (presumably).	`^Z`
`werase` character	The character will erase the last word you typed.	`^W`
`sane`	This command restores your terminal to its default (sane) values.	

That's when it hit me. In some Bourne shells, the caret is a pipe—just like |. So ^ = | my Bourne shell saw the caret and tried to pipe the output of `stty erase` into a command called h. Hence the complaint about there being no h command on my system. I quickly opened my `.profile` file and added a guardian character before the caret—a backslash. That backslash protects the caret from the none-too-subtle advances of the Bourne shell. Now I had this:

```
stty erase \^h
```

And guess what. It worked. This is one of those things I had always taken for granted. Who woulda thunk?

X Terminals, Step One: The Awakening

> If thou art sluggish on arising, let this thought occur:
> I am rising to a man's work.
>
> Marcus Aurelius
> *Meditations*, ca. 170 AD

Snore
Maybe the worst thing that can happen: You get stuck at an X terminal, one of those things from a company like NCD or Visual. I have nothing against X terminals, per se. However, I like my privacy, so I like having a local hard disk. X terminals don't have them, much to the relief of system administrators and to the annoyance of me.

Snort
But that's what the Boss gave you and you're stuck with it. Know this: Your `TERM` type is `xterm`. When you run your `xterm` command, you're not a `vt100`. You're not a `sun` anything. You're an `xterm`. Not that `xterm`s vary dramatically from VT100s most of the time, but if you resize your window (and you will), the VT100 definition will confuse the heck out of most commands. You'll wind up with `more` asking you to press `space` after displaying a paltry twenty-some-odd lines of text. The `xterm` variable tells applications to be on the lookout for changing window sizes.

Need coffee
The X Window System lives in a vacuum. You can tell—it makes a big sucking noise as you start it. That's it, Hoovering up all your system's raw speed. However, X can make you considerably more productive by erecting multiple terminal windows and giving you graphically displayed applications that are a little easier to learn.

X DISPLAY variable
The `DISPLAY` environment variable tells X where to suck, as it were. You need to tell X the name of your host (or its Internet Protocol [IP] address) and the display number you're on. Usually you can get by with sticking a command like this into your `.login` or `.profile` file:

```
% setenv DISPLAY solaris:0
```

Note that `solaris` is the name of my computer. Or, with an IP address, you would use a command like this:

```
% setenv DISPLAY 144.121.32.3:0
```

Or (if you're in the Bourne or Korn shell), the command would look like this:

```
% set DISPLAY solaris:0
% export DISPLAY
```

Now you can go ahead and run `xinit` or `openwin` or whatever command you use to launch X on your computer (those two commands work on IBM RS/6000s and Sun workstations, respectively). X looks at the DISPLAY variable, sees a hostname (solaris) and a display number (0) and runs your application, directing all the windows to that location.

A note on the display number: It's useless 99 percent of the time. There are very few workstations or X terminals with multiple displays (you know—the monitor—the thing you actually look at that has a cathode-ray tube down the middle), so the number after the colon will almost always be 0. In fact, some implementations of X don't like the :0 part and may give you an error when you try to start an X program, like "Display not found." Try it again without the :0. If that still doesn't work, make sure the host system you're trying to connect to (called the client) knows your hostname and address.

A second note for users of Sun's OpenWindows: You may see the error message "OPENWINHOME: not set" or something like it. All you need to do is set this environment variable to the directory that the openwin program lives in. If that directory is in your path, you can find it by typing which openwin or whereis openwin; if it's not, you'll have to search for it with a find command like find / -name "openwin" -print. Then just set OPENWINHOME like any other environment variable. I now have a line in my .profile file that reads

```
OPENWINHOME=/usr/bin/openwin
export OPENWINHOME
```

X Terminals, Step 2: Fix What's Broke

Maybe the nicest thing about the X Window System is that it has the longest dot files there are. .Xdefaults and .mwmrc together can go on for a couple of dozen pages. They're UNIX's answer to Microsoft Windows' .INI files. In fact, they make .INI files look paltry.   **X's dot files**

If you're lucky, your window manager (a program with a name like mwm [for Motif Window Manager] or openwin) has options for making changes to your environment and for saving those changes without editing one of these files. If you're not, you're going to have to do some editing. Rather than printing out a whole .Xdefaults file, I'll take you through a quick star tour of the most important parts.

.Xdefaults Marks the Spot

> Custom doth make dotards of us all.
>
> Thomas Carlyle
> *Sartor Resartus*, 1836

You use a file called .Xdefaults to set up general aspects of X clients (applications)—things like color, size, which fonts they use, which keys do what, and so on. In X-speak, these customizations are called resources. (X has fancy terms for everything.)

One interesting bit of trivia about this file: You can also call it `.Xresources` **and it will have the same effect.**

In order to make programming in X a little bit easier, it comes with some pre-defined components called widgets (if you have an MBA, you'll be right at home with X), which are basically chunks of code that will take care of common functions for a programmer. Virtually every application is composed of widgets these days, but if one isn't, you won't be able to customize it with `.Xdefaults`.

`.Xdefaults`   Just to get us started, here's a small sample of the `.Xdefaults` from my system:

```
*borderWidth:        2
!
! Set up Xclock
!
xclock*borderWidth: 4
xclock*geometry:     50x50
!
! Set up Xterm
!
xterm*curses:        off
xterm*cursorColor:   red
xterm*jumpScroll:    on
xterm*saveLines:     1000
xterm*scrollBar:     on
```

And on and on it goes—you get the idea. The general syntax is

```
application*resource: setting
```

This way, the first thing X sees when it loads is the names of the applications you've customized, then the resources you set. Very simple, no? How you get the application name is usually easy: It's the name of the executable file, usually the command you type.

Getting the resource names can be somewhat more difficult. They're well documented in a lot of places. Try the man **pages first—they're free. If those don't give you enough information (and they probably do—it's just not always clear to someone who doesn't know what they're trying to say), I recommend X**

Window System User's Guide, Volume 3, Motif Edition, written by Valeria Quercia and Tim O'Reilly and published by (you guessed it) O'Reilly & Associates (1990). The O'Reilly book basically expands on the `man` pages with examples and explanations.

Generally, you can set resources in one of two ways: on/off or to a specific value. You'll see that `scrollBar` is turned on, but `saveLines` is set to `1000`. There are more specifics about how to address resources—for example, you can sometimes use a `.` instead of the `*`—but most of them require a lot of breath to explain, and you wind up following the simple examples when you're done.

Probably the most interesting thing that `.Xdefaults` enables you to do is to assign events to mouse buttons and even keyboard keys. For example, if I used the command `ls -l` all the time and wanted a shortcut key for it, I could make an entry in `.Xdefaults` like this:

Keyboard mapping

```
*VT100.Translations:    #override\
  <Key>F3:       string("ls -l") string(0x0d)
```

Now whenever I hit the `F3` key, it will send `ls -l` to the keyboard.

Like all really cool things you can do with UNIX, this one won't work on every system. In fact, it won't work on the Solaris x86 PC I have at home, and Solaris is one *popular* operating system.

Here's a character-by-character breakdown. The `*VT100.Translations:` part really means "when you're in an `xterm` window." The `#override\` part tells your `xterm` that what follows should blow away any default mappings. Next, the `<Key>F3:` part is just the key assignment—you could just as easily have used `F1`, `F5`, `F12`, or anything.

Finally comes the tough part. Use `string()` to get individual keys to send multiple characters. If there are any spaces or special characters inside the `()`, you have to surround the whole thing in double quotes. You can see that the first string is just the command. The second is the hexadecimal code for a carriage return. In other words, `F3` not only prints `ls -l`, it hits `Return` for you, too.

`string()` sends multiple characters

You can remap the buttons on your mouse just as easily—provided you remember that they're numbered from left to right (1, 2, and 3). You get mappings that look like this:

```
*VT100.Translations:  #override\
  <Btn1Down>: select-start()\n\
  <Btn1Motion>: select-extend()\n\
  <Btn1Up>:   select-end(PRIMARY, CUT_BUFFER0)
```

Okay, I'll cop to one thing here: These are actually the *default* mappings for the left mouse button. But they make for good conversation: When you click, it starts a selection, when you drag, it extends it, and when you release, it sticks what you selected into memory as the primary selection and as cut buffer number 0. Neither of these memory areas is the clipboard (`xclipboard`, an occasionally useful tool), so I modified my mappings so that text I selected got dumped into `xclipboard` when I wanted it to. For that, I used this mapping:

```
*VT100.Translations:  #override\
  Button1 <Btn2Down>: select-end(CLIPBOARD)\n\
  Ctrl <Btn2Up>:      insert-selection(CLIPBOARD)
```

What this does When I select text with button 1 (the left mouse button) then click button 2 (the middle mouse button) *while still holding the left mouse button,* my text selection will end and it will be sent to `xclipboard`. (If I just select text with the left mouse button and don't click the middle mouse button, it's sent to that memory area called PRIMARY.) To retrieve what's in the clipboard, all I have to do is point my cursor where I want it to go, hit `Ctrl`, and click the middle mouse button. When I release, `xclipboard`'s contents go there.

Please note how all the lines but the last one end with \n\. In the lingo of .Xdefaults, \n\ means "wait, there's more for this translation section!" (The first line's \ means "begin.") When you want to create translations for something else, just don't include the \n\.

You can also create submappings. These are particularly useful when you have an application you use a lot and you want to abbreviate its keystrokes. Let's take running `vi` in an `xterm` window. In particular, I really want to make exiting into a one-key operation.

```
*VT100.Translations:  #override <Key>F12: keymap(vi)
*VT100.viKeymap.translations: \n\
  <Key>F13: keymap(none)\n\
  <Key>F1:  string(":wq") string(0x0d)\n\
  <Key>F2:  string(":q!") string(0x0d)
```

Legibility Okay, we have a new twist here: The first keyboard mapping is on the same line as the #override. Why? Because there's only one of them. Legibility, basically. The keymap command has the interesting property of making it possible to set up submappings. Now when you press F12 in the `xterm` window, it will run `vi`. Once in `vi` by pressing F12, the F13 key restores the original translation table. F1 sends the `:wq` (write and quit) signal, and `F2` sends `:q!` (quit and don't save changes).

Use your `man` pages to find out more. I hate to admit not being completely infallible, but it's not possible in a 300-plus-page book to write definitively about X. (Well, maybe it's possible, but you wouldn't read about very much else). Fortunately, the `man` pages (in their somewhat cryptic lingo) explain what everything is and does. For example, you'll find all the default mappings in the `man` page for `xterm`. If you want to customize an application, use `man` to find out what's customizable.

Nearly every X application is written using what's called the X Toolkit—a bunch of programming libraries. That means that most of them support at least some of the same options. Some of these options are useful for specifying resources (much as you would in `.Xdefaults`). Anything you specify on the command line overrides what's in `.Xdefaults`. The most important is `xrm`, the X resource manager. You make entries after this option in almost exactly the same way as those that go into your `.Xdefaults` file. For example, you could have a command line like: **The X Toolkit**

```
% xterm -xrm 'xterm*jumpScroll: on'
```

that would be the same as if you had the `xterm*jumpScroll` set on in `.Xdefaults`. Notice the single quotes around the argument.

There's yet another way to save your settings: `xrdb`, the X resource database (see, UNIX commands *do* make sense). You invoke it from a file called `.xinitrc` or `.xsession` (two more dot files). To be absolutely honest, I don't use `xrdb`. Call me a heathen, tell me I don't know what I'm doing. I'm happy like I am. If you're interested, use `man` to learn how it does its magic.

Means, Opportunity, and Motif

> Most of the great results of history are brought about by discreditable means.
>
> R.W. Emerson
> *The Conduct of Life*, 1860

After `.Xdefaults` comes `.mwmrc`, the file that controls the behavior of the Motif window manager. Since Motif is now the "standard" window manager on most systems (except my Sun workstation, *still* [hint, hint]) I'm going to cover the interesting things you can do in it. Other window managers' files work pretty much the same way. **.mwmrc**

There is at least one .mwmrc file on your computer already—the systemwide one. It's called system.mwmrc and is probably stored wherever mwm lives on your system (if you're root, you can quickly find it with the command find / -name "system.mwmrc" -print). If you don't have a file called .mwmrc in your home directory already (and you use mwm), copy system.mwmrc into ~ as .mwmrc. Then edit your own copy.

In case you're wondering, .mwmrc is huge. It defines the menus that will pop up in various windows when you press various keys. In general, though, it makes a fair amount of sense. Here's some of the system.mwmrc file so you can get a feel:

```
# Root Menu Description
Menu RootMenu
{
    "Root Menu"       f.title
    "New Window"      f.exec "xterm &"
    "Shuffle Up"      f.circle_up
    "Shuffle Down"    f.circle_down
    "Refresh"         f.refresh
    no-label          f.separator
    "Restart..."      f.restart
}
```

Okay, here goes the explanation. The thing after the # is a comment. That, at least, is easy to understand. Next, system.mwmrc defines a Menu called RootMenu. (If it weren't defining a Menu, it would be defining Keys or Buttons—those are the only three choices.) The stuff between the braces are the menu items. First comes the title—Root Menu—which will appear at the top of the menu. It's defined by f.title. (I've been curious about what the f. is for. I know that it stands for function, but why is it necessary?)

Anyway, the next item creates a new window—more specifically, a new xterm window. The f.exec command is very important because it's what enables you to create interesting menus of your own. Its arguments come in quotation marks. The next batch of menu items are all standard X actions. I never use them (except Restart . . .) and don't suspect that you will either. In fact, if you're editing your .mwmrc right now, take 'em out. I like simple menus, I hope you do too. I also like a few other choices on this menu. Here's what the menu I use when I'm using Motif looks like:

```
Menu RootMenu
{
    "Root Menu"       f.title
```

```
    "New Window"      f.exec "xterm &"
    "Tools"           f.menu          ToolTimeMenu
    "Telnet Menu"     f.menu          TelnetMenu
    no-label          f.separator
    "Refresh"         f.refresh
    "Restart..."      f.restart
}
```

Later in the same file, I define a couple more menus:

```
Menu  ToolTimeMenu
{
    "Tools and Such"  f.title
    "Analog Clock"    f.exec "xclock -chime -hd slateblue &"
    "Digital Clock"   f.exec "xclock -chime -digital &"
    "Calculator"      f.exec "xcalc &"
    "Editor"          f.exec "emacs &"
    "Help"            f.exec "xman &"
    "Mail?"           f.exec "xbiff &"
}

Menu  TelnetMenu
{
    "Telnet to..."    f.title
    "Solaris"         f.exec "xterm -e 'telnet solaris' &"
    "Cheetah"         f.exec "xterm -e 'telnet cheetah' &"
    "Babyface"        f.exec "xterm -e 'telnet babyface' &"
}
```

The f.menu function (in the first batch of code) creates a *cascading menu*. The term is pretty self-explanatory, but basically it's a menu within a menu: When you select Telnet Menu from the first menu, it pulls up the stuff from the TelnetMenu section of .mwmrc.

Cascading menus

Truth be told, there are about a billion other things you can do in .mwmrc. Most of it's well documented—shortcut keys (which I never use), mnemonics (ditto), and some other tricks—in the man page for mwm. If that's not good enough, get the O'Reilly book I mentioned. It's about as thorough as a user's guide gets.

MORE SHOP TOOLS

> The villain still pursued her.
>
> Milton Nobles
> *The Phoenix, 1875*

Mine has lots   Every shop has tools you touch maybe once a year, if that (unless you're Norm Abram), like the oscillating sander with the special sawdust-sucking attachment. I've got one. My neighbor has one. (More specifically, my neighbor has *mine*, but let's not quibble here.) Everybody needs one, right? Well, okay, maybe not everybody. But it sure does come in handy when you can get it away from your neighbor.

UNIX has lots of commands and files like that, too. They're very handy, but you don't plug them in but once or twice a year. Here are my nominees for most-useful, least-edited files.

A Host of Hosts

> A woeful hostess brooks not merry guests.
>
> Shakespeare
> *The Rape of Lucrece, 1594*

Do you use the `rlogin`, `rsh`, or `rcp` commands? If not, skip to the next section. If you do, you're in for the security-violating ride of your life. You see, there's a file called `.rhosts` that enables you to log in to a computer without supplying a password. That's right: Jump to Go, collect $200, and drive your system administrator insane. Sound like fun? It is.

Using `.rhosts`   Basically, you add to `.rhosts` the names of "trusted" hosts—hosts you'll be logging in from and don't want to bother supplying passwords to. Let's say your user name is `jane` and you have accounts on two computers: `tarzan` and `cheetah`. Say you go to your home directory on `tarzan` and create a `.rhosts` file with this line:

```
cheetah
```

You'll find that whenever you log in to `tarzan` from `cheetah` *you'll never be prompted for a password.* How's that for a security loophole? Great, huh? Well, it gets better.

If you're root and you do this, you've just opened up a security hole wide enough to drive a seven-year-old cracker through. So don't. If you're root, check for `.rhosts` files in the / directory daily. If there is one, DELETE IT. Do it now.

A couple of notes on the `.rhosts` file. First, it requires certain permissions. Specifically, the owner must have read, write, and execute permissions for it to work. You can do this with this command:

```
$ chmod 700 .rhosts
```

Second, it has a built-in way for you to log into your system from another system, even if you have a different username on that system. Let's take the previous example: system `tarzan`, you `jane`. (You saw that coming, I hope.) Only, when you're working on `cheetah`, your username is `janesmith`. Open up your `.rhosts` file and modify the cheetah line to this:

```
cheetah janesmith
```

Now you can't just hang out on `cheetah` and type `rlogin tarzan`. You'll have to type

```
$ rlogin tarzan -l jane
```

The `-l` says "use the following username." It insures that `tarzan` won't look for `janesmith`, not find it, and refuse you access.

Dealing with the Post Office

> Neither snow nor rain nor heat nor gloom of night stays these couriers
> from the swift accomplishment of their appointed routes.
>
> Herodotus
> *Histories,* ca. 430 BC

After buying the house I mentioned at the top of this chapter, I notified the post office that I was moving. About a week after I moved, I started getting some mail from the old address, plus a whole lot of junk mail. UNIX mail has a similar system, only it works better (surprise, surprise).

A file called `.forward` tells the mail system on one computer to send your mail to another computer. All you do is create (in your home directory, of course) a file called `.forward` and add one line that tells where to send your mail. You can even send it to a different user on a different (or the same) computer.

Using `.forward`

Example time: Say your user name is `jane` and you're on `tarzan`. You get renamed to `jsmith` on `cheetah`. In your home directory on `tarzan`, create `.forward` and add this:

```
jsmith@cheetah
```

Now the mail system should know how to forward your mail. (Provided your system administrator added `cheetah` to the `/etc/hosts` file, or at least to the NIS. You're not responsible for dumb system administrators, but you should let them know when they're messing up.) If you're on a larger network, you'll probably need to know your full, domain-style address, which might look like this:

```
jsmith@cheetah.forest.com
```

You'll learn more about E-mail addressing in Chapter 6.

De Plan! De Plan!

> The finest plans have always been spoiled by the littleness of them that should carry them out. Even emperors can't do it all by themselves.
>
> Bertolt Brecht
> *Mother Courage*, 1939

Frivolous   Here's one of those useless files that only UNIX could have. It's called `.plan`. If
.plan   you ever use the `finger` command to find out who someone is, what they're up to, and so on, it will query `.plan` to see if the user has any plans for life. In theory, this file can contain useful information about what a person is working on. In reality, it usually contains a smart remark. (See Figure 2.7.)

Join the crowd: Use a smart remark.

```
# finger john
Login name: john                        In real life: John I. Montgomery -- c
sh
Directory: /usr/people/john             Shell: /usr/bin/csh
On since Jul  9 16:12:39 on pts/6 from localhost
12 days Idle Time
Unread mail since Sat Jul  9 16:11:26 1994
Plan:
to eat as much pizza as I possibly can.
#
```

Figure 2.7 Questions? Comments? Smart remarks?

I'm Just Projecting

Along with `.plan`, hand-in-hand so to speak, goes `.project`. You put one (only one, 'cause UNIX'll only read one) line into a file called `.project`, and when somebody runs a finger command to find out more about you, they'll see a line like this:

```
Project: Project?! I've got lots!!
```

CLOSING UP SHOP

> "This affair must all be unraveled from within." He tapped his forehead.
> "These little gray cells. It is 'up to them'—as you say over here."
>
> Agatha Christie
> *The Mysterious Affair at Styles*, 1920

Logging in to your beautiful UNIX system is just the start. (Literally.) Logging in is really important. It's when things get set up right. It's when you can impress your friends with your customizations. But most people don't even know that there's life after you type `exit`. There is.

I Didn't Mean . . .

> One may know your meaning by your gaping.
>
> John Ray
> *English Proverbs*, 1670

You know `Ctrl+d` will log you out, right? (If you didn't, you just learned.) `Ctrl+d` is the UNIX End-Of-File (`EOF`) marker. It's handy a lot of times—like when you're using the `cat` command to create a file and you use `Ctrl+d` to tell `cat` to stop taking input. Anyway, when a typical UNIX shell sees `Ctrl+d`, it'll translate it to "`logout`." In fact, your shell may even print the word `logout`, just as if you'd typed it.

Ctrl+d to log out

If you're like me, you use subshell after subshell, always forgetting just how far into the shell maze you are. Just keep hitting `Ctrl+d` and eventually you'll probably find yourself at a nice `login:` prompt. This is not what you generally want—unless it's the end of the day. Most of the time, you really mean "`Ctrl+d`, take me away." Unfortunately, it gets to be too late too quickly. Then you have to log back in, fire up the window system, and go for coffee while your system reads all the customizations you made in the first part of this chapter. No fun.

Going too far

So, here are some tricks for making sure that your last `Ctrl+d` won't log you out (unless you really want it to).

- C shell users: start your editors, open your `.cshrcs`, and add the line, `set ignoreeof`.
- Korn shell users: open `.profile` and add the line `set -o ignoreeof`.
- Bourne shell users: Just don't use `Ctrl+d`. Just kidding. Kinda.

The solution for the Bourne shell is complicated because there's no equivalent to `ignoreeof`. I saw one once in a book somewhere (probably *UNIX Power Tools*) and tried it. It didn't work. This is one of those "shortcomings" you hear about when people like me talk about using the Bourne shell as a day-to-day command shell.

Safely Turning Off Power Tools (`.logout`)

> My turn today, yours tomorrow.
>
> Latin saying

Now that you've made your shell impregnable to the advances of even the most nasty overtures of the `logout` and `exit` commands, it's time to take advantage of the unique state they put your terminal into. In other words, let's make `exit` do something interesting.

There's this file, see? It's called `.logout`, see? And you put neat stuff you want done when you log out into it. See? Most people use this file to make their computer say good-bye. Simple people put in one line:

```
echo "Bye. See you tomorrow."
```

How droll. Complex people put in a lengthy discourse on what they did, how well they did it, how long they were logged in for, and so on. In general, this type of information requires you to modify your `.login` or `.profile` file so that you record the time you logged in to a file or environment variable. In many ways, this is an exercise in futility.

Use `.logout` to clean up   Still others use this file to clean up messes they made while working. I'm very messy, so that's what I use mine for: to delete temporary editor files, files with the extension `.tmp`, and anything in my personal `tmp` directory like this:

```
echo "Deleting emacs tmp files"
rm -f *~
echo "Deleting files whose names end in .tmp"
rm -f *.tmp
echo "Clear your refuse container \~/tmp"
rm -f ~/tmp/*
# Display your fortune
/usr/games/fortune
date
echo "Don't forget to `echo ~/todo`"
wait 20
clear
```

Perhaps most interesting are the last three lines. I keep a to-do list in the root of my home directory. Without it, I'd never remember to get any work done—I'd spend my whole day looking at `.mwmrc` and `.Xdefaults` trying to figure out how to get all my key mappings to work. So I have `.logout` read that file, then wait 20 seconds before clearing the screen.

Now Where Was I?

Remember that the C shell and Korn shell keep track of the commands you type? They do that by editing a file called `.history` and putting your commands in there. If you use the C shell, when you log out you lose your history. Unless . . . Edit your `.login` file and add the command `set savehist 20`. This command will create a file called `.history` when you log out. In `.history` you'll find a list of the last twenty commands you entered, and when you type `history` you'll see them.

Saving a history for tomorrow

Naturally, this clever fix isn't perfect. If it were, you probably wouldn't be reading this section. Here's the catch: What happens when you have multiple shells? Like when you're running several terminal windows? When you log out, they'll all try to write `.history`. Last one out of the pool wins: You get its command history whether you want it or not.

Obviously, there's got to be a better way. I've seen a few attempts, but none of them have really impressed me. Why? Mainly because they restore a history arbitrarily—they store all the windows' histories into separate files, then restore one of them, or make you choose which one to restore. In all honesty, I can't say I have a better solution, but I do think that this is one case where automation doesn't help much: I choose one window when I log in as my primary activity window and I manually `set savehist 100` in it. That way I know, when I see my `.history` file, exactly what's in it.

The solution

And now, straight from the home office in Goth, my Top Ten Nasty, Cool Things You Can Do with UNIX (Table 2.5)

Table 2.5 Top Ten Customizations.

10. `alias logout 'echo "You can't go home yet."`
9. `set prompt="`hostname`:${cwd}% "`
8. Modify `.mwmrc` to present menus *you* like.
7. Make `.logout` read your `todo` file.
6. Create a `locate` command (`alias locate 'find / -name \!$ -print'`).
5. Create a `.plan` file with something humorous in it.
4. `set filec` (C shell only).
3. If you use X, map keys to execute commands.
2. Set your backspace key so it backspaces with `stty`.
1. Add the line `president@whitehouse.gov` to your `.forward`.

3 Your Wish: Issuing Commands

> There once lived a poor tailor, who had a son called Aladdin, a careless,
> idle boy who would do nothing but play all day long in the streets with
> little idle boys like himself. This so grieved the father that he died; yet, in
> spite of his mother's tears and prayers, Aladdin did not mend his ways.
> One day, when he was playing in the streets as usual, a stranger asked
> him his age, and if he was not the son of Mustapha the tailor.
>
> Anonymous
> *The Magic Lamp*

Well of course he was. There would be no story if he wasn't. Sheesh [roll eyes].
Anyway, this dude tricks Aladdin into getting the magic lamp for him and
making him court magician. The moral of the story is that, if a big blue dude with
Robin Williams's voice comes up to you and offers you three wishes, take them,
but don't get greedy.

UNIX will do a lot of the work of a genie, too. Make you look good, give you
neat clothes, do funny impressions ("Hey Rocky, watch me pull a genie out of my
hat"). One thing: Rub UNIX three times and no genie comes out, but people will
probably look at you oddly.

The command line is still where most of UNIX's interesting stuff goes on.
Sure, you can do a lot from within OpenWindows or Motif or some other interface
onto the X Window System, but when push comes to shove, you're going to be
typing commands at some kind of prompt. This chapter is about getting the most
from your command lines: editing them, dealing with some of the secret nomenclature that command lines use, and stringing commands together.

Command line = good stuff

COMMAND-LINE EDITING

Cosi è se vi pare
(Right You Are if You Think You Are)

Luigi Pirandello, 1917

I dno't thnik three's anyone amnog us woh hsan't at smoe pnoit made a typo or tow. Heck, even *I* make them occasionally. True, I have spell checkers and copy editors who read behind me to make sure typos don't live long. But those underlauded souls aren't there when I'm typing commands at a shell prompt, correcting my spelling, and performing on-the-fly syntax checks. That's a problem, because UNIX has a terrible time figuring out what's going on if you don't type exactly what it expects. Worse, when you do make a mistake, fixing it can be a real drag—you can either retype the whole line or retype the whole line. Most of the time, anyway.

So much for the bad news. Now for the good news: There are times when, if you know the secret handshake, UNIX will let you recall a command with a typo and fix it.

History

History is the sum total of things that could have been avoided.

Konrad Adenauer, 1950

HISTORY
variable

Most of the credit goes to the history that your shell keeps of your commands. If you have `history` turned on (in the C shell, type `setenv HISTORY 100`; in the Korn shell, try `set HISTORY 100`; in the Bourne shell, you're kind of SOL), your shell will dump every command you type into a file. Sometimes it's called `.history`. Sometimes it's `.sh_history`. Sometimes `.ksh_history`. Use the `ls -a ~` command to see which you have. Anyway, the commands wind up in this file. We've already discussed using the `history` command to type the contents of this file to the screen, and how to recall specific command numbers. Now it's time to recall those commands and modify them.

When you pop your shell into editing mode, you can step back through your `history` file, recalling one command at a time. If you hit `Return`, you execute the command. If you use some command-line editing tools, you can modify that command—fix a typo, substitute a command or filename, whatever you want.

Despite the fact that this capability is incredibly powerful (or maybe precisely because it's so powerful), there's no one, cross-shell method for invoking it. So, the next few sections devote themselves to explaining how to do command-line editing in the three most popular shells.

In case you're wondering, I'll tell you up front that the Korn shell has by far and away the most powerful command-line editing of any shell I've ever seen or used. Why? Because you can use an actual text editor to modify it. By default, the Korn shell uses `vi` or `emacs`, but you can choose any editor you want (at least in theory). This is yet another reason for choosing the Korn shell. Vince Chen, tech editor, beer drinker, and `tcsh` user, also points out that you can set up `tcsh` to do anything you want by explicitly assigning keys in the `.tcshrc` file.

Bourne Not to Edit

This is likely to be the shortest section in the entire book: The Bourne shell has no history file. Without it, you can't have command-line editing. You must invoke `jsh`, `bash`, or `ksh` (the last is the best) if you want command-line editing.

Another idol falls

C Me Edit

> I have a memory like an elephant.
> In fact, elephants often consult me.
>
> > Noël Coward

The C shell is a little better about line editing than the Bourne shell. Which is to say that you *can* get thar from here, but it ain't easy. The keys to C shell editing are the ! and : characters. That should give you a hint about how easy it is to do line editing in the C shell. Table 3.1 lists some of the easier things you can do.

Table 3.1 Basic C shell editing commands.

Sequence	What it does
!!	Recalls the last command you typed
!n	Recalls the whole command number n from the history list
!$	Recalls the last argument of the last command
!:n-o	Recalls arguments n through o from the last command
!:n*	Recalls arguments n to the end of the line from the last command
^x^y	Replaces x from the previous command with y

Not pretty, is it? You already know `!!` and `!n` to recall commands (you probably issued the `history` command before `!n` in order to find out the number of the command you want). Those two sequences operate on the whole history. The next four operate only on the previous command.

The !$ sequence is very handy for lots of stuff. For example, let's say that you copy a file from one directory to another, then you want to edit it. You could just type

```
% cp file1 /usr/file2
% vi !$
```

If all goes well, the shell will politely expand !$ into /usr/file2 and you can begin editing.

The !:n-o sequence is kind of like !$, only it enables you to work on more than just the last argument of the previous command. Instead, you work on arguments n through o.

The C shell starts numbering the elements on a command line with 0 (the first thing on the command line, usually the command itself), and works its way up to 9. If you want to get to an element that would be numbered 10 (actually the eleventh element—remember, the C shell starts numbering from 0) you're out of luck.

Check and delete   Let's say that you want to delete a bunch of files that have dissimilar names. The safest thing is to make sure they are the files you think they are and then remove them, like this:

```
% ls -l file1 adifferentfile anothertestfile
...
```

In the output, you see that anothertestfile has been updated very recently and is very big. You want to take a look at it after you delete the other two files. So the command

```
% rm !:2-3
```

would delete file1 and adifferentfile, but leave anothertestfile for you to work on. If I didn't want to leave anothertestfile behind, I would have said !:2*. The !:n* sequence works just like !:n-o, except that it takes every argument from n on.

Replacing letters   Finally, the double-carat trick, ^x^y, requires nerves of steel and usually more patience than I at least have. It enables you to replace x with y—usually when you've made a typo. For example:

```
% grpe happy sadsack
grpe: command not found
% ^pe^ep
grep happy sadsack
```

This is kind of a silly example, but the basic idea is that I misspelled `grep` the first   **Fixing errors**
time, then told the C shell to substitute ep for pe and run the command again.

I could have done it a slightly different way, with !. Rather than ^pe^ep, I
could have typed

```
% !s:/pe/ep
```

The `s:` part means substitute—it's a bit like `vi`'s `substitute` command.

The ! has many uses in recalling commands, not just recalling the last command (!!) or recalling a specific command number from the history list
(!`commandnumber`). For example, I can use ! to recall the last command that
started with `gr`:

```
% !gr
```

Or I can use ! to repeat the last command that contained hap anywhere in it:

```
% !?hap?
```

There are also variations on the bang theme, which involve various permutations   **Variations on !**
no one will ever remember. I could either ignore them, or put them here in Table 3.2,
all together, so you can cut this page out of the book, thereby infuriating the next
person who reads it.

Table 3.2 How to get a bang out of the C shell.

Sequence	What it does
!s:/*x*/*y*	Recalls the last command, substituting string *y* for string *x*
!*x*	Recalls the last command that started with *x*
!?*x*?	Recalls the last command that had *x* anywhere in it
!! &	Recalls the last command and puts it into the background
!! *x*	Recalls the last command and appends *x* to it
!:0	Recalls the first thing on the last command line (usually the command)
!:1	Recalls the second thing on the last command line (usually a parameter)
!:*n*	Recalls the *n*th thing on the last command line (start numbering with 0)
!:*n-o*	Recalls elements *n* through *o* on the last command line
!:–*n*	Recalls elements 0 through *n* on the last command line
!:*n**	Recalls the elements from *n* to the last thing on the previous com- mand line
!$	Recalls the last element on the previous command line

Generally, I'm not a big fan of large tables, but there are just too many darn things you can do with the C shell's **!** command, and this is the quickest way to present them. Humblest apologies to anyone expecting great writing.

Using :   Once you've gotten settled in with **!**, you'll have to learn more about **:**. (Nobody told you that the C shell is an exercise in punctuation, did they?) You've already seen how **:** can cooperate with **!** to grab particular elements from previous lines. Well, **:** stands on its own as something that's nearly impossible to know from beginning to end without a table. Yes, another table (Table 3.3, namely). If things work out right, this table should fall on the page after the previous one, so you'll only have to razor *one* page out of this book. (Librarians love it when you razor pages out of books—just call the music library at Harvard and ask about Leonard Bernstein.) Unlike **!**, which recalls commands, **:** enables you to edit them. Okay, here's that table I promised:

Table 3.3 Colon all cars.

Sequence	What it does
:e	Returns the part of a filename after a dot, but doesn't work with !
:h	Lops off the last part of a path name
:p	Recalls a specified command, but doesn't print it (used with !)
:q	Exists, but damned if I can figure out a use for it
:r	Lops off the last part of a filename (after the dot)
:t	Opposite of :h—gives just the last part of a path name
:x	See :q

I've given up pretending that I know everything. I had to, because of two of the elements in this table: :x and :q. I understand what they do in principle, and I'm told they're very useful in shell scripts, but I can't figure out any use for them on the command line. You use :q with ! to recall a command, but not to expand any variables. Like :q, :x recalls a command without expansion, but it treats whatever is in a variable like separate words. I'm told these are very useful and easy to understand. As Groucho Marx once said, "It's so easy a three-year-old could understand it. (Quick, run and find me a three-year-old)." Similarly, I'm convinced that :e could be useful, but I haven't had call to even imagine using it.

Anyway, let's look at some of the more useful of these and how they may be used. The **:h** operator is probably the most useful for general purpose command-line work.

```
% cd /usr/people/johnmontgomery
% cd ..
```

```
% history
1 cd /usr/people/johnmontgomery
2 cd ..
3 history
% cd !1:t
% pwd
/usr/people/johnmontgomery
```

The penultimate command recalls command number 1 (!1), then tails it (that's what the t stands for, by the way) with :t. I didn't really need the history command to get this done, but I wanted to show where the number 1 came from.

There are times when you want to recall a command just to print it, not to execute it. Usually you want to make sure that the command you're recalling is what you want. That's not possible with ! alone. What you want is an operator that will expand ! without running it. Like this:

Recall and print

```
% cd /usr/people/barneyrubble
... some more commands ...
% !?peop?:p
cd /usr/people/barneyrubble
```

The cursor then waits politely at the end of barneyrubble. You can hit Ctrl+c to blow away the line, Ctrl+w to erase a word, or Return to execute the line. Whatever. Personally, I think that's one of the neatest things you can do with the C shell.

The last of these colon commands I'm going to deal with is :r. Why? Because I can't for the life of me figure a real (meaning less-than-unbelievably-infrequent) use for it. It returns the root of a filename—the part that comes before the first dot. Why would you want to do that? Well, I can think of one reason:

```
% vi program.c
... do some editing ...
% cc !$:r
```

So you create a C program called program (not very original, are you?), then you want to compile it (that's what cc does). Well, cc doesn't need to know that the program's filename ends in .c—it pretty much has to (at least that's the convention). In fact, some compilers won't work if you specify that final .c. So this is a solution. Since most large programming projects will use the UNIX make utility (which is very clever about joining multiple files together into one program), you probably won't be doing this too much. More likely, you'll use :r like this:

```
% foreach f ( *.c )
? set root=$f:r
? if (! -f ${root}.h) then
?   echo "${root}.h does not exist"
? endif
? end
```

This command takes all the files in the current directory whose names end in `.c` and checks to see if there's a file that also ends in `.h` (a header file, as they're called). You probably won't be doing this too often, but it's handy to know.

Just as a note, I've seen some pretty clever ways to edit C shell command lines. Using a series of aliases or a shell script, you can invoke the `ex` editor to get true editing power. There are, however, some problems with this. The first is that everyone I know who uses `ex` is either a complete UNIX person (has been doing it for a billion years) or has something to prove. The second, and this is more important to me, is that after trying several variations on this theme I found that, although it's interesting, it takes me less time to retype the command from scratch than it does to invoke the editor and make the changes (cursing while I tried to remember `ex`'s commands). Don't bother.

Editing from the Korner

> The seen is the changing. The unseen is the unchanging.
>
> Plato
> *Dialogues*, ca. 400 BC

Best editing in Korn   The Korn shell is by far the coolest of the three shells we're going to talk about in this chapter—at least from an editing standpoint. Why? Well, other shells *say* "command-line editing," but only the Korn shell actually uses the syntax of a popular editor (`vi` or `emacs`). That's right, rather than learning further cryptic and awkward symbol replacement strings, you just type a command and enable character insertion, replacement, appending—you name it. The magic command is `set -o vi`, or `set -o emacs`.

vi or emacs?   Which do you want: `vi`- or `emacs`-style editing? Well, if you're used to one use it by all means. There's really no reason in this day and age to go about learning new editing keystrokes just to show that you can. Besides, that's why the Korn shell has two modes. If you're not used to a specific editor (or you generally use an editor other than `vi` or `emacs`), I'd recommend `emacs`. It's a little easier to learn (what isn't?).

One note before going on: Doing a `set -o vi` or `set -o emacs` doesn't actually turn on `vi` or `emacs`. Instead, it invokes a `vi`-like or `emacs`-like editing facility (called `vi` mode or `emacs` mode). For all the simple stuff, they're the same. For a true commandlineeditophile, it's not enough. Fortunately, you can invoke a full-fledged editor to do your command-line editing. It just takes longer. I'm a speed freak, so I live with the shortcomings of the `set -o vi` command. However, by tweaking an environment variable you can invoke true `vi` or `emacs`. To do it, use something like this in your `.profile` file:

```
VISUAL=/usr/bin/emacs
```

or

```
VISUAL=/usr/sbin/vi
```

or wherever your editor lives. Better yet, use the Korn shell's built-in `whence` command to figure out where your editor lives. That way, should it ever move (or should you move to a different computer that stores `vi` or `emacs` in a different place), your `VISUAL` variable won't be broken. Do it thusly:

```
VISUAL=$(whence emacs)
```

or

```
VISUAL=$(whence vi)
```

That's a tip. Use it. Once your environment is set up for the editor of your choice, all that's left to learn is how to edit.

vi for Power

I'll tell you that once I was a big fan of `emacs`—you couldn't get me to touch another editor with a ten-foot index finger. In fact, I preferred `emacs` to nearly every word processor I'd ever used. It just felt like home. So why am I extolling the virtues of `emacs` at the beginning of a section on `vi` editing? Well, largely because the day came when I went to a new company that didn't have a copy of `emacs`, didn't want my copy of `emacs`, and didn't want anyone installing `emacs` anywhere near their computers for security reasons. (Considering that nearly everyone at the company had the root password, I think they may have been a day late and a dollar short, but who am I?) So that's when I learned `vi`. I never got to be a real `vi` pro—one of those people who can make the Declaration of Independence appear magically on the screen by typing colon-something. But I did come to appreciate the speed with which `vi` ran, the austerity of its interface, and the fact that it was the only text editor around. (In my heart of hearts, I still like `emacs` better, though.)

set -o vi
That said, let's get rolling with vi. Type set -o vi and hit Return. Brace yourself for the consequences. The performance of your computer will suddenly increase fivefold, your mother's coffee will suddenly taste good, and Norman Mailer will appear at your door to tell you that you've won the Publisher's Clearinghouse sweepstakes.

As you've probably guessed, I'm kidding. Actually, nothing dramatic will happen. In fact, it will look like nothing at all has happened. Mostly because nothing has. Yet. Now hit Esc and type a lowercase letter k. You should see the command set -o vi appear. If you remember, the letter k in vi stands for "go up a line." And that's just what you did. Keep hitting k and you will step back through your history file—even if it's from a previous day. That's command-line recall at its best.

Navigation
Now type the letter h for a while and you'll gradually move from the right side of the line to the left. Type l and you'll move back. One character at a time. You're navigating the command line in what vi calls command mode. You got there by hitting the Esc key as I suggested earlier. Table 3.4 lists vi's many navigation aids.

Table 3.4 Twelve lovely vi command mode maneuvering commands.

Character	What it does
h	Moves left one character
l	Moves right one character
k	Recalls the next line up in the command buffer (recalls earlier commands)
j	Moves down one line in the command buffer
+	Does the same thing as j—moves to the next command
w	Moves right one word
b	Moves left one word
e	Moves to the end of the current word
0	Moves to the beginning of the line
^	Moves to the first nonblank character in the line
$	Moves to the end of the line

Typing in vi mode
The opposite of command mode is input mode. That's what you're in at first. Why didn't I tell you about input mode if that's what you're put into first? Two reasons. First, that's what every book and man page I've ever read on the Korn shell does, and I like to be different. Second, what's the big deal about being able to type commands at a command line? I mean, that's why they call it a command line, isn't it?

Well, if you get into the `vi` command-editing mode by typing `Esc` (the same way you enter command mode in `vi`), it only stands to reason that you enter input mode with the same commands you use in `vi`, doesn't it? So type `i` wherever your cursor is on the current line and you should drop out of command mode and into input mode, inserting a character right before the one your cursor's on. Now you can type to your heart's content, adding characters, words, control codes, whatever. Once you've modified the command to the point where you're satisfied, just hit `Return` to execute it. (See Table 3.5 for some `vi` command-editing mode commands.)

Table 3.5 Adding characters with `ksh`'s `vi` mode is about as obtuse as you'd think.

Command	What it does
i	Inserts stuff right before wherever the cursor is right now
a	Appends stuff right after wherever the cursor is right now
A	Appends stuff at the end of the line
s	Substitutes what you're about to type for whatever character the cursor's on

At this point, you're probably hankering for some examples. I know I am. So, here they are. Start by clearing your screen (type `clear` and hit `Return` or `Enter` or whatever they call that key on your keyboard). Now type `set -o vi` to bring you into the Korn shell's `vi`-like command-line editor. Now type a bunch of commands like the ones in Figure 3.1.

```
                              xterm
# set -o vi
# find /usr/people/john -name "test" -print
# fing /usr/people -name "test" -print
ksh: fing:  not found
#
```

Figure 3.1 A `vi`able way to edit.

As you can see, `fing` isn't a command. Fortunately, `vi` edit mode was turned on, so I can hit `Esc` (or type `Ctrl+[`) and hit the `l` key three times to position the cursor on the illicit letter `g`. (See Figure 3.2.)

```
                              xterm
#
# set -o vi
# find /usr/people/john -name "test" -print
# fing /usr/people -name "test" -print
ksh: fing:  not found
# fing /usr/people -name "test" -print
```

Figure 3.2 Outmaneuvered—again!

Now I type s, to substitute the letter I'm about to type (d) for the current letter (g). Then I just hit Return and the command runs.

Better than DOSkey

At this point, you're probably thinking that this is pretty neat. DOS's DOSkey utility isn't nearly this good. Actually, neither is VMS's command-line editing. Offhand, I can't think of a single operating system with the command-line editing power of UNIX, particularly in the Korn shell.

But wait, there's more. There are control-type commands you can make from within input mode. By holding down the Ctrl key and typing some letters, you'll find that you don't have to enter command mode to perform some simple editing chores. Table 3.6 shows a few examples.

Table 3.6 Input mode commands in vi.

Control Key	What it does
Backspace	Deletes the previous character
Ctrl+w	Erases the previous word
Ctrl+d	Quits from the shell

emacs and Gadzooks

Command line-editing in emacs works pretty much as it does in vi, up to a point. That point is the typing of the set command. After that, it's a different world. So run your set -o emacs command to tell the Korn shell that you want to forsake vi as your command-line editor and use the emacs-like editor built into the shell. Now type something on the command line. Anything. Next, hold down the Ctrl key and type the letter b (Ctrl+b). You'll move backward one character (hence the control key combination—b is for back). Notice that you didn't have to hit Esc or do any odd hjkl-style maneuvering. The rest of the maneuvering keys are equally straightforward.

Table 3.7 The wonderfully simple maneuvering commands in emacs.

Control Key	What it does
Ctrl+f	Goes forward one character
Ctrl+b	Goes backward one character
Ctrl+p	Recalls the previous line
Ctrl+n	Goes to the next line
Esc b	Goes backward one word (Don't press the keys at the same time.)
Esc f	Goes forward one word

Figure 3.3 shows what I got by typing `ctrl+p` after typing my `set` command. In and of itself this isn't very interesting. But had you been here watching me type, you would have noticed that I didn't try to use the arrow keys. For a variety of reasons (mainly that different terminals' keyboards send different escape sequences when you press the same arrow key), `emacs` mode doesn't like you to use arrow keys. Unfortunately, you can't watch me type because I'm here and you're not. If you were watching me type, you would probably also notice that I'm wearing a bathrobe and red sneakers right now, so not watching me type has its advantages, too.

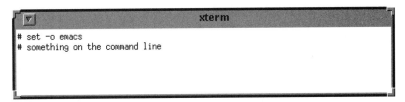

Figure 3.3 Ah, but does it do Windows?

After moving around for a while, you'll probably want to start doing some editing. Don't bother pressing `i` for insert as you would in `vi`—you're already in insert mode. Just add the text you want wherever the cursor is. Table 3.8 shows some of the keystrokes for deleting text in `emacs`.

Deleting text

Table 3.8 How to kill words and characters in `emacs`.

Control Key	What it does
Backspace	Deletes the character behind the cursor (may work with the Del key, too)
Ctrl+d	Deletes one character in front of the cursor
Ctrl+w	Deletes the previous word
Esc Backspace	Deletes the previous word, too (Don't press the keys at the same time.)
Esc h	Also deletes the previous word
Esc d	Deletes one word forward

As you've probably noticed by now, the `Esc` key has an interesting counterfunction. It's kind of like the `Ctrl` key (except that you don't press it at the same time as the key that follows), but it extends the operation of the like `Ctrl` key combination. If `Ctrl+h` deletes the previous character, `Esc h` will delete the previous word. And so on. Serious `emacs` users often call the escape key the "meta" key because it metamorphoses the next key you press into a more powerful version of itself. (Well, maybe that's not why they call it the meta key, but it's something like that. There are some aspects of UNIX lore that are too arcane for me.)

Doing lines   So far, we've navigated through characters and words. Now let's deal with the largest chunk available to us in command-line editing: the line. I'm not going to waste a lot of time talking about killing lines and jumping around lines—I'm just going to give you yet another table (Table 3.9). I hate to do it because tables are boring and smack of poor writing, but sometimes they're the best tool for conveying information.

Table 3.9 The line killers.

Control Key	What it does
Ctrl+a	Moves to the beginning of the line (not really mnemonic, is it?)
Ctrl+e	Moves to the end of the line
Ctrl+k	Deletes from wherever you are to the end of the line
Ctrl+c	Deletes the whole line

One keystroke the Korn shell `emacs` line editor gives you is so important it gets its own table (3.10).

Table 3.10 The most important keystroke.

Control Key	What it does
Ctrl+y	Undeletes whatever you just deleted (in theory)

Of course, what would life be without some disappointment: Ctrl+y doesn't always work. I spent one evening trying to figure out what I was doing wrong. Seeing as I had only deleted about three characters, it was a pretty poor way to spend an evening, but I learned that I was, as they say, SOL (really out of luck). Seems there are just some terminals you can't Ctrl.

One of the nicest things about `emacs` command-line editing is that you can search through your command history. Yes, no longer do you have to type `history` and then manually search through all the commands on the screen. By typing `Ctrl+r`, then one word or sequence of characters from the command you want to recall, and then `Return`, you'll recall the most recently typed command containing that string. Figure 3.4 shows the results.

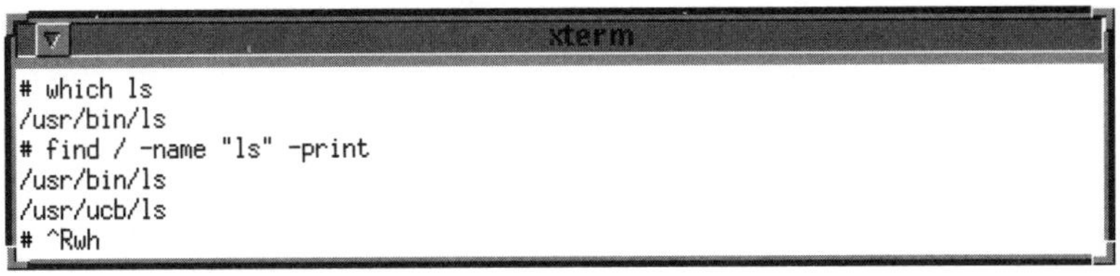

```
xterm
# which ls
/usr/bin/ls
# find / -name "ls" -print
/usr/bin/ls
/usr/ucb/ls
# ^Rwh
```

Figure 3.4 Search and destroy. Now!

The best way to figure out how `Ctrl+r` works is to experiment. Actually, that should go without saying about most of the stuff in this chapter, but this is a good place to reiterate it.

If you think you're done, think again. We still have to cover filename completion. If you remember that the C shell has a command (`set filec`) that turns this capability on, you're *good*. The Korn shell's `emacs` mode has virtually the same thing. Here's how it works.

Filename completion

You're typing along and you realize that you have to type the name of an incredibly long file. Rather than typing the whole thing, you type just enough of it to distinguish that filename from the rest of the files in that directory, and hit `Esc` twice. If you've done your job right (that is, typed enough of the file's name that you've uniquely distinguished it from the rest of the files in that directory), the Korn shell will finish the file's name and put a space after it so you can type more command options or other filenames. If the filename that the Korn shell sees is actually a directory, instead of a space it'll put a slash (so you can continue typing more subdirectory names).

If you haven't done your job right and there are two or more possible completions of the filename, the shell will complete as much as it can (the part the filenames share), then beep to get your attention so you can supply more characters to make the filename unique. For example, if you have two files in a directory, called `superman` and `supperman` (although why you'd have either of these is a little beyond me), and you typed

```
$ cat sEscEsc
```

the shell would respond with

```
$ cat sup
```

and a beep. You'll need to supply either the **e** or the other **p** to make the filename unique. Then you can hit `Esc` twice again:

```
$ cat suppEscEsc
```

and the shell will respond with this:

```
$ cat supperman
```

And everybody's happy.

Using Esc*   Don't try to turn the page yet—you can't `Esc` that easily. There's another trick you should know: `Esc*`. `EscEsc` does a fine job of completing *one* filename, but what happens when you want to expand your horizons and deal with all the filenames that begin with a particular prefix? Typing `Esc*` will show you all the filenames that complete what you've started typing. To go back to our `super` vs. `supper` example, if you typed

```
$ cat sEsc*
```

when you hit `Return`, you'd see

```
$ cat superman supperman
```

What's the   If you're thinking, "What's the difference between this and just typing `cat s*`?"
diff?   you're right. There is no effective difference. Except that the `Esc*` routine expands the filenames so you can see what you're about to do. If you decided to delete all the files that began with the letter `s`, rather than typing an `ls s*` command first, you could type `rm sEsc*` and see how it expanded. As with so many things in UNIX, it's just another way of accomplishing the same goal.

There are some other keystrokes you should be aware of. (See Table 3.11.) They come from `emacs`land and probably aren't too very useful, but they're there and what good would this book be if I didn't try to be so totally exhaustive that it makes you want to hurl?

Table 3.11 Neat Korn shell `emacs` editing miscellany.

Control Key	What it does
`Ctrl+t`	Transposes the characters to the right of the cursor
`Ctrl+u`	Repeats the following command four times
`Ctrl+v`	What version of Korn shell are you using?
`Ctrl+]` *n*	Searches for character *n* on the current command line
`Esc c`	Converts the word after the cursor to all caps
`Esc l`	Converts it to all lowercase
`Esc .`	Inserts last word in previous command here
`Esc _`	Ditto, although why you'd use the underscore . . .

And if you're wondering what to do with some of this stuff, here are some examples. Probably the most important of these keyboard shortcuts is `Esc .`. It can be used in anything from a simple series of commands such as

```
$ ls figu*
figure1 figure2 figure3 figurine
$ rm Esc .
```

to more complex groupings of commands where you insert filenames partway through a command line.

> The `Esc c` and `Esc l` commands are really appealing, but in practice they're not very useful. I mean, how many of us accidentally type a word in the wrong case? Sure, it happens, but it's not an everyday occurrence. File it for future notice and don't bother wasting much brainpower employing it. Similarly pointless is `Ctrl+v`. It's nice to know if you want to show off, but once you're done, forget it again. `Ctrl+u` seems like it should be useful (it's certainly interesting), but I don't think I've ever even thought, "Gee, it sure would be nice if I could repeat this exact command four times." I'm sure somebody can point to a situation, but it's not one I've ever seen.

Trasnpoes lettres

`Ctrl+t` is an oddball: It's a command I should find very useful, but I never remember to use it. I'm a fast typist (about 120 errors—uh—words per minute). Unfortunately, there are two times a day when my fingers are willing, but my brain is asleep—before lunch and after lunch. I'm continually trasnposnig letters when I shouldn't be. Generally, I backspace over them and correct the problem. It's just faster. `Ctrl+t`, if I learned to use it, would be much better than deleting my hard-won keystrokes. But I've never gotten my fingers to forget the backspace-repair rule. Why? Because only the Korn shell's `emacs` mode (and `emacs` itself) uses `Ctrl+t`. When I'm working in the C shell or Bourne shell or any other shell, I don't have access to it.

> I'm irregular—most people don't switch from shell to shell every day (unless they're system administrators). If you use the Korn shell, take the time to learn `emacs` mode's `Ctrl+t` command.

A NOTE ON WINDOW SYSTEMS

> Violence is necessary; it is as American as cherry pie.
>
> Rap Brown, 1966

Before X came along there were some other graphical operating environments for UNIX which have largely passed into the annals of history. By now, most everyone

History again

who reads this will be using some variant of the X Window System. X, one of the products of work at MIT's Project Athena, brought semi-Macintosh-like cut-and-paste features to UNIX terminal windows. It gave us a cute little clock we could stick on our screens to continually remind us that there are still six hours left in the day. It also brought us about twenty different window managers. You got your `uwm` (universal window manager), `awm` (a window manager), `twm` (Tom's window manager—one of my favorites), SunView and OpenWindows (both from Sun, thank you very much), and, of course, today's standard `mwm` (Motif, which I still don't like as much as `twm`, but I was outvoted). I say there are twenty because I figure that for every one I know there are three or four I don't.

X's rules   Anyway, the reason you're probably reading this is to hear my words of wisdom about windows on UNIX. There aren't any. I mean, windows are great— I couldn't do my work in UNIX without them. Most of the software I use for work these days requires X. Some of my best friends are windows. But every graphical environment has its own rules.:

- One of the most general rules is that you select text in any window with the left mouse button. Unlike most PC-based graphical environments, once you select it, it's automatically put into the clipboard. Now, to paste, just position the cursor where you want and center-click. (This may not work with your terminal window. If it doesn't, try running the command `xterm &` in that window, and practicing the copy-to-clipboard-and-back routine in the resulting `xterm` window.)

- Right-clicking generally brings up a menu of possible actions. In OpenWindows, the environment on most Sun workstations these days, it brings up a menu with all sorts of programs to launch, games to play, and demos to run. Under Motif, the menu (by default) is simpler, but no less powerful. Right-clicking generally brings up a menu that has an Exit or Quit option.

All these actions are controlled by files with names like `.Xdefaults` and `.mwmrc`. Look for them, open one, and play with the contents. Mostly it's color information (what color should text, foreground, background, borders, menus, and such be), but they do contain some useful stuff about customizing menus. If you're really good, you can even modify one to include your own menus for running commands just the way you want (see Chapter 2).

If you're using a windowed terminal session (probably called `xterm`), try right-, center-, and left-clicking in the window. Now hold down the `Ctrl` key and try your clicks again. Then try all those clicks with the `Alt` key held down. Finally, try them with the `Shift` key. Now repeat the process with `Ctrl+Alt`,

Shift+Ctrl, Shift+Alt, and **Shift+Ctrl.** Why? Because you'll usually see some menus pop up (standard **xterms** are sensitive to this type of clicking). Now repeat all these clicks with every window that pops up on your screen. You may be surprised at some of the menus you see.

The best thing is to play around. Save your default files, then open 'em up and edit the heck out of 'em. If worse comes to worst, just restore your saved backup files (you *did* make backups, didn't you?).

Everyone heralds graphical user interfaces (or GUIs—haplessly pronounced **Gooey** "gooeys") as the future of computing. They probably are, simply because they take a fraction of the time to learn that a standard command prompt takes. Who likes to spend time learning how to use a computer when they have a job to do? Aside from me, that is.

But GUIs have some drawbacks. First and foremost, a sufficiently intuitive interface will put authors of computer books out of work. That alone should be enough to cause a boycott. But there's more: They take up lots more memory than a simple command prompt, they're generally slower than a command prompt (compare **vi** to a graphical editor some time), they're tougher to program for than a simple command prompt (that's changing slowly), and most of them need a command prompt to get going.

Aside from that, they're great. If you're really interested in them, there's probably a manual that came with your particular computer system that explains the ins-and-outs of using your GUI. Maybe next year I'll write a book just on using a GUI.

NEAT WAYS TO STRING COMMANDS TOGETHER

> I get by with a little help from my friends.
>
> John Lennon and Paul McCartney
> "A Little Help from My Friends," 1967

Let's get back to the command line, where we belong. Start thinking dollars and percents. Think about **!s** and **:s.** It's time to see what we can do with the commands we've learned so far. I have never met a command that can't be used in conjunction with UNIX's I/O redirectors. You remember <, >, and |, don't you? They're baaaaack. And this time they mean business. That's because last time I didn't tell you about some of the *most* interesting things you can do with them.

You probably remember what these little things do, but in case you don't:

The greater-than sign (>) directs output from the command on the left into a file (whose name goes on the right). For example, consider this string:

```
% ls > directory
```

Normally `ls` dumps its listing of files to the screen, but this time they went into a file called `directory`.

The less-than sign (`<`) forces the command on the left to take as input whatever is in the file on the right. It's a lot less frequently used than `>`, but no less useful. For example, consider this:

```
% ls > directory
% vi directory
... edit it and take out some files ...
% rm < directory
```

Pretty clever, no? Rather than deleting the files one by one, I dumped the contents of the directory into a file, edited the file to remove the names of the files I didn't want to delete, then forced `rm` to take its input from `directory`.

Last but not least, there's the pipe (`|`). Where would we plumbers be without it? Oh, wait. I'm an author. Darn, I always wanted to be a plumber. Then I could wear a shirt with my name sewn over the left breast pocket. Maybe I can do that anyway . . .

What's a pipe?   Oh, you're still here? You probably want to know what a pipe is, then. Well, it takes the output from the command on the left and forces it into the command on the right. Whereas `>` creates a file with the word you type to its right, `|` assumes that the thing on the right is a command that knows how to accept input. The `|` is probably the most useful all-purpose tool there is. Here's one example:

```
% env | grep X
```

It's simple: The `env` command prints out all my environment variables, but before they get to the screen (called **standard output**), they're grabbed by the pipe and stuck into the **standard input** of the `grep` command, which searches for the letter X. This command is really useful to help you search for the environment variables that control your X Window System.

This is probably as good a place as any to deal with standard input, standard output, and standard error. Standard input is where input standardly comes from: the keyboard. No surprises. Standard output is where output usually goes: the screen. Again, no surprises. Standard error is where error messages go. Mostly, that's the screen. Some commands (mainly system administration ones) only dump their errors to a special terminal or window called the console. The console is the terminal that's connected to a console port on the back of the machine. It's used to boot the machine, and on some UNIXes it's the only terminal that root can log in from. A clever but annoying security precaution.

Standard error is one of those annoying things that can really get in the way of a nice, clean screen. That's because, even if you redirect standard output (or standard out, or stdout to C programmers) to a file, standard error (standard err or stderr) will still go to your screen. That's right: > won't capture standard error (unless it's defined the same as standard output, which it almost never is). I ran into this problem running benchmarks on some systems: I'd go away, figuring that the benchmark would redirect its results into a file. When I'd come back, I'd see that error messages had scrolled all the way up the screen. That's when I learned about redirecting standard error. **Capturing errors**

Use >& to capture stdout *and* stderr into the filename that follows (for C shell users, only—there's no equivalent for the Bourne or Korn shells). If you have a program that you want to run and you want to capture everything, use this combination of operators.

Every once in a while, you want to redirect just stderr into a file—stdout will still go to the screen. Why? Sometimes, it's just a good way to get rid of pesky error messages—to view the unadulterated output. Sometimes you really want to capture the error message. In any event, the Bourne and Korn shells—but not the C shell—enable you to do just this with 2>. Use it like this:

```
$ x11perf > x11perf.results 2> x11perf.errors
```

With this command you'll get one file with the results (x11perf.results) and another with all the errors (if there are any).

> **C shell users: You can circumvent this shortcoming by redirecting stdout, then capturing stderr. Try something like this:**
>
> ```
> % ( x11perf > x11perf.results ) >& x11perf.errors
> ```
>
> **See what you get. The first redirector captures all the stdout from x11perf, leaving stderr to get dumped to the screen. The second redirector (which you'll remember from above) captures stderr.**

Unfortunately, >& captures *all* the output. You don't git nuffin. That's why most UNIXes include a command called tee. Add a command called ball and another called club and you could play golf. Or one called crumpets and you could dine in the late afternoon. **Tee and pipettes**

You use tee with pipes to direct the output to the screen as well as to a file. But tee won't capture stderr—only stdout. Use it like this:

```
% x11perf | tee x11perf.results
... see the results of the x11perf benchmark ...
```

```
% cat x11perf.results
... see the results of x11perf again ...
```

And that is how `tee` works.

After < and > come << and >>. They have pretty drastically different uses from < and >. The most obvious difference is between > and >>: > writes stdout to a file, creating that file if it doesn't exist and destroying it if it does; >> also writes stdout to a file, creating it if it doesn't exist, but appending the output if the file does exist.

In general, it's a whole lot safer to use >> than >, simply because > can destroy a file's contents unless you set noclobber. The C shell has a special mode called noclobber that you can invoke with the command `set noclobber`. When noclobber is on, > won't destroy a file. In general, noclobber makes it difficult to destroy a file accidentally. If you use the C shell, I recommend you put `set noclobber` into your `.login` file. (If you don't use the C shell, you don't have a noclobber to set.) The superguru tip is that you can override noclobber by using >! instead of just >.

Similarly, C shell users can use >>& to append stdout and stderr to a file, and Bourne and Korn shell users can use 2>> to capture just stderr and append it to a file.

The << redirector is something of a different beast. You can't really think of it in any appendy way as you can with >>. In fact, its function is totally different from <. You use < to read stuff from a file. You use << to read stuff from a keyboard. More specifically, the syntax is <<c, where c is a character. Used like this, << will read your input from the keyboard until you type character c, at which point it'll stop.

When to use <<   When would you want to do this? An excellent question, and the answer is, probably not too often. You can use it (and probably will use it most often) when you're writing a shell script that deals with an interactive program, only you don't want to be around to interact. One good example is `ftp`, the file transfer program: It requires you to supply it with all sorts of information as it goes along, like your username, password, and the name of the file you're going to retrieve. But it always asks for that same information in a predictable way, so you can use << to create a shell script that will automate a file transfer (if you know exactly where that file is on the remote machine). You get the idea.

4 Files and What's in Them

Let each man exercise the art he knows.

Aristophanes
The Wasps, 422 BC

In our description of nature the purpose is not to disclose the real essence of the phenomena but only to track down, so far as it is possible, relations between the manifold aspects of our experience.

Niels Bohr
Atomic Theory and the Description of Nature, 1934

The lawn had reached its optimal height (I was having problems finding the house from the street), so I decided it was time to mow. I went into my garage to retrieve the lawn mower. As I opened the door to the garage, I was struck by that wonderful *garage* smell. A smell of insecticide, fungicide, herbicide, weed killer, gasoline, and other remembrances of my youth. I closed my eyes and inhaled deeply. I must have blacked out momentarily, because I began to think of all the detritus in the garage—boxes, furniture, yard care products—as files. The garage was a file system. I began to explore.

I moved boxes around, making notes about what was in some of them. I reorganized, reshuffled, and restrained my back. But in the process I began to think about how files work under UNIX, and what's in them. Each box contained something. When it was something of mine, I opened and browsed. When it wasn't, I set the box aside, unexamined. (Well, maybe just a *little* examined.) Everything in that garage fit into a box. Just like everything in a UNIX file system is a file. Heck, even processes are files on some of the more recent UNIXes.

So that's why there's this chapter: to explore UNIX's garage.

SECURITY, PERMISSIONS, AND OWNERSHIP

Should the whole frame of Nature round him break,
In ruin and confusion hurled,
He, unconcerned, would hear the mighty crack,
And stand secure amidst a falling world.

Horace
Odes, Book 3, Ode 3

When I was in elementary school, one teacher told me that before the Europeans arrived in North America, the residents didn't have locks. Instead, each family had a unique design that was painted on a stick. To keep others from taking their belongings, they'd lay the stick across. Basically, everybody respected the honor system. UNIX security is just slightly more secure than that.

Owners and groups

Each file has an owner, and that owner is a member of a group (or a bunch of groups). When you create a file, a bunch of information is laid down on the disk along with whatever you put into the file. The information includes who created the file (you), what group you were in when you created it, and who is allowed to access it. The first two are straightforward, the third—file permissions—is a little complicated. If you read Chapter 1, you probably already know this stuff, but if you're starting from scratch here, take a sec and read on.

If you type `ls -l` to look at the long listing of a file, you'll see that the line starts with something like this: -rwxrwxrwx. Each letter is part of a code: r = read, w = write, and x = xecute (who said pragrummahs couldn't spell?). Those letters are set automatically when you create your user security mask (your "umask"). As you can see, there are three repeating groups of three letters here, each with an r, w, and x. The first group of three contains your rights as owner of the file; the second contains the rights for your group (your system administrator creates groups either by editing the /etc/passwd and /etc/group files [the first holds user information, the second group information] or by using a system administration utility such as IBM's System Management Interface Tool [SMIT]); and the third contains the rights for everyone else on the system. In this case, everybody has all the rights. Geez, that's not very secure. How do you change it? With numbers.

Calculating permissions

Go back to the groups of three, and think like this: Each r scores 4 points, each w scores 2, and each x scores 1. Maximum score per group: 7. (Sounds like me playing basketball.) Minimum score: 0. If you wanted to change the rights on this file so that you could read and write it (but not execute it) and no one else had any rights at all, you'd add up the score for the r (4) and the w (2) for the first group, for a total of 6, while the second and third group would each score 0. Then you'd put the three scores into a command to enact your wishes:

```
% chmod 600 filename
```

The command chmod stands for "change mode" (UNIX thinks of permissions as modes—read mode, write mode, and execute mode).

> **Permissions are read from left to right. For example, if a file's permissions are 077 and you're the owner, you can't do anything to it. Yes, even though you're the owner, and you're in the right group, *and* you're one of all the users on the system. This is a clever security measure: If you want a particular group of users *not* to have access to a file, make yourself a member of that group (with the newgrp command—the command that enables you to switch from one group to another), then create it, then set the permissions to 707 (rwx–rwx). Now, that group *and only that group* can't get into the file. (If you have any questions about switching from one group to another, see the man page on newgrp.)**

Directories also have the same type of rwx file permissions, except they mean something slightly different. If you have read access to a directory, you can see what's in it. If you have "write" access to a directory, you can delete, rename, or add files to it. If you have execute permission, you can look into, read, and access files in the directory.

Controlling who can access a file you create is done (in part) through the umask command. By default, any directory you create gets permissions of 777, and any file gets 666 (Aaaah—Satan on my system!). That's fine if everybody on your system is *really* nice and doesn't bear you a grudge. But ever since you got that raise and promotion you didn't deserve, they've been out to get you. You need to shut them out a bit more. You could just set the permissions by hand every time you create a file. And you could get to work by pushing your car, too. There's an easier way, natch.

Wearing a umask

The umask command *removes* rights that you specify from the default rights (it *subtracts* from the default r, w, and x values). A directory, by default, has 777. But you want it so that when you create a directory no one outside your group is able to delete files from it, so you need to remove their write access. Let's see, the w gets 2 points, so you could do this:

```
% umask 002
```

Now when you create new directories, the world will have no write access. They will also have write access taken away from any *files* you create. If you wanted to take away all of the world's rights, you'd use this:

```
% umask 007
```

Now any directory you create will have no world permissions: 777 – 007 = 770. But what about files: 666 – 007 = 66-(1). Now that doesn't work. Fret not: UNIX rounds negative numbers up to 0, making this 660.

There is one exception to all rules about file permissions—the superuser can get into all of them. Usually the superuser has an account named root, but root can create other superuser accounts. This is a reminder: Just because you've secured the permissions on a file doesn't mean no one can read it.

The best thing to do with `umask` is to set it to a good value, such as `027` in your `.profile` or `.login` file so that it's always set the way you want. If you need to change it for a particular project, do it manually: It's always better to get an anguished call from someone who can't get into a file they're supposed to be in then to get a nasty call from someone who got into one they weren't.

My Bits Are Sticky

"I've a right to think," said Alice sharply, for she was beginning to feel a little worried.

"Just about as much right," said the Duchess, "as pigs have to fly."

Lewis Carroll
Alice's Adventures in Wonderland, 1865

One problem with generic permissions is that if users have write permission on a directory, they can delete and rename files in it. If you don't want them to do that, you have little choice but to exclude them from the directory—unless you set the directory's **sticky bit**:

```
% chmod 1777 sticky_directory
% ls -ld sticky_directory
drwxrwxrwt  2 john   users     32 Jul 30 10:01 sticky_directory
```

Notice that there's now a `t` where there would be an `x` in the other permissions. That one letter (the result of adding a fourth digit to the directory's permissions) means that users can't delete or rename files that belong to others.

Out of Octal

Mathematics may be defined as the subject in which we never know what we are talking about, nor whether what we are saying is true.

Bertrand Russell
Mysticism and Logic, 1917

Now that you're comfortable with using `chmod` and its octal numbers (or maybe you aren't), it's time to learn how *not* to use them. In addition to accepting numbers, `chmod` accepts letters—letters that are only slightly less cryptic than the numbers. First off, you don't really need to remember that there are three groups of three letters—each group has a letter to explain itself. (See Table 4.1.)

Table 4.1 Who's who to chmod?

The letter	Who it is
u	yoU, the User of the file (really the Owner, but there's already an *o*)
g	Group
o	Others (everybody who's not you and is not in your group)
a	All (everybody)

Simple—it's even more efficient if you're dealing with setting a permission for all the different types of users. Next, why bother remembering that odd octal math? Just use the letters in Table 4.2.

Table 4.2 What's what to chmod?

The letter	What it means
r	Read access
w	Write access
x	Xecute access (there's that spelling thing again)
X	Reverse status of execute bit
s	Set user or group ID (more on that in a second)
t	Set the sticky bit

Two of these deserve some explanation. First, that capital **X**. Seems that the lowercase **x** will do what you tell it: Specifically add or remove execute access. But, on those odd occasions when you want to change the execute status of a file without knowing what it already is—say you just created a shell script you want to edit—you can use the **X**. This is one of those odd bits of trivia you may get asked, but otherwise don't worry about it. The **s** bit is a little more useful.

As you already know, you belong to a group. You may belong to several groups, actually—more recent versions of UNIX have made this fairly standard. It's useful to belong to several groups if you're involved in several projects. For example, if you're in accounting, but you're also a project leader on a new software project as well as a manager, you might belong to three groups: accounting, newsoft, and manage. Using the chgrp command (as in "chgrp accounting"), you can switch from group to group. Each group has access to different directories and different files (as befits that bureaucracy we call an office).

Multiple groups

When you create a file on a BSD system, whichever group is your primary group is made the owner of that file. On an old System V system, whichever group owns the directory you're in owns the file. On SVR4 and most more-recent UNIXes, you can set a bit on the directory so that any file created in it is owned by the person who created it, and whichever group they were in when they created it is stored as the owner's group. By setting the **s** bit on a file, you're making it sensitive to which group you're in. A long explanation of a simple subject.

But how do you set all these? Glad you asked. Table 4.3 has the answers.

Table 4.3 And what to do when you get there.

The letter	What it does
–	Removes the permission
+	Adds the permission to whatever's already there
=	Sets the permission to what you specify

Now you're probably wanting some examples. To change a file so that it's executable by you, just type

```
% chmod u+x shellscript
```

If you're thinking that this is a longer way to type `chmod +x shellscript`, you're right: `chmod` assumes that you mean u if you don't supply a "who" letter. Alternately,

```
% chmod g-x shellscript
```

will make it so that other members of your group can't execute a file. Most of the time, + and – are fine—you can do a lot with them. But they have a drawback: they will just modify whatever is already there. In the previous example (the one with **g-x**), you may have left read and write permissions on the file for your group. To top that off, a member of your group could just change to another group and then execute your shell script: You didn't remove the `other`'s execute access.

You should get in the habit of specifying exactly the permissions you want. For that, use the = sign. Like this:

```
% chmod g=x shellscript
```

Now nobody can get into your file—its permissions will look like this:

```
------x--
```

Daunting, isn't it?

The = has another use, too: You can set one group's permissions to equal another's. Say you've been working on a bunch of shell scripts and files that describe what they do. Now they're ready for prime time and you want your group to have access to them, too. You could go through all the `readme` files and add the `rw` bits, then through all the scripts and add `rwx`. But that would take too long—you already have these permissions yourself and you can just copy them from point A to point 2. Thusly:

Equating permissions

```
% chmod g=u *
```

And bingo, the group's permissions will match yours.

The Hole

> No man acquires property without acquiring with it a little
> arithmetic also.
>
>   R.W. Emerson
>   *Representative Men*, 1850

Pssst. Hey buddy. Wanna buy a secret? Okay, for you, it's free, but you owe me. [Look both ways, lean in conspiratorially. Lower voice.] UNIX isn't very secure.

Whoah. Now *there's* a news flash. Let me give you a simple example—one that's probably all over your system. Most of the time, there's nothing you can do about it, either. Let's say that `joebob` creates a file and sets the permissions to `444` (everybody can read it). That means that I can't open it with a text editor and modify it. I can, however read it, which means I can copy it. Once I copy it, it's mine. (When you move a file, it still belongs to the original owner, but when you copy it, it belongs to you.) Then I can edit it and make all my changes. And I can put it back with the `mv` command. UNIX will ask, "`override protection 444 for filename?`" And I just have to answer `y`. Done.

Open house

Why did this happen? Because I have write access to the directory. If you're not careful, your directories will give everybody write access. You probably should check all your directories to make sure the permissions look something like `711` (`drwx-x-x`). And set your `umask` properly, too.

Plugging it

DELETING, COPYING, RENAMING, AND MANAGING FILES

> Three removes is as bad as a fire.
>
> Benjamin Franklin
> Preface to *Courteous Reader*, 1758

This should be a pretty brief section, seeing as you already know a bit about most of what's in it. You know that you use `cp` to copy files, `mv` to rename them and move them to other places, and `rm` to delete them. Okay, fine. We'll skip that. Mostly. And we'll get on to the truly interesting stuff, like how you can make sure you never lose a file again, and how to make copies of files that take up no space, and how you can delete files that have impossible names. But first, the mostly I was talking about two sentences ago.

Duck! It's The Basics

> Which is the more difficult, to be born or to rise again?
> That what has never been should be, or that what has been, should be again?
> Is it more difficult to come into being than to return to it?
>
> Pascal
> *Pensées*, 1670

I come not to praise rm I'm not going to eulogize `cp`, `mv`, and `rm`. I'm going to show you how to make them better. First off, if you've gotten this far, you already know what these commands do and probably are even familiar with some of their options. But you probably aren't using them as fully as you should.

For example, when was the last time you deleted a bunch of files using a wildcard, then realized that there was one file in there you didn't want to delete? Saaaay, yesterday? Okay, you never have to do that again. You can go back to Chapter 2 and read about **aliases**, but I'll give you the lowdown. If you're a C shell user, add a line like this to your `.cshrc`:

```
alias ri rm -i
```

And if you use Korn shell, make it

```
alias ri=rm -i
```

And now never use the `rm` command again—use `ri` instead. If you use the Bourne shell, create a directory called `aliases`, add it to your path, then create a shell script in it called `ri` that includes the command `rm -i`. Same as the aliases (just a little slower to execute).

Alternately, when was the last time you wanted to delete a bunch of files and found that they had annoying permissions that forced you to answer "y" to a bunch of confirmation questions? Day before yesterday, huh? Create an alias (or script) called `rf` and make it (you guessed it) `rm -f`. This is a delete with extreme prejudice.

Also see Chapter 2 for information on how to make `rm` copy your files to a temporary holding area so they aren't deleted immediately.

You should also know the `rm -r` command—one that recursively removes all **Death to files** files and directories you specify. It's one of UNIX's most powerful, yet simple, commands. With it you can destroy an entire computer's data. Never, *ever* try typing `rm -r /*`—it's death.

Like `rm -r`, there's also a `cp -r` command that does about the same thing. It's a decent way to move one directory structure to another place if you have to. Some systems don't have it, however (mostly older ones). If that's your case, try using the `rcp` command. It always has the `-r` switch. It takes the same syntax as `cp` (except it can copy to and from computers on your network, too).

Dan Watts, my technical editor, raises a good point (as always). Using `cp -r` has the nasty side effect of converting soft-linked files into real files, which take up more room. (Links are UNIX's way of having one file in two places at the same time.) It also changes the ownership of the files. A hint on how to get around this is to use the `tar` command:

```
% tar cf - somefiles | (cd /somewhere; tar xf - )
```

The command creates a `tar` file to the standard output, and pipes it to a pair of commands in parentheses. The first of these commands does a `cd` to some other directory and then it `untars` standard input.

Here's yet another trick for copying across a network and saving network bandwidth (at the expense of CPU cycles, unfortunately):

```
% rsh somehost '( cd /dir1; tar cf - files | compress )
  ' | \ uncompress | tar xf -
```

This runs a `tar` command on the remote host, sending the `tar` file to standard output, which is in turn compressed. This is all executed using the CPU on the remote host. The compressed output is then sent across the network to standard output of `rsh`, a command we'll talk about at length in Chapter 7. Next, we pipe the output to the `uncompress` command, which in turn pipes its output to `tar`. The `uncompress` and `tar xf` are run on the local host. If you have a lot of data to move across the network and you don't have the disk

space to store the `tar` file on disk and then copy that file, this is a very useful trick. Combine this into an alias or put it in a shell script and you can make a very powerful remote copy command.

You probably know that you can use the `cat` command to act like `cp`. You usually don't have to, but it's useful if your `cp` somehow becomes corrupted. Use it like this

```
% cat < file1 > file2
```

and `cat` will dump the contents of `file1` into `file2`. Simple (but not as simple as `cp`).

Renaming files   Finally, we come to `mv` (short for move)—an underrated yet cheerful command. Like `cp` and `rm`, it's straightforward. Straightforward, that is, until you have to rename one group of files to another name. Let's say you have a bunch of files that end with the extension `.txt`, and you want them to end with the extension `.doc`. How do you do it? Using `mv *.txt *.doc` won't work—`mv` doesn't work that way. Instead, you have to use a compound command containing a command you haven't seen yet:

```
% ls -d *.txt | sed 's/\(.*\)\.txt$/mv & \1.doc/' | sh
```

Now I suppose you want me to *explain* this. Sheesh, you're so demanding. Okay: the `ls` command lists all the files in the directory and the `-d` does it as a single column. That's piped to `sed`, a special editor that deals with streams of data (like what the `ls` command is dumping out). In this case, we're performing a substitution (s/), changing every occurrence of *.txt (\.*\)\.txt$) and replacing it with a bunch of other things—the command `mv`, the original filename (that's what the `&` is), then the original filename with a `.doc` in place of the `.txt`. All that gets piped to `sh` so that it's executed. I owe this to someone at Silicon Graphics—I wish I could remember his name—who also demonstrated some of the neat things that their computers can do.

A friend's scripting trick   Someone at Apple's A/UX division showed me a variant on this using `vi`. First open `vi` in the directory you want to rename the files in. Now issue the following commands:

```
:r !ls *.txt
:%s/.*/mv & &/
:%s/txt$/doc/
:w !sh
:q!
```

And we're off. First we list *.txt, and dump that into the current buffer. Now we add an mv command to the beginning of every line. Next, we change the txt to doc. Finally, we execute what's in the buffer. Then, just quit without saving. It does exactly the same thing as the command line, but you can edit the command before it's run. Never use it myself, but I have it written on a sheet of paper in my office in case I should ever need it.

Never Do What You Can't Undo

> Whenever a man does a thoroughly stupid thing, it is always from the noblest of motives.
>
> Oscar Wilde
> *The Picture of Dorian Gray*, 1891

I live by that motto. Mostly. Except when I'm signing contracts. Then I tend to get intimidated by that pseudo-English that lawyers write. I'd dearly love to force all lawyers to read Strunk and White's book on grammar. But I'm not here to discuss the litigious nature of the American public. I'm here to talk about control systems for files.

Actually, these tools are called revision control systems and are, as you probably suspected, used largely by programmers. But DON'T TURN THE PAGE YET. Programmers know a lot that we (the unwashed masses) don't. They were the first to discover UNIX, for example.

Version control isn't just for programmers

The basic idea of revision control systems is to make sure that you never do something that can't be undone. Conversely, you can never undo something that can't be redone. (Unless you delete the whole dang revision control structure, but you'll *never* do that.) Instead of just creating a file on Monday, then editing it on Tuesday and Wednesday, then making some changes on Thursday that you regret Friday, forcing you to start from scratch, revision control systems force you to check files in and out, like you do at a library. At every stage along the way, the revision control system records the changes. If you need something undone (or accidentally delete a file), you can fix it.

There are two main utilities used for revision control: the Source Code Control System (SCCS) and the Revision Control System (RCS). The basic difference is that SCCS tracks the first version of the file and all its changes, while RCS tracks the most recent version of a file and all its changes. If you're unfamiliar with the concept of versions, it's pretty self-explanatory: When you change a file, your changes are entered into the revision database, and your changed file gets a new version number. The advantage of RCS over SCCS is that RCS will get the most recent version of your file faster. The disadvantage is that if you need an earlier version, it will take longer than with SCCS to rebuild. On with the show.

SCCS and RCS

First, RCS Let's get down and dirty with RCS. First, create a directory in your $HOME and name it RCS. Now create a file (call it file1). There are two commands you need to know from here—ci and co. Use ci to check file1 into the revision control system: ci file1. The original is deleted (just like when you return a book to the library), and a new version goes into RCS. To get it back out, use the co command: co -l file1. (The -l option tells RCS that you want to edit the file—if you don't use it (co file1) RCS will assume you want a read-only version.

There are two more useful commands. First, you're probably going to need some time to get used to the RCS system, so you're probably going to forget what you checked out. To see what you have checked out, use the command rlog -L -R ~/RCS/* (or $HOME/RCS/*).

The other useful command is the one that enables you to undo what you just did: rcs -u file1. It means, "tell the revision control system that I want to undo my changes to file1." Since you're really just editing a copy, rcs tells RCS to pretend you never checked it out. Now delete file1 and you're done.

The key to any revision control system is checking files in and out frequently. It's like saving a document you're working on—you should get into the habit of dropping files back into RCS or SCCS so that they can track your changes. If you don't, you're no better off than if you hadn't tried.

Vince, one of my technical editors, says: "One *major* problem with RCS and SCCS is that they only work on text files. If you use some apps that generate binary files (like FrameMaker, or some drawing programs), neither RCS nor SCCS will work. Despite that, we can't live without RCS."

Now, SCCS The other system (and the one that I use when I'm not feeling too lazy) is SCCS. For me, the SCCS commands make a little more sense. Table 4.4 gives you a quick overview.

Table 4.4 Is thisccs getting monotonousccs?

Command	What it does (or should do)
sccs create file1	Creates file1
sccs edit file1	Checks file1 out for editing
sccs get file1	Checks file1 out (read only)
sccs get -rn file1	Checks out version n of file1
sccs check	Tells you what files are checked out in your name
sccs delta file1	Checks file1 back in (okay, so this one doesn't make a lot of sense)
sccs unedit file1	Undoes whatever changes you made since you checked file1 out

I prefer SCCS because I know it—it was what was on the system I learned on. Your system may not have both and you may just have RCS. No worries: They're each as good as the other. Use them right and you'll never have to worry about accidentally deleting a file again.

The Missing ln

All things by immortal power,
Near and Far
Hiddenly
To each other linked are,
That thou canst not stir a flower
Without troubling of a star.

Francis Thompson
The Mistress of Vision, ca. 1900

This is probably another of those cheesy subheadings that only I would dare use. UNIX has a method for making "copies" of a file called **links**. The idea is that if you have a file (or even a directory) in one place on your computer and you want it to be in another at the same time, rather than copying it you link the second location to the first. You can keep doing that, making as many links off the original file as you want (but after making a few links of links, you'll find that UNIX gives you an error when you try to link to a link, so avoid it if you can).

Links have a couple of advantages over regular copies. First, they take up almost no space on the disk—just an inode or a directory entry to store the link information. Second, links *are* the original files: When you edit a link, you're editing the original.

Links can be better than copies

There are two kinds of links: hard links and soft (or symbolic) links. The technical difference continuously escapes me, but there are a couple of things you should know about each one:

- Hard links are the default. If you say `ln file1 link1`, it'll be a hard link. You need to say `ln -s file1 link1` to make a soft link.

- Although they're the default, hard links are so limiting they're less commonly used than soft links. If your system supports soft links, it's a lot more likely that people will create soft links rather than hard ones.

- Hard links can't cross file systems. (A file system is a logical subdivision of a hard disk. File systems break the hard disk into smaller, more manageable pieces. You can think of a hard disk as a filing cabinet and a file system as a file in that filing cabinet. You can have multiple files in one filing cabinet, each holding different types of information, or you can have one file [like the file for an important client] that spans several filing cabinets.) Want to link `/usr/people/john/file1` to `/usr1/smith/file2`? Well, chances are you can't, because `/usr` and `/usr1` are probably different file systems.

- Hard links can't link directories. If you want to link an entire directory tree to another tree, you're SOL (seriously out of luck) with a hard link.

- Hard links are available with every version of UNIX. Soft links aren't.

- Hard links *are* the file they're linked to. If you delete the original file, a hard link will remain and be fully usable—the file system generates a pointer that turns the hard link into a real file. If you delete the original behind a soft link and then try to access the soft link, you'll get a "file not found" error.

Simple syntax   The syntax of linking is just like copying—nothing new to learn here—except that to link one directory to another, the syntax is the same as if you were linking two files to each other. The one thing I caution you about is this: If you create a soft link, never delete the original file or directory. It's not particularly injurious, but it can confuse people.

Is there any way to know if a file you're working on has links to it? Not if they're soft links. With hard links, you can see if a file has a link with `ls -l` (right after the permissions will be a number—if it's greater than 1, the file has links) or with `ls -F` (links will have @ after their names).

 Warning: Don't get the link order wrong! If you type `ln link1 file1`, the `ln` command will typically delete the file `link1` if it exists, and then it will create the link. This means that if you get the order wrong, you've just deleted the real file.

JoeBob's File Market: Filenames for All Occasions

The nothing of a name.

Edgar Allen Poe
Tamerlane, 1827

Everybody's system has files on it with names that just don't make sense. Like `$testfile`. Or `test!file`. Or, better yet, a file with a space: `test file`. These are perfectly legit filenames, and the UNIX file system has no problem storing them. Of course, opening one of these in an editor can take some extra characters. So here's how to deal with filenames that have special characters in them: Rename them to something useful.

**Kill 'em with **   Mostly you can do this with wildcards and the backslash. For example, a file named `test!file` could be renamed to `filetest` with the command

```
% mv test* filetest
```

and you'd never have a problem with it. Or you could try

```
% mv test\!file filetest
```

and get the same results. Filenames with spaces are the worst because the UNIX command line will think that they're multiple files. For example, trying to type

```
% mv test file testfile
```

looks fine to us because we know there's a file in the directory called `test file`. The command line doesn't. You need to try something more clever, like

```
% mv test* filetest
```

to get what you want.

If that doesn't work, try specifying the full pathname to a file:

Or use the full path

```
% rm ./\$testfile
```

This works particularly well with filenames that include a dash or a slash. The `./` just means "look in the current directory." As a last resort, try this:

```
% rm -i *
```

As this command asks you (file by file) what you want to delete, say n to everything but the nasty file.

If worse comes to worst, move everything in the directory to another directory, then move up a level and use `rm -r` to destroy the entire directory in question.

> **I've heard tell of people that delete files by inode number or use other such fancy tricks. I don't recommend them. Three such methods got passed on to me when I was doing the research for this book. I destroyed my file system with one (the file system repair utility, `fsck`, wouldn't repair it and I had to reinstall the operating system), and I created large holes in my file system with the other two (that `fsck` did repair). Unless you're the superuser, you can create a lot of havoc using such commands. If `rm` won't take it away, chances are nothing will. Despite that warning, I'll explain how to do it in the next section.**

My Node, Inode

> Two hackers, lost in the woods, consult a topographic map. After much heated debate the younger one scans the horizon, sticks out his arm, points at a nearby hilltop and yells, "Over there! Over there!"
> "What?" sighs the other hacker.
> "I got it! Don't you see? According to this map, we're over there!"
>
> Pensées Pinecliffius

Do not attempt this at home

Okay, so what's an inode? Oh yeah, sure, you know all about how a file system creates inodes and stores information about files in them, but I mean *really*, what's an inode? Basically, it's a place on the disk that stores the location of the file—a kind of database. At its simplest, an inode is just a number. Figure 4.1 shows an example of an inode, in case you're interested in looking at a stupid number, which you're probably not.

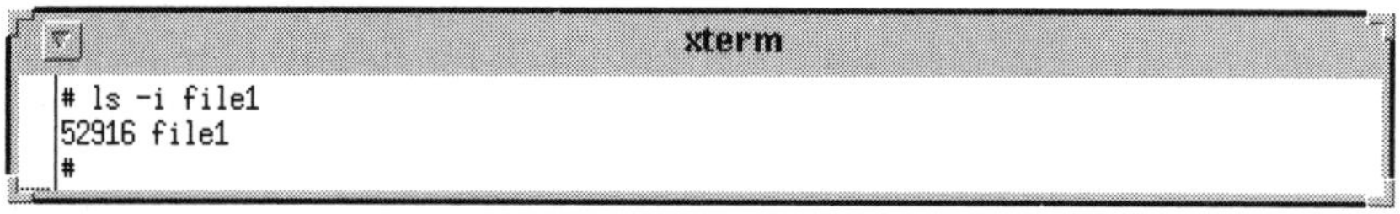

```
xterm
# ls -i file1
52916 file1
#
```

Figure 4.1 If you node what Inode . . .

I am a trained professional

When you have a file's inode number (which `ls -i` supplies), you can delete it. It's a completely nasty way of removing a file and should be used very rarely—so rarely that I didn't put it with the rest of the tips for deleting files. Use this trick only if every other deletion trick fails and you *really want that file gone*. First, unmount the file system the file is on. You'll find that you can't do that unless you're the superuser (thank UNIX for small favors). Let's say that the file's called `file1` (with an inode of `52916`) and resides on `/usr`. You'd type this:

```
% su
...
% umount /usr
% clri /usr  52916
...
% fsck /usr
...
% mount /usr
```

So what happened? You `su` to become the superuser, then you unmount `/usr`. Next, the `clri` command removes inode `52916` from the inode table of `/usr`.

That leaves a gaping hole in your file system. You try to repair it with the file system check command (`fsck`). If it works, you mount /usr again. If it doesn't, you're in deep trouble.

FINDING FILES

> "Are you lost, daddy?" I asked tenderly.
> "Shut up," he explained.
>
> Ring Lardner
> *The Young Immigrunts*

I'm sitting in an unairconditioned room, surrounded by enough computer equipment to heat a small country, during the hottest July on record. I am sweaty and probably smell bad. All of that I can live with. But my file done left me. TWAng. It's all over now. Twangtwangthump. I got the lost-file blues. Twangadeedang. I—

Oh, hello again. Just practicing for the local talent show. And yes, I *do* need a lot of practice. So what do you do when you've created a file and don't remember where it went? Or when you just need to find an executable that's not in your path? Well, you use the `find` command—it's UNIX's electronic mother ("mom, where did I put ___"). We've used it before (see Chapter 2) with a C shell alias like this:

```
% alias locate 'find / -name \!$ -print'
```

But that's just the tip of the berg: `find` probably has more options than my boss has ways to torment me. Among the more popular are those in Table 4.5.

Table 4.5 You didn't think I'd let you escape so easily, did you?

Option	What the heck it does
-name	The next word better be a filename in quotes.
-atime	When was the file last accessed?
-mtime	When was the file last modified?

And just about all of them need -print as their last argument, or else find will happily find your file and not ever tell you. (Kind of like one of those people who answers "yes" to the question, "Do you have so-and-so's phone number?")

Actually, it's simple   Find commands nearly always look like this:

```
find where what
```

"Where" is usually a directory like / or /usr or . (dot is the current directory). "What" is a little more complicated. Usually you specify what to find with −name:

```
% find / -name "joebob.o" -print
```

will find all files named joebob.o;

```
% find . -name "\*.o" -print
```

will find all files whose names end in .o; and

```
% find /usr -name "[a-zA-Z]*.o" -print
```

will find all files whose names begin with a letter (either lowercase or uppercase) and end in .o. The one trick to −name is quoting what comes after it. If there are any wildcards, you need quotes; otherwise the shell will barf on your command. In the second example above, a simple backslash protects the *. In the third line, we're searching for a file whose name begins with either a lowercase or an uppercase letter (as opposed to a number) and ends in .o. For that, we need double quotes.

Finding by date   Probably second most often (after finding a file by filename), you'll want to search for a file that you recently modified (and now lost). For that, use −mtime. This command thinks in days before today, so −mtime 2 finds files modified two days ago. Some twists: −mtime −2 finds files modified between two days ago and today, and −mtime +2 finds files modified more than 2 days ago. Das examples:

```
% find -mtime +4 -name "*.o" -print
% find -mtime +4 -mtime -6 -print
```

But how about when you want to see when a file was accessed—when somebody just opened it up for a look inside—rather than when somebody actually modified it? find has an option for that, too (or why would I be writing this?): −atime. It works the same as −mtime—no worries.

There's also −ctime, but it's so ludicrously obscure you'll probably never need it. It checks (get this) when the inode information on a file was last modified. I have yet to see anyone use this option.

Next come the somewhat-less-useful switches for finding files: `-user`, `-group`, `-type`, `-size`, and `-newer`. The quickest way to present these is in a table, so I will (Table 4.6). They're aren't worth much more effort.

Table 4.6 To know an obscure `find` switch is to love one.

Option	What you hope it tells `find`
`-user`	The file belongs to the username you specify next.
`-group`	The file belongs to the group you specify next.
`-type`	The file is an f (plain, ordinary file), d (directory), b (block device, like a disk or tape drive), c (character device, like a terminal), p (pipe—don't worry about it), l (symbolic link—a file that isn't a file, but links to where a file lives), or s (socket—generally a network thing).
`-size`	The file is however large you specify in (usually) 512K blocks.
`-newer`	The file you're looking for is newer than the file whose name you specify next.

Moving right along. What happens when you want `find` to *do* something with something it finds? Something other than print the filename, I mean? Well, nothing unless you specify the `-exec` switch. The `-exec` switch enables you to tell `find` to run a command after it finds a file. It's a great way to get into totally hot water: If there's one problem with the syntax of your `find` command you can munge myriad files without knowing it.

There are three things you need to know about `-exec`: (1) Every `-exec` statement will end with a "quoted" semicolon (usually `\;`). (2) The characters { and } are very special to `find`—together they represent the name of the file that `find` found. ("The file that `find` found" . . . I kind of like that. Anyway . . .) (3) Finally, `-exec` is not a panacea: There are many operations that it won't perform (for example, you can't have two sets of `{}` in one `-exec` argument), and its syntax can be confusing.

Running commands with `find`

Despite all that, here's a good use for `-exec`:

```
% find . -name '*~' -exec /bin/rm {} \;
```

The purpose of this command is to remove the temporary files `emacs` creates (their names end with ~). Basically, this will find any file whose name ends with a tilde and execute `/bin/rm` (remove) on it. The space before the escaped semicolon (`\;`) is vital: otherwise it won't work.

> **If you do decide that you want to use `-exec`, put it as close to the end of your command line as possible, preferably right before the `-print` statement. Why? Because you want every other test to run *before* exec executes its**

command—otherwise you're executing the command more than you need to and your `find` command will take longer to run than you want. Oh, and before you run your true –exec command, place the command `echo` between –exec and the command you want to run. This will force –exec to print out what it's going to do, so you can debug things and head off potential nightmares.

Question and answer time: "So what happens when you want to find two files whose names are completely different?" You can use an "or" on the command line to make this possible. Or makes its appearance in the form of –o, like this:

```
% find /usr -name "file1" -o -name "file2" -print
```

This line will find both `file1` and `file2`. The `find` command reads the "or" like this: Find a file whose name is either `file1` or `file2` (and start looking from the /usr directory).

Complex finds
"So what happens when you want to find two files that were modified after a certain date?" You can chain together your search criteria pretty easily, but you need to group them so that `find` knows which ones are most important. The command line would look like this:

```
% find / -mtime -3 \( -name "file1" -o -name "file2" \) -print
```

Some notes on this line: First, why do the two names go in parentheses and not `mtime`? Because `mtime` is the more general criterion, and it's faster to search from the general to the specific. For example, if you have a filing cabinet that's alphabetized and you're looking for the Smith records, you first find the drawer with the letter "S" on the front, then open it, then go into a folder with "Sm" on it, and so on. If you started with the first ("A") drawer looking for the Smith file, you'd have to wade through many drawers before you found it. Second, why are the parentheses preceded by backslashes? These are "quotes" to protect what's in parentheses from the shell. Without them, the `find` command would never see the parentheses—the shell would try to evaluate what's inside (and fail, by the way). Third, why is there a space before and after the \(and the \). If you don't put that space in there, `find` won't find the ( )s. (The irony of `find` not finding something should be lost on no one.)

"How about finding a file that was modified no more than 72 hours ago that bears the name `file1`?" Okay, you've seen `find`'s "or," now meet it's "and":

```
% find / -mtime -3 -name "file1" -print
```

Done. The "and" is nothing—don't put anything and `find` thinks you're "anding" your criteria.

"Okay, smart guy, how about finding every file *not* named `file1` for a change? Got you there, didn't I?" Nope. Use the `!`:

```
% find / \! \( -name "file1" \) -print
```

Done. Note the quoted `!` and `( )`. Also remember the spaces before and after the `( )`.

These are all the patterns to `find` commands. You can string together all sorts of criteria as you wish—just remember to enclose like elements in parentheses and always include your `-print` at the end.

PRINTING

> Print is the sharpest and the strongest weapon.
>
> Joseph Stalin, 1923

Read any other book on UNIX and they'll make out like printing is some kind of arcane art requiring chicken lips and voodoo dolls. It isn't. I can think of little that's easier than printing. Falling off a log, asking my accountant to do my taxes. Yup. UNIX printing is right up there on the easy scale. You could say that, on a scale of easy to hard, printing is easy. (Setting up your printer may not be so easy, but actually printing is pretty easy.) So I'm not going to waste a whole lot of time on it.

Here's the quick-and-dirty: If you have a System V system, your printing **It's easy** command is `lp`. Just type

```
% lp file1
```

to print `file1` to whatever the default printer is. For BSD systems, it's similarly simple:

```
% lpr file1
```

This just doesn't qualify as difficult in my book.

Which printer is your default? Well, that's usually controlled either by a **Ain't my** variable called `PRINTER` (on BSD systems) or `LPDEST` (on System V systems). You **default** can `echo` these variables to see what your shell thinks is your default printer, or you can just set them in one of your dot files (`.login` or `.profile`, probably). I recommend setting them both, no matter what version of UNIX you're running— it makes your dot files more portable, and it removes any doubt.

Q who are U?   So how do you know what your printers are called? I mean, it's not a lot of good knowing that you can set an environment variable if you don't know what to set it *to*, now is it? For that, you have the `lpstat` command. Type `lpstat -p -D` to see all the print queues on your system with a brief description.

Print queues? What are they? This raises an interesting point about UNIX printers. UNIX printers have to be shared with multiple people. In order for that to work, UNIX needs a method for tracking the different files that different people print and a method for lining them all up so they get printed in the order requested. To do this, UNIX has a print queue **system, which queues up print jobs to different printers. One queue can actually be directed to several printers, and one printer can be a member of several queues.**

You can also send files to different print queues from the command line (you don't have to reset the environment variables each time). You'd do this with

```
lpr -Pprinter file1
```

or with

```
lp -dprinter file1
```

Notice that System V uses the incredibly non-mnemonic –d (for destination, I suppose) switch. Don't you just love it?

Killing jobs   If you print something and then change your mind, try the `cancel` command (System V), as in

```
% lpstat -u
lp-112               512 john        on lp
% cancel lp-112
lp-112: canceled
```

or the `lprm` command (Berkeley):

```
% lpq
lp is ready and printing
Rank      Owner      Job    Files          Total Size
active    john       112    test.doc       512 bytes
% lprm 112
dfA112solaris dequeued
cfA112solaris dequeued
```

In both cases, notice that I used a command to find out the job number that the queue system assigned my file, then I killed that number.

So Much for the Basics

> Though the adjective may agree with the noun in gender, number and case, nevertheless the adjective and the noun may not agree.
>
> Voltaire

This is the easy stuff. You can also wreak some havoc with your printer, adding clever titles to your burst page and clever formatting. Some of that is done with the lp or lpr command, some of it is done with a command called pr—a print formatting command. Let's cover the ground we know first. **Advanced printing**

A burst page gets printed on most queues—it's the page that comes out looking really ugly and has information about the queue that the file was printed on, who submitted it, and what the filename was. With both lp and lpr, you can change the title that gets printed on that page. For lp, try lp –t "This is a test title" file1; for lpr, try lpr –J "This is a test title" file1. Nothing too interesting here, but it's useful to be able to customize this stuff.

More interesting is the pr command. The quickest way for you to get an idea of all of pr's capabilities is to read the man page. It's one of the better ones. Basically, pr takes Plain-Jane text files and makes them slightly less plain. It takes a file, formats it, and dumps it to standard output. You can either capture that output into a file and then print the file, or pipe the output of the command directly to an lp or lpr command. See Table 4.7 for some options for pr. **Formatting**

You can use pr like this, for example:

```
% pr -l 20 -h "Mucking with files" -m file1 file2 file3 | lp
```

This merges file1, file2, and file3 into columns (on really short pages) and prints them.

Table 4.7 Making pretty output.

Option	What it does
–l *n*	Sets page length to *n* lines. Default is 66.
–w *n*	Sets page width to *n* characters. Default is 72.
–o *n*	Indents all lines by *n* characters. Good for creating a left margin.
–h *"text"*	Makes *text* the header on each page. Good for creating nice headers.
–m	Merges and formats files into columns (one file per column). Good for making quick-and-dirty multicolumn output.
–d	Double spaces

SEARCHING

> Attempt the end, and never stand to doubt;
> Nothing's so hard but search will find it out.
>
> Robert Herrick
> *Hesperides, Seek and Find*, 1648

Lost? Confused? Need guidance? The spiritual counselor Swami Grep is here to help. He doesn't necessarily know where to look, but he knows how to find all the answers.

There are three standard UNIX search programs: `grep`, `fgrep` (or fast grep), and `egrep` (or extended grep). Of these three, you'll probably never use `fgrep` because, despite the clever name, it's the slowest of the lot (although it does have some interesting capabilities). That leaves `grep` and `egrep`.

The three **greps**: Larry, Moe, and **egrep**

> grep /grep/ vt: To rapidly scan a file or file set looking for a particular string or pattern. By extension, to look for something by pattern. "Grep the bulletin board for the system backup schedule, would you?"
>
> Eric Raymond, ed.
> *New Hacker's Dictionary*, 1992

Who dreams these up? The name `grep` is actually an abbreviation (in true UNIX form) for **global regular expression print**. Now that you see it spelled out, it makes *perfect* sense, doesn't it. It doesn't? Well, it doesn't for me, either. What the heck is a regular expression and why would anyone want to print one globally? The first one is simpler to answer than you might think. A regular expression is just a pattern that you want matched. We've seen 'em before with wildcards like [a-z], which would match all the lowercase letters but no numbers or uppercase letters. There are lots of others, and they each deserve a brief moment (since we're working in a book, they each get 15 words of fame, not 15 minutes). Table 4.8 covers the important ones.

There are a few others, but I don't have call to use them very much and I doubt you will either. If you do, see the man page on `regex` (short for regular expressions).

 If you want to match either the left or right brackets, use the form [ ] [ ]. That's because a right bracket as the first character of the set represents a right bracket, not the end of the set. Just thought you'd like to know.

Table 4.8 Isn't *that* special?

Special Character	What it means
.	Matches any single character.
*	A character followed by * matches zero or more occurrences of the previous character.
\	Escapes the next character.
^	At the beginning of a regular expression, the ^ matches the beginning of a line.
$	At the end of a regular expression, the $ matches the end of a line.
[*n*]	Matches the set of *n* characters or numbers.

For all of that garbage, what the grep commands do is very simple: They find stuff inside files. They can search binary files or text files just as easily, although you'll probably have a hard time creating the string to search *for* in a binary file, not being a computer and all. So what's the difference between all the different forms? Well: **Search but not destroy**

grep The simplest command and probably the one you'll use most.

fgrep The slowest of the three greps, fgrep is useful when you want to make an exact line match (the **–x** option), or when you want to use a file to hold all the different patterns you're searching for (the **–f** option). Usually, though, it's best left on the shelf.

egrep The grepfast of champions. It's very fast but can be a resource hog (or so I've heard—I have yet to see a system crash because of egrep). It's got a lot of the best features of fgrep and grep, but it uses what are called extended regular expressions. That basically means that you add a few more characters to the special characters list above. I don't use it a lot, but those that do swear by it (and, on occasion, at it).

So what do you need to know about the grep commands? How about a quick lesson on how to use them? We'll use grep for the initial examples. Mostly the syntax works just fine for fgrep and egrep. Most commonly, you want to find a string like the one in Figure 4.2 in a single file.

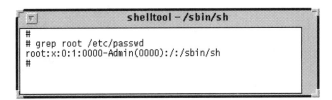

Figure 4.2 A grep a day keeps the root away.

But there will be occasions when you want to search the output of another command for a particular string, and `grep`'s great at that, too. (See Figure 4.3.)

```
                      shelltool - /sbin/sh
#
# ps -ef |grep sh
    root     3     0 80 19:09:27 ?        1:00 fsflush
    root   170     1 58 19:10:13 console  0:00 -sh
    root   176   170 50 19:10:29 console  0:00 /bin/sh /usr/openwin/bin/open
win
    root   189   181149 19:10:41 console  0:00 sh /usr/openwin/lib/Xinitrc
    root   288   200 80 17:47:43 ?        0:01 /usr/openwin/bin/snapshot
    root   207   206 17 19:10:50 pts/0    0:00 sh
    root   211   210 12 19:10:51 pts/1    0:00 sh
    root   215   214 24 19:10:52 pts/2    0:00 sh
    root   220   218  4 19:10:55 pts/3    0:00 /sbin/sh
    root   222     1 80 19:10:56 console  0:01 shelltool -Wp 1 0 -Ws 593 738
-WP 315 701 +Wi
    root   224   222 14 19:10:57 pts/4    0:00 /sbin/sh
    root   297   224  3 17:51:26 pts/4    0:00 grep sh
#
```

Figure 4.3 `ps` the salt, will you? `sh`-ure.

And how about those occasions when you want to match everything but what you specify? Well, `grep` has a solution for that, too, shown in Figure 4.4.

```
                   shelltool - /sbin/sh
# ps -ef |grep -v root
      UID   PID  PPID  C   STIME TTY        TIME COMD
     john   304   215 52 17:53:52 pts/2    0:00 -csh
     john   310   304  5 17:54:00 pts/2    0:00 sh
     john   311   310  4 17:54:01 pts/2    0:00 sh
     john   312   311 24 17:54:02 pts/2    0:00 csh
     john   316   312  9 17:54:03 pts/2    0:00 ksh
     john   318   316 11 17:54:21 pts/2    0:00 vi
#
```

Figure 4.4 Oh, no, not again!

And, of course, you never know when you'll be confronted with a caseless society, so being able to ignore case (see Figure 4.5) is very important.

```
                     shelltool - /sbin/sh
# ps -ef |grep -i JOHN
     john   304   215 52 17:53:52 pts/2    0:00 -csh
     john   310   304  5 17:54:00 pts/2    0:00 sh
     john   311   310  4 17:54:01 pts/2    0:00 sh
     john   312   311 24 17:54:02 pts/2    0:00 csh
     john   316   312  9 17:54:03 pts/2    0:00 ksh
     john   318   316 11 17:54:21 pts/2    0:00 vi
     root   327   224  3 17:57:09 pts/4    0:00 grep -i JOHN
#
```

Figure 4.5 A case for no case.

There are other options, too, that are useful, but I generally have to look them up in the man page because I don't use them all that often. Just so you don't have to look in the man, here they are in Table 4.9.

Table 4.9 Fast and loose with `grep`.

Cause	Effect
`-n`	Precedes each line with its line number
`-b`	Precedes each line with its disk block number (totally useless 99 percent of the time, invaluable the rest)
`-c`	Counts the matching lines, but doesn't print them
`-l`	Names the files with matches, but doesn't print the matches
`-s`	Suppresses error messages (`grep` only, System V only)
`-x`	Matches entire lines only (BSD UNIX only)
`-w`	Searches for the pattern as a word (BSD UNIX only)
`-e` *pattern*	Uses *pattern* as the search pattern (`egrep` and `fgrep` only)
`-f` *filename*	Reads the patterns you want to search for from *filename*

One problem with `grep` is that it doesn't always display the name of the files in which it finds matches. That's right: If you issue a command like `grep tissue Kleen*` and there's only one file in the current directory that begins `Kleen`, `grep` won't print out its name. (If it finds matches in more than one file, it *will* print their names out before printing the matches.)

Okay, so now you know a bit about `grep`. That's the simple stuff. Let's get into some more complex searches using some of these regular expressions we talked about before. Let's say I went into my boss's home directory and wanted to search through all the files in his `performance_review` directory for mentions of my name. (Now why would I do a thing like that?) Well, I don't know if he called me `john`, `John`, `montgomery`, `Montgomery`, or `ass`. So, I create a simple `egrep` statement like the one in Figure 4.6 . . .

Using regular, old expressions

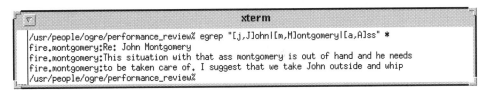

```
/usr/people/ogre/performance_review% egrep "[j,J]ohn|[m,M]ontgomery|[a,A]ss" *
fire.montgomery:Re: John Montgomery
fire.montgomery:This situation with that ass montgomery is out of hand and he needs
fire.montgomery:to be taken care of. I suggest that we take John outside and whip
/usr/people/ogre/performance_review%
```

Figure 4.6 Gosh darn. I'm in trouble now.

and find out that I should be updating my resume. Why did I use `egrep` here? For a couple of reasons: First, I was searching a lot of files, and `egrep` is just faster at doing that than the other `grep` commands. Second, I needed to look for a bunch of different strings, and `egrep`'s syntax is a little clearer (I think) than `grep`'s for this. Let's take the command apart:

```
% egrep "[j,J]ohn|[m,M]ontgomery|[a,A]ss" *
```

First we have the `egrep` command itself. No problem. Now double quotes. These are important in any case when you have a string with a space or special characters in it. It's good practice to get into the habit of adding quotes around every string you're searching for, but it's not necessary with simpler strings. Now the `[j,J]` bit—what's that? It just tells `egrep` that either a lowercase or an uppercase j is acceptable. The vertical bar (`|`) is `egrep`'s "or"—it just means "find this or that or the other thing." And finally, the `*` means "search every file."

Fancy egrep   Another thing you can do with `egrep` is have optional stuff. Say that I was called Monty by some people. (In fact, I am.) I can make `egrep` search for `Montgomery` or `Monty` using `|` or I can do it more efficiently using `egrep`'s extended syntax with the Ms, as in Figure 4.7.

```
/usr/people/ogre/performance_review% egrep "[m,M]ont(gomery|y)?" *
fire.montgomery:Re: John Montgomery
fire.montgomery:This situation with that ass montgomery is out of hand and he needs
fire.montgomery:him for a while. And I hate the way people call him monty.
/usr/people/ogre/performance_review%
```

Figure 4.7 I'm monty to some, and Monty to others, but never Mont.

So what's going on here?

```
% egrep "[m,M]ont(gomery|y)?" *
```

Well, the only new twist is the `()?` syntax. What this tells `egrep` is that if it stumbles across either `gomery` or `y` or neither, to print the line.

A simple way to think of the difference between `[]` and `()?` is that `[]` means "either" and `()?` means "either or neither."

The other strength of the `egrep` program is its capability to search for a list of patterns that it finds in a file. For example, I could have created a file called `trouble` containing

```
John
john
Montgomery
montgomery
monty
Monty
ass
Ass
```

then used the `egrep -f` command to search all files using the patterns in `trouble`. (See Figure 4.8)

```
                                    xterm
/usr/people/ogre/performance_review% egrep -f trouble *
fire.montgomery:Re: John Montgomery
fire.montgomery:This situation with that ass montgomery is out of hand and he needs
fire.montgomery:to be taken care of. I suggest that we take John outside and whip
fire.montgomery:him for a while. And I hate the way people call him monty. And I think
trouble:John
trouble:john
trouble:Montgomery
trouble:montgomery
trouble:monty
trouble:Monty
trouble:ass
trouble:Ass
/usr/people/ogre/performance_review%
```

Figure 4.8 All in a file's work.

As you can see, having the pattern file in the same directory as the other files I'm searching doesn't work too well, but you get the idea. This method is great for checking a bunch of files for the presence of a bunch of terms, and I use it all the time to make sure I'm being consistent.

SORTING AND COMPARING

> Shall I compare thee to a summer's day?
> Thou art more lovely and more temperate:
> Rough winds do shake the darling buds of May,
> And summer's lease hath all too short a date.
>
> William Shakespeare
> *Sonnet 18*

I just read an advertisement in the local paper for a "Life-Size Candyland Game" suitable for children in grades K through 5. I wanted to go. I asked around. Most of my friends wanted to go. I'm not sure what this says about most of my friends and me, but we're going to go. Anyway, shortly after reading that ad, I tromped back out to the garage to continue unpacking. Everything was a mess (and I thought the packing job was really good, too). As I was fiddling with boxes and miscellaneous loose pieces of furniture, I wished I had a "Life-Size `sort` Command." Then I could just push it over to all these boxes and have everything neatly sorted in no time at all. Then I could use my "Life-Size `diff` Command" to figure out the difference between a box labeled "Kitchen stuff" and one labeled "More Kitchen stuff."

I'm weird   My dream may never come true. Heck, I may never get unpacked. But at least I'll be able to share the joys of UNIX sorting and diffing with all my friends. (Except they all just left for the "Life-Size Candyland Game" without me. Serves me right for having friends who would be interested in the damn thing anyway.)

What a Mess

> Technology . . . the knack of so arranging the world that we don't have to experience it.
>
> Max Frisch
> *Second Stop*, 1957

The creators of UNIX knew that they'd need a command to arrange things alphabetically or numerically. Being the clever sorts they are, they named it `sort`. It works pretty much as you'd expect:

```
% sort filename
```

This gives you a very nice output (the file's not changed, though), with everything sorted from left to right, alphabetically. Actually, ASCIIbetically: first numbers, then capital letters, then lowercase. For example, remember the file called `trouble` that I created for the `egrep` script I was using to determine if my boss wanted to fire me? Forgot it already? Me, too. It's in Figure 4.9.

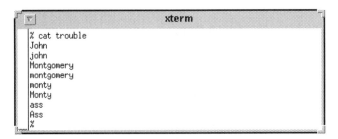

Figure 4.9 You're out of order!

That's all well and good, but what happens if I want it listed in order? I might try the one in Figure 4.10.

```
% sort trouble
Ass
John
Montgomery
Monty
ass
john
montgomery
monty
%
```

Figure 4.10 Ah! Order from chaos.

Well, this is okay, but not great. After all, `Ass` is more closely related to `ass` than it is to `John`. (I hope.) So what can I do? How about employing the `-f` ("fold lower-case [sic] letters into upper case [sic]" according to the `man` page)? Basically `-f` makes everything appear uppercase to `sort`. (See Figure 4.11.)

On hangers, too?

```
% sort -f trouble
Ass
ass
John
john
Montgomery
montgomery
Monty
monty
%
```

Figure 4.11 Much better.

Okay. Now we're on a roll.

But what happens if I have numbers in the file, like in Figure 4.12?

```
% sort numbers
1
10
2
20
45
5
500000
9
%
```

Figure 4.12 Numbers are just funny-looking letters.

What we have here is a problem. It's pretty clear that 500000 is a bigger number than 9. In fact, I can almost guarantee it. Must be the new new math. The problem is that sort thinks that these numbers are words, and it reasons this way: since the letter a would precede the word about in a dictionary, the number 2 should precede 20 but come after 10. See, sort sees 10 as 1+0 and 2 as just 2. Since 2 is greater than 1 . . . Well, you get the point.

Sorting numbers

Now let's fix it. Use the –n (for numbers) switch, as shown in Figure 4.13.

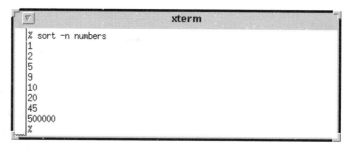

Figure 4.13 Now we're counting.

But all of this is kid stuff—sort is really a lot more powerful. Able to leap tall buildings, etc, etc, etc. For example, you can sort on something other than the first word on a line, because sort understands fields as words separated by spaces (or any other character you specify).

```
% sort -t\" +1 -3 testfile
John"Montgomery"100
Dad"Montgomery"456
Albert"Morris"112
%
```

Figure 4.14 Me, Dad, and numbers.

So, the –t option in Figure 4.14 tells sort that a double quote is going to be my field separator. The +1 option tells sort to start by looking at field 2 (here, the last name), and the –3 tells sort to stop sorting with field 3 (sort starts numbering with 0). So, sort looked at this file, saw that there were two Montgomerys, then sorted them based on column 3, then it proceeded to sort Morris after Montgomery, even though his field 3 is a lower number than Dad's. See?

Backwards march

Now let's reverse things. Specifically, let's reverse the way sort searches on that pesky field 3. (See Figure 4.15.)

```
┌─────────────────────── xterm ───────────────────────┐
│▽                                                     │
│ % sort -t\" +1 -r -3 testfile                        │
│ Albert"Morris"112                                    │
│ Dad"Montgomery"456                                   │
│ John"Montgomery"100                                  │
│ %                                                    │
└──────────────────────────────────────────────────────┘
```

Figure 4.15 `sort`—bass-ackwards.

Dang. Something went wrong here: The whole search is backwards. Sorry, but that's just the way `sort` is: There's no clever way to reverse-search only one field. You'll have to use `awk`.

There are three other things you can do with `sort`: Remove repeated lines, make `sort` know the months of the year, and merge two files. The first of these, removing repeated lines, is easy as falling off a log: Just add the –u option. The second is also simple: The –M option takes care of it. Let's dispense with both of these at once, in Figure 4.16.

Three sort tricks

```
┌─────────────────────── xterm ───────────────────────┐
│▽                                                     │
│ % cat testfile                                       │
│ January                                              │
│ March                                                │
│ June                                                 │
│ June                                                 │
│ June                                                 │
│ July                                                 │
│ June                                                 │
│ January                                              │
│ April                                                │
│ May                                                  │
│ August                                               │
│ December                                             │
│ September                                            │
│ % sort -u -M testfile                                │
│ January                                              │
│ March                                                │
│ April                                                │
│ May                                                  │
│ June                                                 │
│ July                                                 │
│ August                                               │
│ September                                            │
│ December                                             │
│ %                                                    │
└──────────────────────────────────────────────────────┘
```

Figure 4.16 A monthly problem.

Now on to bigger and brighter things. Say I wanted to merge this file full of months with a file full of other months? I'd use –M with –m, like Figure 4.17 does.

The catch to the –m (merge) option is that the two files have to have been sorted already.

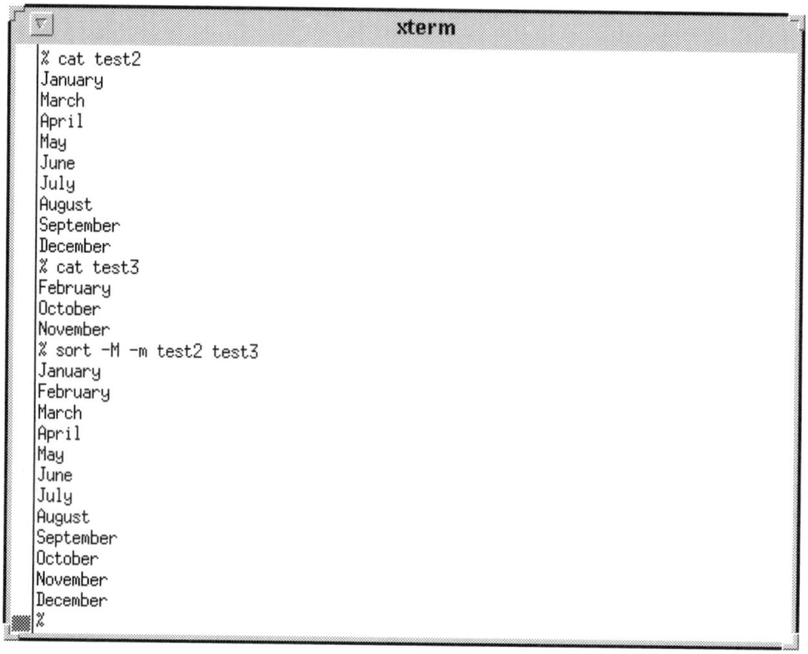

Figure 4.17 One whole year.

What's the `diff`?

> We've got a cat called Ben Hur.
> We called it Ben till it had kittens.
>
> Sally Poplin

Continuing on with the theme of events in my personal life that make me reflect on UNIX commands, not too long ago my cat, Jake, attacked me. He was staring out the kitchen window, growling and hissing. I went to see what he wanted to attack. Just as I saw the other cat on the other side of the window, Jake decided that what he *really* wanted to attack was my left forearm. I had never seriously considered just what 16.5 pounds of muscular, male feline could do to a bunch of tender, defenseless skin. Now I know.

Not for the faint of heart   Anyway, the following day I saw that the wounds were infected. Normally, you probably wouldn't laud anyone for that, but considering the fever I was running by the time I noticed the infection, you should be praising me for remembering my name. I went to the doctor, who gave me a tetanus shot and prescribed penicillin. He also drew a dotted line around the swelling area on my forearm, so I could "monitor the progress of the infection." (What fun.) "Don't shower for a few days," he added cheerfully.

This (the dotted line, not the edict not to shower) made me contemplate `diff`. After all, when your fever is blazing and you would really have preferred that your tetanus shot were administered with a .45 Magnum, you keep your wits about you however you can. The dotted line is the infection on day 1. The large, pussy, red area is the infection on day 2. My eyes are the `diff` command, telling me the difference.

Okay, it took a while, but we're finally back to UNIX. There are several types of `diff` commands (kind of like the `grep` brothers). There's `diff`, `diff3`, `sdiff`, `bdiff`, `cmp`, and `comm`.

Table 4.10 Feeling diffident?

Your command	UNIX's wish
`diff`	Mom to most of the other `diff`s.
`diff3`	Compares three files instead of `diff`'s two
`sdiff`	Makes `diff` pump its output out side by side
`bdiff`	Does for big files what regular `diff` does for small ones
`cmp`	Tells you whether two files are different, but not how
`comm`	Uses columns to show where two files agree and where they're different

We can eliminate `bdiff` right here because I've *never* used it. In theory, you use it to `diff` two files that are too big for `diff`, but I've never found one. I'm sure they're out there, though. Anyway, its syntax is just like `diff`'s, because basically what `bdiff` does is to break the big files down into smaller ones, then call up `diff`. We can also part ways with `cmp`. Although it's sometimes useful to know whether two text files are different (but not *how* they're different), it's rare. At least rarer than the other stuff. (One note: `cmp` is good for comparing binary files [programs]—it'll tell you that they're different, but spare you the line-by-line, character-by-character of *how* they're different, which you don't need to know anyway.)

If you need bdiff, you'll know

Now, an overview: `diff` works pretty much like you'd expect, but its output can be a little jarring. (Try reading Figure 4.18.)

I mean, who's to say what < and > mean? And can you imagine using that to determine the difference between a couple of big files? Clearly, `diff` is good when the output you're expecting is pretty minimal. When you need a better way to look at your results, try `sdiff`: It denotes differences with a |, like in Figure 4.19.

You could get pretty much the same results with `comm`, as in Figure 4.20.

Column 3 is where they agree, column 2 holds the elements unique to the second file on the command line, and column 1 contains the elements unique to the first file on the command line.

```
┌─────────────────────────────────────────────────────────────┐
│ ▽ │                      xterm                              │
├─────────────────────────────────────────────────────────────┤
│ % cat jar1                                                   │
│ pickles                                                      │
│ relish                                                       │
│ ketchup                                                      │
│ mustard                                                      │
│ pesto sauce                                                  │
│ % cat jar2                                                   │
│ pickles                                                      │
│ relish                                                       │
│ ketchup                                                      │
│ mustard                                                      │
│ fireflies                                                    │
│ % diff jar1 jar2                                             │
│ 5c5                                                          │
│ < pesto sauce                                                │
│ ---                                                          │
│ > fireflies                                                  │
│ %                                                            │
└─────────────────────────────────────────────────────────────┘
```

Figure 4.18 Fireflies or pesto?

```
┌─────────────────────────────────────────────────────────────┐
│ ▽ │                      xterm                              │
├─────────────────────────────────────────────────────────────┤
│ % sdiff jar1 jar2                                            │
│ pickles                                       pickles        │
│ relish                                        relish         │
│ ketchup                                       ketchup        │
│ mustard                                       mustard        │
│ pesto sauce                                 | fireflies      │
│ %                                                            │
└─────────────────────────────────────────────────────────────┘
```

Figure 4.19 `sdiff`ed again.

```
┌─────────────────────────────────────────────────────────────┐
│ ▽ │                      xterm                              │
├─────────────────────────────────────────────────────────────┤
│ % comm jar1 jar2                                             │
│               pickles                                        │
│               relish                                         │
│               ketchup                                        │
│               mustard                                        │
│       fireflies                                              │
│ pesto sauce                                                  │
│ %                                                            │
└─────────────────────────────────────────────────────────────┘
```

Figure 4.20 So that's what `comm` does.

diff's options So much for the introductions. Off with the clothes. Two of diff's most useful options are –b (ignore trailing blanks) and –i (ignore case). Of all diff's options, you'll use these two the most. The next-most-often-used option is –c, which gives three lines of context (usually by printing two lines before and a line after the different lines). (See Figure 4.21.)

Sometimes, you probably want to make one file look like another for whatever reason. You could just copy the first file into the second, but God forbid you should do what's easy. Instead, diff gives you a way to make the second file look like the first, by creating an ex script with the –e option. This is shown in Figure 4.22.

```
# diff -c jar1 jar2
*** jar1        Sun Aug 14 10:50:27 1994
--- jar2        Sat Aug 13 19:23:14 1994
***************
*** 1,5 ****
  pickles
  relish
- mustard
- pesto sauce
  ketchup
--- 1,5 ----
  pickles
  relish
  ketchup
+ mustard
+ fireflies
#
```

Figure 4.21 Put it in context.

```
% diff -e jar1 jar2
5c
fireflies
.
%
```

Figure 4.22 Pesto chango.

You could simply direct the output to a file and then give **ex** that file as a script name. This would look something like Figure 4.23.

```
% cat jar1
pickles
relish
ketchup
mustard
pesto sauce
% diff -e jar1 jar2 > script
% echo w >> script
% ex - jar1 < script
% cat jar1
pickles
relish
ketchup
mustard
fireflies
%
```

Figure 4.23 One minor change . . .

Unfortunately, the **-e** option doesn't add the final **ex** command w to write the file. So I just echoed one and appended it to the file. You can also run these commands, only on the **ex** line add **> jar3** (or some other filename) so that you're not blowing away your first file. You can then circulate this output file to all the users who might have copies of the old file, and have them run it through `ex` to get the latest version.

Three files   On to `diff3`. I've created yet another file full of foodstuffs (maybe it's time I ate some dinner), and I want to see what it has that `jar1` and `jar2` don't. Figure 4.24 should tell me . . .

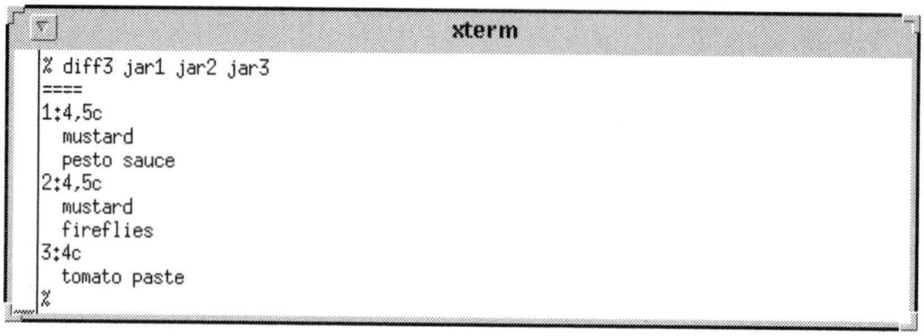

```
xterm
% diff3 jar1 jar2 jar3
====
1:4,5c
  mustard
  pesto sauce
2:4,5c
  mustard
  fireflies
3:4c
  tomato paste
%
```

Figure 4.24 Yum: Tomato paste.

. . . but I'll be damned if I can tell the difference based on this butt-ugly output. Sheesh: I thought `diff` was bad. If `diff` is bad breath, `diff3` is severe halitosis. Garlic, onion, and coffee. Let's try to figure this out:

```
====
1:4,5c
  mustard
  pesto sauce
2:4,5c
  mustard
  fireflies
3:4c
  tomato paste
```

What does it all mean? Well, every little bit means something—even the four equals signs at the top. That means that all three files are different. It's just a forewarning about how different the files are. You could also see `====1` (the first file is different), `====2` (second), and `====3` (third). The next line is `diff3`'s shorthand for letting us know which file to change and where the changes need to be made: `1:4,5c` means that in file 1, lines 4 and 5 need to be changed. The next two lines tell us what they are right now. In file 2, only line 5 is different; but in file 3, there is no line 5. That's why we see mustard up there twice: Files 1 and 2 have it, but file 3 doesn't.

Now you know how to read the output of `diff3`. It supports the `-e` option, just like `diff`—only this time the script will make the first file into a combination of the second and third files.

DEVICES

> All for one, one for all, that is our device.
>
> Alexandre Dumas
> *The Three Musketeers*, 1844

UNIX governs all the hardware in your system with device drivers. These are usually small programs that know on one end how to talk to the piece of hardware in question (a terminal, a tape drive, a disk drive, whatever) and on the other how to talk to UNIX. The concept is pretty simple—they're translators. You can (and, truth be told, must) talk to devices all the time—although you usually don't know it.

Most of your devices live in a directory called `/dev`. Do a cd to `/dev` and take **Look in /dev** a look. They're really pretty unassuming files. So why do you care? Mostly, you don't. The time will come, however, when you have to do something clever, like mount a floppy disk drive or copy files onto a tape, and you'll wish you knew more about device names. So, rather than bothering you with arcana about devices, I'll give you my best shot, in Figure 4.25, at which devices do what and what they're all usually named.

```
                                    xterm
solaris# ls
arp         fd1       lp1       ptyp9     rfd1b     term         ttypa
conslog     fd1a      mbio      ptypa     rfd1c     ticlts       ttypb
console     fd1b      mbmem     ptypb     rfd1d     ticots       ttypc
cua         fd1c      mem       ptypc     rfd1e     ticotsord    ttypd
cua0        fd1d      null      ptypd     rmt       tty          ttype
diskette    fd1e      profile   ptype     rootprop  tty00        ttypf
dsk         icmp      ptmajor   ptypf     sad       ttya         udp
dump        ip        ptmx      rawip     smc       ttyd0        vt00
eisarom     isdn      pts       rdiskette sound     ttyp0        vt01
fb          kmem      ptyp0     rdsk      sp        ttyp1        vt02
fbs         kstat     ptyp1     rfd0      spx       ttyp2        vt03
fd          ksyms     ptyp2     rfd0a     stderr    ttyp3        vt04
fd0         llc1      ptyp3     rfd0b     stdin     ttyp4        vt05
fd0a        lo0       ptyp4     rfd0c     stdout    ttyp5        vt06
fd0b        lo1       ptyp5     rfd0d     swap      ttyp6        vt07
fd0c        lo2       ptyp6     rfd0e     syscon    ttyp7        wscons
fd0d        lo3       ptyp7     rfd1      systty    ttyp8        zero
fd0e        log       ptyp8     rfd1a     tcp       ttyp9
solaris#
```

Figure 4.25 Left to my own devices.

Feeling Floppy

> The fat's in the fire.
>
> John Marston
> *What You Will*, 1607

Your floppy drive (if your system has one—if it's a workstation it probably does) is probably called something like `/dev/floppy` or `/dev/fd0` (for "floppy disk 0"). There are usually a lot of `fd`s in `/dev`—`fd1`, `fd2`, `fd3`, `fd0a`, and so on. There's probably also a directory called `/dev/fd`. These are variations on a theme. The first floppy drive on your system is `/dev/fd0`. The second is `/dev/fd1` (analogous to the `B:` drive in a DOS-based PC). The files in the `fd` directory are the same as their counterparts in `/dev`.

Mount a floppy   To mount a floppy drive (or any drive, for that matter), you need two things— the name of the device (which we have: `/dev/fd0`) and a *mount point*. Counter to what you could imagine, the mount point has nothing to do with sex: It's usually just a directory. I create a directory called `/floppy` and mount my floppy drive there with a command like this:

```
% mount /dev/fd0 /floppy
```

This works just fine. I can now mount a 1.44 MB floppy drive in my UNIX computer just as though it were a hard drive. But it'll have to be formatted with a UNIX file system.

Don't format it   I can't imagine anything more useless than a floppy disk with a UNIX file
as UNIX   system on it. Instead, it's a much better idea to format your floppies as DOS floppies (using the File Allocation Table (FAT) file system type, which is the lingua franca of the floppy disk world) and mount them as DOS floppies. You can do that with these commands (after you insert a disk into your floppy drive):

```
% fdformat -d -H /dev/fd0
% mount -F pcfs /dev/fd0 /floppy
```

Although these are Sun's versions of these commands, most UNIX variants have something like them. Sun's `fdformat`, for example, is just a special diskette formatter that puts a PC file system (in this case, a high density file system) onto the diskette. These are a worthwhile pair of commands to know about, so save them somewhere.

 The problem (and heinous it is) is that you have to be the superuser to mount a floppy drive. Isn't that the stupidest thing you've ever heard?

Tape-Tied

> A robber convicted of theft shall be shorn like a hired fighter, and boiling tar shall be poured over his head, and feathers from a pillow shall be shaken out over his head.
>
> Law of Richard the Leonhar . . . er . . . Coeur de Lion
> *Third Crusade*, 1189

Now let's talk about tapes. Tapes are horrible. Not because the tape itself is bad, but because you never know what the tape in your system is called. Worse, there are a million tape formats. Basically, I get the shivers whenever somebody gives me a tape that wasn't created on the same type of machine that I'm going to restore its files to.

Let's do tape names first. Most tape names end in the letter `t`, then a number. **What's in a** For example, the default quarter-inch cartridge (or QIC, pronounced "quick") **name?** tape drive on an older Sun system is `/dev/rst8`; on a newer (Solaris 2.3) one it's `/dev/rmt/8`.

On some systems you'll get lucky and find it's called something like `/dev/tape`. Anyway, look for a bunch of files with names that end in `t` then a number, or for a directory called something like `/dev/rs` or `/dev/tape`. Then just start checking out the tape drives in there. (Sun users can sometimes also use the graphical tapetool, but I've not had much luck with it.)

Tape devices come in two varieties: rewinding and nonrewinding. The basic difference is that a rewinding device driver sends a "rewind" message to the tape drive and the tape is rewound when you're finished with it. Some software comes on a tape that is broken into two parts: On the first part of the tape is a small installation program, which you `tar` off (see the explanation of this command in a couple of paragraphs) using a nonrewinding tape device. The installation program then takes over and finally rewinds the tape when it's done. Nonrewinding tape drives usually go under the same name as the regular tape drive, only there's an `n` at the beginning, as in `/dev/nrst8`. Just good to know.

The easiest way to know if you have the right tape drive is to try this command on every conceivable device:

```
% tar tf /dev/rst8
```

(Substitute the device name you want for `/dev/rst8`.) If this is the first time you've met the `tar` command, it's UNIX's tape archiver, and it writes a universal (albeit extremely inefficient) format onto the tape. Even if the tape you have in the drive wasn't written with `tar`, this command should cause the tape drive to spin for a bit. Watch it and see if it spins. If it does, you've probably found your drive.

A bit more on `tar`, because it's an incredibly useful tool. First, in Table 4.11, its options.

Table 4.11 There's `tar` on my shoe.

Option	Effect
x	Extracts files from the `tar`red device.
c	Creates a new `tar` archive
f	Uses the following device name as the input
v	("Verbose") Prints the names of files as you write or read them
t	Reads `tar` archive and print out its "table of contents"

There are other options, but these are the most general-purpose ones. If somebody gives you a `tar`red tape, use the command

```
% tar xv
```

to extract the files. If you want to `tar` up a file (or a whole directory), use

```
% tar cv
```

You'll notice that I omitted the device name on both these commands. That's because `tar` knows about the default tape device. If you don't know what your tape drive's device name is, try using the `tar` command without any options. You'll probably find that it works.

> Before extracting a `tar` archive (with the `tar x` command), you should run a `tar tv` to see exactly where `tar` is planning on putting the contents of its archive. You can have some nasty surprises if `tar` uses hardwired directory names—including the destruction of existing files. If you see filenames that are fully specified (they'll begin with /), you might want to extract them with the `R` option (`tar xvR`).

Ten Little Endians

> Si finis bonus est, totum bonum erit*
>
> Gesta Romanorum, ca. 1472

*If the end is well, all will be well.

Sometimes you'll be given a tape written on a different kind of machine. My first (and most exasperating) experience with this was when I used a Silicon Graphics workstation. Somebody sent me a bunch of files on a tape created with tar on a Sun workstation. Whenever I tried to read it, I got a simple error message telling me that tar couldn't read the tape. What was wrong?

The big tar trick

I scratched and puzzled, and finally gave up and called a friend with another SGI. He told me that there were two types of tar archives: big-endian and little-endian. I can't remember which workstation used which format, but basically what was going on was that one workstation wrote each bit in a byte from low to high (0, 1, 2, 3, 4, 5, 6, 7), and the other wrote them from high to low (7, 6, 5, 4, 3, 2, 1, 0). I later found out that he had oversimplified things a bit. Dan Watts explained it to me like this: Some tars write words (16 bits at a time) low byte first, some write them high byte first. So it was occurring on a byte level, not a bit level. We're splitting hairs here a little, but if you're into being strictly accurate, you should know.

Anyway, to solve this problem, my friend suggested a creative use of the dd command, the data dumper for UNIX. It'll read just about anything, because all it's doing is reading bytes. In addition to reading bytes, it can convert them into various different formats (great if you happen to have IBM mainframe EBCDIC tapes). This is the command:

Using dd

```
% dd if=/dev/rst8 conv=swab | tar xvf -
```

So dd reads its input from /dev/rst8 and swaps every two bytes with each other; its output then goes to tar, which extracts it. The – after tar tells tar to take its input from standard input.

One last tar trick: If you want to copy a directory structure from one place to another and keep all your symbolic links in place, you can use tar. For example,

```
% cd /usr/people/john
% tar cvfb - 20 . | (cd /usr1/people/john; tar xvfBp -)
```

copies /usr/people/john to /usr1/people/john. The first tar creates an archive of the current directory (.) and writes it in 20-byte blocks (the b and the 20) to the standard output (the -). The stuff in the parentheses first changes to the destination directory, then untars what's coming in on standard input. The B says to expect a special blocking factor, and the p says to make sure that all the permissions of the files it's extracting are the same as what it's being fed.

5 Editing Files

> "When *I* use a word," Humpty Dumpty said, in rather a scornful tone,
> "it means just what I choose it to mean—neither more nor less."
> "The question is," said Alice, "whether you *can* make words mean so
> many different things."
> "The question is," said Humpty Dumpty, "which is to be master—
> that's all."
>
> Lewis Carroll
> *Alice's Adventures in Wonderland*, 1865

When in the course of human events it becomes necessary to make changes to a configuration file or write a quick note to yourself, you'll probably find that you use an editor. The kind of editor you're probably thinking of is a pretty, What-You-See-Is-What-You-Get (WYSIWYG) editor, like the word processors you'll see on PCs and Macintoshes. Don't hold your breath. UNIX's editors at best require you to memorize a bunch of keystrokes, and at worst make you need to keep a cheat sheet nearby just so you can write your name.

In UNIX you'll encounter three types of horrors (pronounced "editors"): line editors (like ed and ex), screen editors (like `vi` and `emacs`), and stream editors (like `sed` and `awk`). All three serve different purposes. Line editors are the dinosaurs of UNIX editing. They only let you work on one line of text at a time, and if you want to make changes to it you'll have to remember some serious commands. Today they're mainly good only for running scripts you write. Screen editors are easier to use because they let you work on a screenful of data at a time, but they still need some coaxing from oddball commands. Stream editors are something entirely different. They're noninteractive, and you use them to make massive changes to the appearance of streams of input (a stream of input can come from a file or a program, so stream editors are particularly nice for tailoring your commands' output).

This chapter has two parts: Pretty Editors, which are the screen editors you'll probably be using the most; and Ugly Editors, which covers everything else (or at least a chunk of everything). This is not a complete guide to any of these editors, but instead it's a kind of pull-yourself-up-by-your-own-bootstraps-and-do-some-neat-stuff kind of chapter. Hope you like it.

PRETTY EDITORS

> Write drunk, edit sober.
>
> Anonymous

Where would files be without editors? Nowhere, I say. The two most popular are `vi` (which is one of the oldest) and `emacs` (which is one of the best). I'm not going to waste a lot of time trying to convert you to one of them—I'd just receive flaming hate mail from all the users of the other. To be honest, I use both. They're both good. And `emacs` is simply easier to use. So there.

`vi`

> Words pay no debts.
>
> Shakespeare (who certainly should've known!)
> *Troilus and Cressida*, 1601

But we'll start with `vi`. You've already had your primer, remember? In Chapter 1? Okaaay. We'll just run through that really quickly. Start `vi` by typing `vi file1`. There, you just opened a file. There are three modes in `vi`: control mode (where you can't actually type characters and have them appear on the screen), insert mode (where you can pretty much only type), and status line mode (where you type long commands). When you start `vi`, you're in control mode. To get into insert mode, type `i` (for insert). After that, you can type. To get back to control mode, press the `Esc` key. Take a look in Appendix C for all the keyboard shortcuts and you'll see the bulk of `vi`. How's that for a lightning review?

I'm not going to bother running through all the combinations of keystrokes and what they do. Instead, I'm going to concentrate on `vi`'s file-manipulation capabilities, including

- How to fix misspellings and typos in your files

- How to cut and paste from one file to another

- How to write just part of a file

At the end, I'll throw in some bonus tricks, just because I feel like it. Look for

- How to make different files have different margins (and other neat stuff)
- How to make a search run a command
- How to write macros

But first, misspellings. There are two kinds of misspellings: typos and honest-to-gosh-I-don't-know-how-to-spell-this-word misspellings. Both are very easy to fix.

Auto spelling

I have a tendency to spell the "teh" and windows "windoes." (The latter always leads me to ask, "So who doesn't?") There is a cure for this condition—vi's abbreviation function. With vi's abbreviations, you can have one, short word stand for another, long word or even a phrase. Compare this to some of the expensive word processors on the market that are just now coming out with such features (with names such as "autocorrect" and "autotext"), and you realize just how far ahead of its time vi was.

Get into a vi session:

```
% vi file1
```

Now type :ab teh the. Now every time you type teh it will immediately be replaced with its proper spelling. I actually have a whole bunch of words that I mispell. In fact, the copy editor reading this book probably deserves hazardous duty pay. Anyway, there's an annoying prerequisite to using the abbreviation function—you have to fix up vi each time you start it by setting up all your "abbreviations."

vi's init file

That's why vi has its own initialization file, called .exrc. Why not .virc? Because vi isn't really an editor. Well, it *is*, but it's really just a *vi*sual mode of the ex editor. So it reads much of what you put into .exrc. To set up your abbreviations, go to your home directory, and type

```
% vi .exrc
```

and start adding abbreviations. Try adding these for starters:

```
ab teh the
ab hte the
ab adn and
ab Unix UNIX
ab jm John Montgomery
```

Clearly, you shouldn't type "`ab jm John Montgomery`"—you should use someone else's name. I suggest your own. Anyway, you get the point. You can even put
in multiline abbreviations using vi's `Ctrl+v` command to insert a "literal" keystroke (the `v` stands for "verbatim").

**Inserting
special
characters**

See, when you press `Ctrl+v` in vi's insert mode, it tells vi that it shouldn't
interpret the next character you type—it should just print it on the screen. That's
how you get escape characters to appear on the screen. You can also insert actual
carriage returns. For example:

```
ab address John MontgomeryCtrl+vReturn1 Oak WayCtrl+vReturn
```

(Oh—when you see "`Ctrl+vReturn`" up there, it doesn't mean that you should
spell these things out. Just hold down the `Ctrl` key and press `v`, then release them
and press your `Return` or `Enter` key.) Now when you type `address` in vi,
you'd see this:

John Montgomery
1 Oak Way

So that's one way to outfox vi and your own fingers. But what about those
times when you honestly don't know how to spell a word? UNIX has a `spell`
utility that has a sizable dictionary of commonly misspelled words. To use it, just
type:

```
% spell file1
```

and `spell` will deliver a nice list of all the words it doesn't know. Of course, they
may be spelled just fine and are just unknown to the dictionary, but that's another
problem.

**Calling a shell
command from
within vi**

Say you don't want to exit from vi in order to spell-check something. There is
a way. From within vi, try typing this:

```
:1,50!spell
```

This command summons the command line (that's what the colon does) and then
sends lines 1 through 50 of the file you're currently editing to the `spell` program.
The `!` is vi's way to access shell commands. There are lots of things you can do
with `!`. So long as we're on the subject, I'll give you a few quick examples, in Table 5.1.

And this is *just a sampling* of all the great hits on this album. Be daring and try
your own.

Table 5.1 Playing with bangs.

The Command	What it does
`:%!sort`	Sorts the contents of your buffer
`:%!ls`	Dumps an `ls` command's output into your buffer (sometimes useful for shell scripts)
`:12r!ls`	Dumps an `ls` command's output into your buffer, appending it after line 12
`:%!grammar`	Sends your current buffer into the `grammar` command (which most UNIXes don't have)

Dealing with buffers

For a while now, I've been talking about "buffers." If you've hacked around a UNIX system, you probably have a good sense of what a buffer is. If you haven't, you probably don't. So . . . When you open a file in `vi`, you're actually reading the contents of that file into an area of memory that `vi` sets aside for it. That area is called your main buffer. There are 26 other buffers in `vi` (named after the letters of the alphabet, all 28 of them). You can get to these little buggers by using their "name" preceded by a double quote. For example, if I wanted to delete a word from the main buffer and store it in the "a" buffer, I'd type:

`"adw`

The `a` is for buffer a, the `d` is for delete, the `w` is for word. (Actually, `dw` is a standard `vi`-ism for "delete word.") Any command you use to cut or copy text can be augmented this way to make it stick whatever it cuts or copies into a buffer.

By using a buffer's capital name, you can make UNIX append characters to a buffer (as opposed to overwriting what's already in the buffer). So, if you type

`"Adw`

You'll append the next word to buffer `a`. (The uppercase/lowercase distinction only matters when it comes to appending versus overwriting the contents of a buffer.)

Now, to pull stuff out of a buffer, just use the "pull" command:

`"aP`

This tells `vi` to pull the contents of buffer a and insert them before wherever the cursor currently is. If buffer `a` contains lines (rather than words), you'll start inserting on the line before wherever the cursor currently is.

You can use these named buffers to cut and paste from one file to another. Open the file you want to cut from, cut what you want cut, and paste it into a buffer. Now open a second file (`:e filename`) and paste what you want wherever you want it. Or, you could open both files at once when you start `vi` just by specifying both their names on the command line. When you close the first file, you'll be staring at the second.

Extracting a portion of a file

Sometimes there's a better way to do this. Say you just opened a really big file and you just want to take a bit of it out and have that as its own file. Rather than cutting lines from the first file and pasting them into the second, you can select the lines from the first file you want to write. Just type something like

```
:1,25w file1
```

to write lines 1–25 into a file called `file1`.

Up above, I promised three other tricks, too: how to make different files have different margins and tabs and so on, how to make a search run a command, and how to write macros. They're all pretty simple. First, you probably know about commands such as `set autoindent` (or `set ai` for short) and `set wrapmargin` (or `set wm`). These are **local variables** for `vi` (and for `ex`) and they determine how `vi` will handle the file in its buffers. When you turn `autoindent` on, for example, every time you press `Return`, `vi` will automatically indent your line to the same degree as you indented the previous line. It probably sounds pretty useless if you're used to writing letters home, but if you're a programmer, it's very useful. Similarly, `wrapmargin` tells `vi` when to wrap very long lines of text from an input file. There's also a `set tabstop` command that looks like this: `set tabstop 5`. This command sets tabs at every five spaces rather than the default eight.

Special file setups

So what? So you have to type these commands every time you open `vi`. Or you can put them into your `.exrc` and have them apply to every file you edit. Or you can use mode lines at the top of your files to set them on a per-file basis. Say you wanted `autoindent` turned on and you wanted your tabs set to every three spaces. Try adding this to the top of your file:

```
# vi:set autoindent tabstop 3
```

Other neat things to put on a mode line: turn on line numbering (`set number` or `set nu`), ignore case when running searches (`set ignorecase` or `set ic`), and make `vi` save your file automatically when you exit (`set autowrite` or `set aw`). There are more than a few others, but they're relatively obscure. One thing to keep in mind about mode lines: You may have more than one, but they must appear at the top of the document, and `vi` expects each one to start with a pound sign.

Next, here's how to make a search run a command:

```
/shlomo/d
```

This command will delete any line that contains `shlomo`. The only difference between this and a standard search is that I appended `/d` to the end. Another variant would be to add `+d`, which would delete the line *after* one that contains `shlomo`. You can also set up a search to delete from one point to another; for example, to delete from wherever your cursor is up to and including `shlomo`, you'd type

```
.,/shlomo/d
```

Or you can delete from, say, `Lovitz` to `shlomo` (including both endpoints) like this:

```
/Lovitz/shlomo/d
```

And finally, you can move text, too. To move all the text between `Lovitz` and `shlomo` to line 45, you'd type

```
/Lovitz/shlomo/m45
```

And that is the extent of what you need to know to use a search to run deletions and the like.

> **Don't be too surprised if some of these tricks don't work: Not all `vi` implementations support them. You'll have to try yours to find out.**

Writing macros

Now for the really interesting stuff—how to write macros. Actually, `vi` doesn't really have "macros" in the sense that `emacs` or Microsoft Word has macros. It has keymaps. You can redefine any key to make it perform any combination of keystrokes. For example, say you use `vi` to create answers to a lot of E-mail you get. You generally want to include a few lines of the sender's message, but you want to precede them with a > character so that everybody will know that these are the product of someone else's demented mind, not yours. You could issue the command

```
:%subst /^/> /Ctrl+vEnterEnter
```

which puts the sequence > before each line. (Remember, you don't type the letters E-n-t-e-r—you press the Enter or Return key.) Well, it gets pretty tedious to do this for each and every message. So instead, try defining a macro to do it:

```
:map v :%subst /^/> /Ctrl+vEnterEnter
```

Now when you press the v in command mode, you'll make this substitution globally. And that's all there is to writing macros in vi. The v key isn't used by vi already, so it's safe to remap it. Actually, you can remap any key there is, but remapping an unused one is a good place to start. Here are the other keys that aren't used: g, K, q, V, Ctrl+a, Ctrl+k, Ctrl+o, Ctrl+t, Ctrl+w, and Ctrl+x.

You should have no problem mapping these control keys, but some control keys need protection from vi's ex mode. For example, if you want to remap the backspace key (although *why* you would . . .), you'd have a hard time, because every time you press it, you'd delete the last thing you typed. You must protect it with Ctrl+v, as we did above with the Enter key.

You can place any mapping into your .exrc file (just omit the initial colon). You can even use multikey maps. For example, say you wanted to create your own section of mnemonic shortcuts, but all the good letters are taken by vi already (isn't that always the case?). You could just precede any one of them with an available character, like the @ sign:

```
:map @w Ctrl+vEsc:1,25w tmpCtrl+vEnter
:map @q Ctrl+vEsc:w!q!Ctrl+vEnter
```

And so on.

When you're using sequences that require you to press the Enter key to complete them (like :wq), always remember to add the sequence Ctrl+vEnter to the end. Otherwise they won't run. Of course, that can be an advantage, as I'll show in the next example.

The # is for function keys

The only symbol you really shouldn't use like this is the pound sign—that's reserved for your function keys. Say I wanted to make vi do a "Save As" function with the F12 key, I could type:

```
:map #12 Ctrl+vEsc:w
```

and without any filename or Enter sequence on the end of the line, this command line would wait for me to type something in. There's a lot more to vi that

I'm not going to get into, but this should give you an idea of where you can start searching for its power.

There's one shortcut that applies to all of vi's range-based commands: the mark. You can set a kind of bookmark anywhere in a vi document by typing m followed by a letter, like this: ma. This will put a bookmark wherever the cursor is at the moment. You can then move the cursor to someplace else and set another mark (mb), and issue a command like

```
:'a,'b s/oldword/newword/
```

to substitute newword for oldword between the bookmarks a and b. Or you can write the lines from a to b using this command:

```
:'a,'b w testfile
```

Very simple, very clever, very nice.

emacs

> If you wish to be a writer, write.
>
> Epictetus
> *Discourses*, ca. 110 AD

Your system may not have this editor, but it's well worth getting a copy if you can. It's easy to use and extremely powerful. It's so powerful that I can't begin to touch all its features here. I will, however, share a few of the ones I like best.

If you're not familiar with emacs, get familiar. Fire up emacs and try hitting Ctrl+h t. This will bring up the emacs tutorial (Ctrl+h by itself brings up emacs help). The on-line help should get you familiar with the basic keystrokes (or you can look in Appendix C).

I'm going to have some fun by showing you how to play with some of emacs's advanced features, including how to split your windows, record macros, make your text come out pretty, and fix spelling mistakes.

But first, three of emacs's most important features: how to complete commands, how to repeat commands, and how to undo commands. There are two kinds of commands in emacs, the short ones (like Ctrl+x Ctrl+c to quit) and the longer, meta commands. You access meta commands by typing the meta key plus x, then the command name. Curious what the heck the meta key is? Well, emacs isn't particularly good about letting you know. Usually, your meta key is your Esc key. (You press Esc and release it before typing x.)

Anyway, the meta sequences tend to have rather lengthy names like replace-string and buffer-menu. Typing out these long command names is anathema to most UNIX people, so emacs will expand them at your wish. Just type the beginning of the command and press Tab, and emacs will complete as much of the command as it can. If you've typed the beginning of a command that begins like another command (maybe they both begin with the same word), emacs will expand the part they share, then wait for you to give a hint about how you want the command to end. Once you type enough so that emacs can choose a unique command name, it will complete the command for you.

When you know your emacs commands well enough, you can abbreviate them a lot. Rather than typing in a whole command name, you can just type in the unique part and press Enter. Then emacs will complete the command and run it.

Once you get your commands the way you want them, you'll probably find yourself wanting to run the same command over and over. For example, say you've done three things wrong—made three edits you really didn't mean. You can undo them one at a time with the sequence Ctrl+x u Ctrl+x u Ctrl+x u. But that's a lot of typing. How about if you could use a modifier to make emacs repeat Ctrl+x u three times? Well you can, with Ctrl+u. By default, if you press Ctrl+u Ctrl+x u, emacs will repeat Ctrl+x u four times. Ctrl+u makes emacs repeat the next command you type, four times by default. But you can also make Ctrl+u do something as many times as *you* want. In this case, you want to undo only three events, so you'd type Ctrl+u 3 Ctrl+x u. (By the way, some versions of emacs don't support more than one undo—a pain, but true.)

In other words, undo is Ctrl+x u, and repeat is Ctrl+u *n command* (where *n* is a number and *command* is any emacs command).

Just like vi, emacs lets you insert "special" characters. Remember how in vi you used Ctrl+v to insert the next thing you type? Well, in emacs it's just Ctrl+q—to "quote a character." Now doesn't that make more sense?

Dealing with multiple windows

One of the nicest things about emacs is that you can split your windows. Say you want to be looking at two documents at once so you can compare them, just type Ctrl+x 2. This splits the window into two parts, with a horizontal line (you get two short, fat windows). Now you can type Ctrl+x Ctrl+f to open a new file in one of the windows. (Ctrl+x Ctrl+f supports filename completion just as the rest of emacs supports command name completion, by the way. Just thought I'd let you know.) Or you can split your windows vertically, with Ctrl+x 5. Why 5? Dunno. (I just said it was better than vi, not by how much.)

Now you can step through your windows with Ctrl+x o. Your cursor will drop from one window to another. If you find that one of your windows isn't big enough, you can resize it. First select it (use Ctrl+x o until you're in it), then press `Ctrl+x ^`. It will get one line bigger. Keep it up until it's big enough for you. The only problem with this is that you're robbing the other window of its space. Windows can get pretty small—down to one line long—and therefore pretty useless pretty quickly. It's the only drawback to having multiple windows. If you split your windows vertically (with `Ctrl+x 5`), you use `Ctrl+x }` to make a window larger.

Finally, when you're sick and tired of having too many windows cluttering up your screen, use `Ctrl+x o` to get into the one window you want to keep and press `Ctrl+x 1`. This deletes all the other windows and grows the window you're in to fill the screen.

Macros in `emacs` are much simpler than macros in `vi`. (Not simple in the sense of Simple Simon, but simpler to create.) Unlike `vi`, where you define your macros by knowing in advance what key combinations you want, `emacs` records your macros. You use the sequence `Ctrl+x (` to start recording and `Ctrl+x )` to end it. Once you've started the recorder, just do what you want done. Then `Ctrl+x )` to stop the recorder. Now you have a macro of your very own.   **Macros**

To use the macro, you've got to name it. You name a macro with the command `Meta+x name-last-kbd-macro`. When you press `Return`, `emacs` will prompt you for a name. Just about any name is valid, so long as it doesn't include spaces. Press `Return` again and you've named your macro. Now you can call it up just like you would any other `emacs` command: `Meta+x macro-name` (where *macro-name* is the name of your newfound macro).

You can even save your macros for your next editing session. After you've created and named your macro, open your `.emacs` file (the `emacs` initialization file) by typing `Ctrl+x Ctrl+f ~/.emacs`. Now type `Meta+x insert-kbd-macro`. Never mind the gobbledygook that gets stuck in your `.emacs` file—it's a programming language based on LISP. It's also your macro. Next time you start `emacs`, you'll have your macros right there.

Next on my hot list of fun things to do with `emacs` is making my text pretty. There are only two tools `emacs` has that I use with any great frequency for this purpose: auto-fill mode and line centering. Let's look at the second first because it's so simple.   **Making pretty text**

To center a line in `emacs`, put your cursor in the line you want and type `Meta+x center-line`. What could be simpler? You can center a bunch of lines by blocking them. You do this by setting a **mark** (`emacs`'s term for dropping a little bookmark into your text) at one end of the text you want to block, then moving your cursor to the other end. Set your mark by hitting `Ctrl+Space`, then use your cursor keys (or page up and page down keys, or whatever) to get to the end of the text. You've just blocked that text. Now if you press `Meta+x center-line`, you'll center all those lines.

The emacs mark (which you set with Ctrl+Space) and point (which is where your cursor is) are an incredible innovation in UNIX editors. One of the things I do most often with the point and mark is to set the mark at one location in my document, then go someplace else to do a little more editing (I just don't set the mark again). Then, when I have new insight on what I was editing in the first place, I type Ctrl+x Ctrl+x—the command to exchange the point and mark. I'm immediately whisked back to where I set the mark in the first place.

Fixing margins   Once you've centered all the lines you want, you can do something else useful. You know how a typewriter has a right-hand margin, and when you get to it a bell rings? Well, most UNIX text editors don't. You can keep typing on one line until you run right off the screen. You've got to see that you're out of room at that right margin, then press Return to start a new line.

Except with emacs, which has what's called an auto-fill mode. You tell emacs where you want your right margin set, then issue the auto-fill command, and emacs will fix everything for you. Here's an example. When I used to work for a weekly computer newspaper, they measured their article lengths in lines (probably still do—most magazines use words instead. Why? I don't know.). A line to them was 43 characters. (Why 43? Again, I don't know, it just was. I was young and foolish and just accepted what they told me.) Anyway, I told emacs to set the right margin at 43 characters, then engage auto-fill like this:

```
Ctrl+x f 43
Meta+x auto-fill
```

Then, when I'd start editing, every line would automatically wrap when I exceeded 43 characters. (Actually, emacs counts characters. When you reach 43, it starts to watch for you to press Space or Tab, and when you do, it starts you on a new line.)

This worked great. Except when I'd go back and do some editing—emacs only checks on line length like this when you're typing. If you delete a few words from one line, you can get a ten-character line, and you can concatenate two lines and get an eighty-six-character line. You're back to looking ugly. Fortunately, emacs gives you a command to enact its beautification process in retrospect: Meta+q. If you set your right margin with Ctrl+x f n (where *n* is a number), you can use Meta+q to force existing paragraphs into that mold.

Spellling   Finally, the last thing I promised to talk about: spelling. Unlike vi, emacs has a built-in spell checker. You invoke it by either selecting a region and typing Meta+x spell-region or, to spell-check your whole document just typing Meta+x spell-buffer.

You can also make `emacs` fix spelling errors on the fly with its abbreviation mode. There are two ways to set up abbreviations: for the current session, or for all your sessions. To do it just for the current session, type

```
Esc x abbrev-mode
```

This is called a "meta" key sequence (remember, I never meta key I didn't like?) because it begins with the `Esc`, or "meta," key. The `x` tells `emacs` that what comes next is going to be a long command. Once you execute this command, the word `abbrev` appears on the mode line. Now you're free to define abbreviations. For example:

```
Ctrl+x-jm
```

Type it, and `emacs` will very politely ask you what you want it expanded into. Type this:

```
John Montgomery
```

Each time you press `Enter`, `emacs` knows that you're ending the line.

If you want to do that for every `emacs` session you ever have (and who wouldn't), put your changes into your `~/.emacs` file, like this:

```
(setq-default abbrev-mode t)
(read-abbrev-file "~/.emacs-abs")
(setq save-abbrevs 't)
```

You're nearly ready. If you used `emacs` to create this `.emacs` file, exit and restart `emacs` so it reads the changes. When you reenter `emacs`, you'll see `abbrev` on the mode line. That's a hint: This is no regular editing session. Use `Ctrl+x-jm` again, and `emacs` will ask you how you want it expanded. Type in the expansion: `John Montgomery`. Keep doing that for every abbreviation you want. Now type

```
Esc x write-abbrev-file
```

to save your changes. The program will ask for a file name. Type `~/.emacs-abs`. And that's how to fix your misspellings with `emacs`.

UGLY EDITORS

"My name is Ozymandias, king of kings:
Look on my works, ye Mighty, and despair!"

Percy Bysshe Shelley
Ozymandias, 1817

Editors like `vi` and `emacs` are great when it comes to actually creating documents—you know, writing your magnum opus. But they're not so great at quickly making bulk changes to lots of files or at filtering certain strings out of input streams. For those chores, we have some other editors: `ex` is a useful editor when you have a script you want to run to make formatting changes, for example; `sed` is terrific when it comes to changing the output of a command; and `awk` . . . well, `awk` is a kind of column-oriented, stream-manipulating . . . uh . . . um . . . *thing*. These three tools (particularly `sed` and `awk`) belong in your toolbox.

`ex` Marks the Spot

A man may write at any time, if he will set himself doggedly to it.

Samuel Johnson
Boswell's Tour to the Hebrides, 1773

Ivan: "The goose flies north for the winter." Vasili: "The stream flows hot and chunky." Ivan: "Do you have the papers?" Hmm. Is this some kind of code? Perhaps. Then `ex`—the extended editor (a line editor)—should be right at home with it. If you don't know what a line editor is, imagine driving on a twisty road at 55 mph, but you're only able to see the next 2 feet in front of the car at any turn. With `ex` you can edit only one line at a time, and usually it only shows one line—if that. Its standard error message is "?," and most of the commands are routinely abbreviated to one letter and a couple of numbers. It's like someone asked Hemingway to design a text editor. Figure 5.1 shows what it looks like.

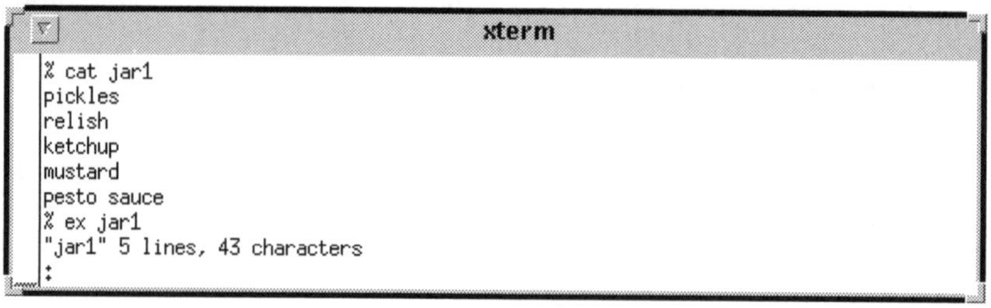

```
% cat jar1
pickles
relish
ketchup
mustard
pesto sauce
% ex jar1
"jar1" 5 lines, 43 characters
:
```

Figure 5.1 A face only a mother could love.

All that said, knowing a little defensive `ex` can help you in two ways. First, there will probably be times when `vi` won't run for one reason or another (usually a messed-up terminal setting). UNIX will dump you into `ex` instead. Oh joy. Second, `ex` can be useful for batch editing—opening multiple files and performing some change or changes on all of them from a shell script, for example. **It is and isn't so bad**

So let's fire up `ex` and step through a few basic maneuvers. It tells you that it's ready to accept a command by providing you with a colon to type at. What now? Well, let's take a look at Figure 5.2 and see what's inside this file.

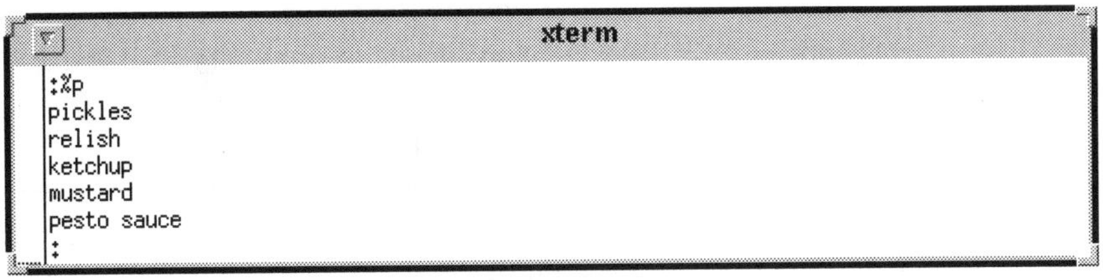

Figure 5.2 So what's inside?

Intuitive, isn't it? `%p`. Okay. What the heck does it mean? Well, the `%` tells `ex` that whatever command we're about to run should be applied to the whole buffer (the buffer we're working on is the file we're editing). The `p` means print. Now it makes sense, no? You can even see some of the logic, probably.

Rather than stepping through a whole bunch of examples, I'm going to cut to the chase. Tables 5.2 and 5.3 should explain the most common ways to move around the buffer and the most common commands. **Fast learning**

Moving around is pretty simple: You just type the number of the line you want to move to, or use the + or – keys. Then `ex` will obligingly print the contents of the line you've moved to. So, in the example above where I used `%p`, I didn't

Table 5.2 Moving around in `ex`.

Cryptic abbreviation	What it affects
1	The first line in the file
$	The last line in the file
x	Line *x* (No relation to Generation X)
x,y	Lines *x* to *y*
.	The current line
%	All the lines in the file
+	The next line
–	The previous line

Table 5.3 Doing stuff in `ex`.

Abbreviation	Command	What it does
q	quit	Quits
w	write	Writes the contents of the buffer
x	xit	Exits and writes the file (same as w then q)
a	append	Opens a new line after wherever you tell it to
i	insert	Opens a new line before wherever you tell it to
p	print	Shows the specified lines on the screen
d	delete	Deletes the specified lines
c	change	Replaces the specified lines with what you type
co	copy	Copies the specified lines
m	move	Moves the specified lines to a new location

need the p to get `ex` to print. Similarly, if I type 2,4, then `ex` will print out lines 2, 3, and 4 for me. If you're ever curious about what line you're on, just type #; `ex` will let you know, and will keep printing line numbers until you type # again.

The default action is to print out the lines you specify. That works fine when you're working interactively, but if you write an `ex` script, you're best off clearly stating what you want `ex` to do. In fact, you probably shouldn't use the abbreviations of the commands (like p for print) if you can avoid it. It may take less time to write, but if somebody else (maybe somebody who doesn't know `ex`) has to decipher your script, having full and explicit commands can be helpful.

The command I use most often in `ex` is q. Why? Because I most often wind up in `ex` because my terminal is set incorrectly when I try to run `vi`. I get an error message like, "hp8735: Unknown terminal type. I don't know what kind of terminal you are on—all I have is 'hp8735' [Using open mode]." This is `vi`'s way of saying you're in trouble. Usually I see that there is some typo in my terminal definition (I really meant vt100, not hp8735) so I quit, fix it, and use `vi`.

How to use commands

Most `ex` commands are very simple to use. A command such as 1a, for example, tells `ex` to append what you want to type after line 1. The command 8i means "insert before line 8." Typing 5,6c tells `ex` to "change lines 5 and 6 to what I'm about to type." And something like 4,90m$ tells ex to move lines 4 through 90 to the end of the file.

That's simple. There's also a search function (using the /, just like `vi`), which can help you move stuff around, too. Just typing /mustard will search the file forward for the word mustard (?mustard searches backwards for it) then prints the line containing mustard. Since the / (or ?) moves you to the line containing your search string, you can use it in any command that needs a line address. So /mustard/d tells ex to find the line containing mustard and then delete it. And 4,/mustard/m/ketchup/ tells ex to select from line 4 to the line containing mustard and move that block to after the line containing ketchup.

Simple, really. So now let's see how to write an ex script. Basically, you edit a file, put one command on a line, save the file, and use this syntax:

Write an ex script

```
% ex - filetobechanged < exscriptfile
```

The - tells ex to completely suppress user feedback (no typing allowed) and then to change filetobechanged according to the script in exscriptfile. If there's an error, ex will respond with the incredibly clear warning ?. Which is like sending your car to a garage where they do just fine if you tell them *exactly* what you want done, but scratch their heads if you make a mistake while you're telling them. Create a shell script called exscript containing these lines:

```
/root/m$
w
q
```

It's a simple script that will move the line containing "root" to the end of the file we're about to specify. Now type ex - /etc/passwd < exscript. (Why you'd actually do this is a different matter—this is really for an example only.) The one caveat is that you may not have rights to save the /etc/passwd file.

It is a sed, sed day

> Summer is icumen in,
> Lhude sing cuccu!
> Groweth sed, and bloweth med,
> And springth the wude nu—
> Sing cucu!
>
> Cuckoo Song, ca. 1250 AD

The sed editor, short for "seditious" editor, is a lying, cheating, stealing kind of editor, destined to do no good. Just kidding. Actually, sed stands for "stream editor," and it's designed to filter and change files and output quickly. Think of sed kind of like a perpetual-motion vending machine: You put stuff in one end, tell it what to do, and out the other end comes what you want.

The sed editor is a variant of ex (well, of ed—the first editor, actually, but who's counting), only it's totally noninteractive. That's right: It's like ex except

Meet my ex

you can only run scripts through it. There's also a difference in how it handles its output. As you saw, when you use **ex** with a script, it writes its output to a file. But **sed**, on the other hand, writes to standard output. If you want to capture **sed**'s output, you'll have to use an output redirector (> or |, for example). In techno-babble, this means that **sed** is stream-oriented and **ex** is line-oriented. In normal-babble, **sed** is usually going to be faster at making mass changes to large files or to the output of a particular command.

So what can you do with **sed**? Well, let's take some simple examples.

```
solaris# who
root          console     Aug 10 19:10
root          pts/0       Aug 10 19:10
root          pts/1       Aug 10 19:10
root          pts/2       Aug 10 19:10
root          pts/5       Aug 14 19:05
root          pts/6       Aug 14 19:05
root          pts/7       Aug 14 19:05
johnsh        pts/8       Aug 14 19:07    (localhost)
johnksh       pts/9       Aug 14 19:07    (localhost)
john          pts/10      Aug 14 19:07    (localhost)
solaris# who | sed 's/root/whataboob/g'
whataboob        console     Aug 10 19:10
whataboob        pts/0       Aug 10 19:10
whataboob        pts/1       Aug 10 19:10
whataboob        pts/2       Aug 10 19:10
whataboob        pts/5       Aug 14 19:05
whataboob        pts/6       Aug 14 19:05
whataboob        pts/7       Aug 14 19:05
johnsh        pts/8      Aug 14 19:07    (localhost)
johnksh       pts/9      Aug 14 19:07    (localhost)
john          pts/10     Aug 14 19:07    (localhost)
solaris#
```

Figure 5.3 Having fun yet?

Okay, **sed** is really good for making fun of people. The command in Figure 5.3 (**sed 's/root/whataboob/g'**) should look a little familiar—the syntax is borrowed from **ex**'s substitute command. In this example, **sed** simply read what was given to it (the output of the **who** command) and made a substitution. The single quotes, as usual, protect the **sed** command from the shell's otherwise notoriously invasive nature.

Changing words

Say you regularly misspell *occurrence*. I do. If you don't have an abbreviation set up in your .exrc file (**ab occurence occurrence**), you could use **sed** to make the global substitution with a command like this:

```
% sed 's/occurence/occurrence/g' misspelledfile
```

The substitute command is probably the one you'll be using the most, so let's spend a minute on it. First of all, know that **s** will only change the first occurrence of a string if you don't give the g option at the end of the line, as I did in the example. There are three other possible options: p, which produces the input buffer if any substitutions were made; w filename, which writes the input buffer to filename if any changes were made; and finally, n, a number that tells s to change the *n*th occurrence of a string (*n*'s got to be less than 512).

You can also make transformations in sed, such as changing case. This capability complements the s command by changing only parts of a word. (See Figure 5.4.)

Changing case

```
solaris# who | sed 'y/o/O/'
r00t       c0ns0le      Aug 10 19:10
r00t       pts/0        Aug 10 19:10
r00t       pts/1        Aug 10 19:10
r00t       pts/2        Aug 10 19:10
r00t       pts/5        Aug 14 19:05
r00t       pts/6        Aug 14 19:05
r00t       pts/7        Aug 14 19:05
j0hnsh     pts/8        Aug 14 19:07   (l0calh0st)
j0hnksh    pts/9        Aug 14 19:07   (l0calh0st)
j0hn       pts/10       Aug 14 19:07   (l0calh0st)
solaris#
```

Figure 5.4 Yes, a capital time.

The y command is sed's "transfer whatever appears between the first / and the second / with what appears between the second / and the third /" command. Again, pretty simple.

You can even string multiple commands together on the same line:

```
% sed -e 's/occurence/occurrence/g' -e 'y/ABC/abc/' testfile
```

The –e option tells sed that this is one of several commands to execute. Yet again, simple. Of course, if sed were much more simple, there'd be no section in this book on it.

For example, most sed commands can be given a range upon which to work their magic. Like ex, sed knows about line numbers, the end of input, and so on. The one caveat is that, if you give sed a bunch of files to work on, it starts numbering with 1 at the top and keeps numbering on straight through to the end: It doesn't start with 1 again at the beginning of each file. Similarly, the $, which means "end of file" in ex, means "end of everything" in sed.

Shooting ranges

"But wait—there's more": sed also knows about addressing lines through "regular expressions." Don't worry too much about regular expressions—you've already been using them without knowing it. A regular expression is just a search (mostly). (Well, not totally, but thinking of it that way is easier than trying to understand the arcana of regular expressions.)

Your address?   Anyway, you can use line addressing to tell sed where to (or not to) make its changes. For example, say you wanted to change only the section of a file between SUBHED1 and SUBHED2 (pretty standard notation in the magazine world for subheadings). You could use a sed script like this:

```
% sed '/SUBHED1/,/SUBHED2/s/string1/string2/g' column.jan
```

Look complicated? It's not—sed is going to start by looking for SUBHED1, then initiate a substitution, changing all occurrences of string1 to string2. When it reaches SUBHED2, it'll stop. We could also make sed perform this operation on all lines *not* between SUBHED1 and SUBHED2 by placing a ! in a strategic location— after the second address's last /:

```
% sed '/SUBHED1/,/SUBHED2/!s/string1/string2/g' column.jan
```

So now you know how *not* to do things with sed. Get it? I just showed you the logical "not" operator for sed—it's a joke. A really, really lame one.

Addresses can also work in slightly different circumstances. For example, you can mix and match regular expressions and line numbers or use only one address (which will make sed work only on a line with that address).

There are many more commands in sed than just s and y. Now's probably a good time to introduce some of them in short form. Namely, in Table 5.4.

Table 5.4 Some of sed's faves.

Command	Purpose	Example
a	Append text after matched lines	/SUBHED1/a\ Append this text after subhed1.
c	Replace text of matched lines	/SUBHED1/,/SUBHED2/c\ This will be a really short section.
d	Delete the matched lines	/SUBHED1/,/SUBHED2/d
i	Insert text before matched line	/SUBHED1/i\ Insert this text before subhed1.
p	Print the matched lines	/SUBHED1/,/SUBHED2/p
q	Quit when match occurs	/SUBHED1/q
r	Append file at match point	/SUBHED1/r jar1
w	Write match to file	/SUBHED1/,/SUBHED2/w jar2

You can also make multiple commands work with one address. Say you want to really munge one range of text—do a couple of insertions and a substitution, for example. Rather than respecifying the range each time, you can use braces, like this:

```
% sed '/SUBHED1/,/SUBHED2/{
i\
This is the text to insert.
s/string1/string2/g
i\
And this is more text to insert.
}' jar1
```

The only catch is that the first { must appear right after your range with no spaces, and the last } must appear on a line of its own, with no command preceding it.

After seeing this **sed** script spanning multiple lines, you're probably thinking about replacing carriage returns and how **sed** does stuff like that. If you weren't, then you are now. To **sed**, a carriage return (also called a newline) is a pretty simple thing—you just have to escape it properly. Say you wanted to change each occurrence of the word *relish* with "r

e

l

i

s

h." You could use a command like

```
$ sed 's/relish/r\
e\
l\
i\
s\
h/g' jar1
```

and **sed** would see the backslashes as newlines and make the appropriate output. Notice that I've switched to the Bourne shell here (you can tell by the $ prompt). That's because the C shell, which I normally use, doesn't handle the backslashes properly—you've got to double them up to protect them.

The one catch is that I haven't found a way to substitute something for a newline—I can't search for a newline and replace it with something else. Live and learn, I guess.

While we're on the subject of dealing with multiple lines, let's talk about how to change multiple lines at once. Say you have a phrase that you know appears on multiple lines and you want to make a substitution for it: **sed** has a command, **N**, that can do just that. Take a look at Figure 5.5.

Returned carriages

Subbing multiple lines

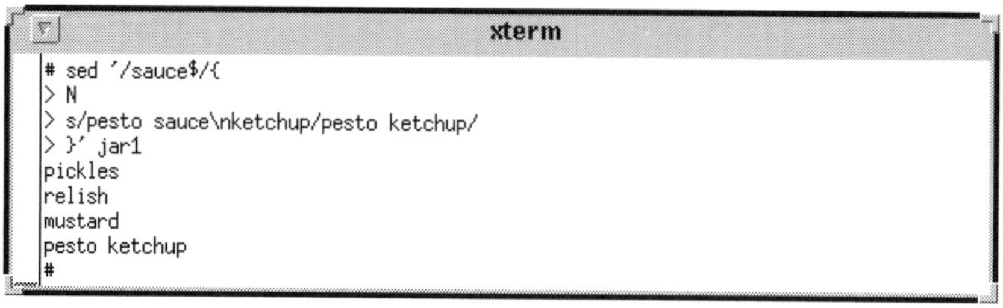

Figure 5.5 Yum.

Notice where the lines break and how you use \n to mean newline here (as opposed to just \). It's one of those differences you've just got to learn.

Spaced out   I'm not going to pretend that I've now told you everything there is to know about sed. I haven't even begun to scratch the surface. I haven't even mentioned that sed is multidimensional. That's right, it has two spaces: the pattern space and the hold space.

Pattern space is where sed does its dirty work. So far, all the commands we've dealt with work primarily in pattern space. Hold space is a good place to stash lines or text you want to put someplace else in a file. It's like a clipboard. There are five commands for moving stuff into and out of hold space. Table 5.5 show 'em all.

Table 5.5 Hold on.

Command	Purpose	Example
h	Copies pattern space into hold space	/SUBHED1/,/SUBHED2/h
g	Moves hold space into pattern space	/SUBHED3/,/SUBHED4/g
H	Like h, only it appends	/SUBHED1/,/SUBHED2/H
G	Like G, only it appends	/SUBHED3/,/SUBHED4/G
x	Exchanges input buffer and hold buffer	/SUBHED1/,/SUBHED2/x

They're pretty simple to use. I haven't had much call to use them, and the times I have have been in scripts so convoluted it would take a page to explain what the heck is going on.

Scripting with   There's one last thing to learn about sed: how to make it use scripts. Rather
sed   than typing long command lines, you can create sed scripts and invoke them with the -f option, like I've done in Figure 5.6. Just omit the single quotes that you usually use around the sed script.

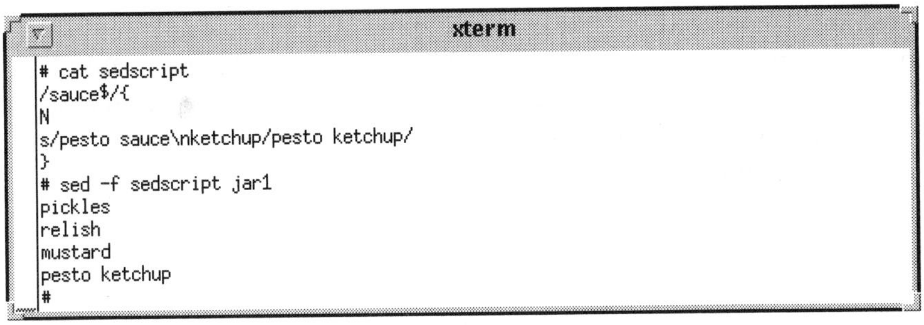

```
# cat sedscript
/sauce$/{
N
s/pesto sauce\nketchup/pesto ketchup/
}
# sed -f sedscript jar1
pickles
relish
mustard
pesto ketchup
#
```

Figure 5.6 No quotes.

A Bird of a Different Feather: awk

> Awkwardness has no forgiveness in Heaven or earth.
>
> R.W. Emerson
> *Society and Solitude*, 1870

There are times when grep isn't enough. It's not always sufficient to find lines that contain strings. Sometimes you want to find lines that contain strings and just print one or two items from those lines. That's where awk comes in handy.

The awk editor is one of my favorite tools, if for no other reason than that I like doing a large bird imitation when I say the name. No other UNIX tool gives me that same satisfaction. And so what if people look at me strange? Like a spreadsheet, awk deals with data in rows and columns. To it, a row is any line terminated by a newline character, and a column is any word separated from other words by a space (or a character you specify). As if that weren't enough to deal with, awk is also a programming language. Now don't turn the page. Come on, if I learned it, so can you. **It's a programming language *and* an editor**

One note for all you people out there expecting an in-depth tutoring on how to learn programming with awk: You aren't going to get it here. A pattern-matching programming language like awk deserves a book of its own.

First of all, I'm not going to bother teaching you syntax rules and all that kind of stuff. It's not that it's useless, but I don't do well without examples. (For that very reason I nearly flunked philosophy. It seems that, "Can you give me an example?" is not considered a categorical imperative—or maybe the professor just didn't know. I got even: I cheated on the final and cited Machiavelli.) So let's have some examples.

First of all, awk works best with data that has some kind of formatting. For example, I keep all the names and phone numbers of my contacts in a text file with this format: **Formatted data**

```
Firstname Lastname Company Phone Fax
```

Five columns separated by spaces. I use grep to locate people and company phone numbers, but every once in a while, someone asks me a question like, "How many people do you know named Diane?" There are a couple of ways I could find that out. The easiest would be by piping a grep command into the wc (word count) command like this:

```
% grep Diane rolodex | wc -1
```

The wc command would count all the lines with Diane in them and give me a number. Or, I could use awk. Granted, it's not as efficient, but you'll see what it can really do in a second. But first, take a look at Figure 5.7.

```
solaris:/test - 82 - Thu Aug 11 19:27:50 PDT 1994 - biff is n
% awk '$1 == "Diane" {print $1, $2}' rolodex
Diane Higgins
Diane Johnson
Diane Jones
Diane Pabst
Diane Smith

solaris:/test - 83 - Thu Aug 11 19:27:50 PDT 1994 - biff is n
%
```

Figure 5.7 Reinventing the wheel using stone.

Congratulate me: I've just managed to do with a tremendous amount of effort what I could have done with three words. Okay, so maybe awk isn't the best searching tool, but it has its place. For example, the grep command above would find every line that had Diane in it. What happens if I just want to know about a person whose *last* name is Diane? Suddenly grep seems lame and awk seems like a very useful tool. Figure 5.8 shows what it can do.

```
# awk '$2=="Diane" {print $1, $2}' rolodex
Lisa Diane
#
```

Figure 5.8 Aha, so there is a use for this tool after all!

Now let's take a look at what these commands are actually doing. Once you know that, you'll understand just about everything there is to know about awk. First of all, every awk "program" is surrounded in single quotes to protect it from the shell. That's easy. Second, awk's columns are numbered from left to right starting with 1: $1, $2, $3, and so on ($0 would be the entire line). So $2 is the last name.

There are two types of equals signs in awk: = and ==. The = sets whatever is on the left equal to what's on the right—it's an assignment operator. The == checks the thing on the left to see if it's already equal to what's on the right—it's a checking operator. So the section $2 == "Diane" is just saying "is the second column of the line Diane?" Actually, that's not quite right. Actually, $2 == "Diane" says "if $2 is equal to Diane." The if is implied.

awk's two =s

The second part of the awk program is surrounded in braces {}. This is the action to take if the part that's not in braces comes back true. In this case, we're just printing two columns. If we had just said {print} it would have been the same as {print $0}—print the whole line.

Braces

The awk editor can also read its program from a file. To turn this rather odd search into an awk script, I could just open a file in vi and add the lines

```
# weird.awk - An odd searching awk script
$2 == "Diane" {print $1, $2}
```

I'd then invoke it with the command

```
% awk -f weird.awk rolodex
```

and save a little typing the next time I wanted to run the command. Also, awk is generally useful for moving stuff around in files. Like switching columns:

```
% awk '{print $2, $1}' rolodex
```

You could even completely reverse the columns like this:

```
% awk '{ for (i = NF; i > 0; --i) print $i}' rolodex
```

Although the call for that isn't too frequent.

Sometimes, though, it's useful to know averages. Like, say you have a file with the name, team, and batting average of every major league baseball player, and you wanted to find out what the average batting average was across both leagues. Say each player's average is stored in column 4. You could just use a formula like this:

Mathematical calculations

```
% awk '{ s += $4 } END {print "average is", s/NR}' baseball
```

So what's new here? First of all, we have two activities separated by an END statement. The first statement sums everything in column 4 (remember, you need to add up everything then divide by the number of elements to get the average).

Once you have that number, you stick it into a variable called s. Now you just divide that by the number of rows, which awk stores (handily) in a variable called NR. There's also an NF for the number of fields (columns).

In fact, there is a whole slew of variables awk keeps that you can use. They are listed in Table 5.6.

Table 5.6 awk's friends.

Variable	What it varies based upon
FILENAME	Name of the file being read
FS	Field separator (default is a space)
NF	Number of fields in the current record
NR	Number of the current record
OFS	Output field separator—what you see when awk reports its results (default is a space)
ORS	Output record separator—again, what you see (default is a return)
RS	Record separator—what's in the file (default is a return)

But what can you do with these odd variables? Well, a lot, actually. Like, say you have an address list that's made out to be printed on labels. You know, the name's on the first line, the street on the second, city and state on the third, and such? Well, you can tell by looking that each group of three lines is one record—all related data. awk isn't as bright as you, however, and needs to be told. The secret is to reset the record separator (RS) to be a blank line (you *do* have blank lines separating your addresses, don't you?). You'd do it with syntax something like this: '{RS = ""}'

But that doesn't get you very far. It just means every blank line separates a record. You now have each record spanning three lines, with each element separated by a space, which means you'll have some odd results if you try printing anything. Ah, the joys of awk.

Record and field separators So, what you need to do is set not only RS, but FS, the field separator, too. If you just wanted to cull the names from this address list, you'd have a script like the one in Figure 5.9.

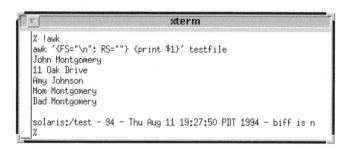

Figure 5.9 Oops.

Okay, what went wrong—why is it printing one line of my address but not of anyone else's? Good question. That one held me up for a day when I was trying to do this with a ten-thousand-record mail merge I'd gotten from the home office in Newton, Massachusetts. It was a day well spent, I will say. Any day that I don't actually do what I'm paid for is a day well spent.

Back to the subject. The problem is the absence of a crucial `awk` script element: `BEGIN`. This element is illustrated in Figure 5.10.

```
% awk 'BEGIN {FS="\n"; RS=""} {print $1}' testfile
John Montgomery
Amy Johnson
Mom Montgomery
Dad Montgomery

solaris:/test - 95 - Thu Aug 11 19:27:50 PDT 1994 - biff is n
%
```

Figure 5.10 In the BEGINning . . .

And suddenly there was light. It was dim light, as I was going on what the man page said about `awk`. Considering the complexity of this particular tool, I was surprised that the man page was all of about four pages long. Then I found out why: There was damn little information in it for someone who wasn't already fluent in `awk`.

As nearly as I can figure, `awk` will actually read the first line of the file *before* it does anything else unless you have the `BEGIN` statement in there as the very first thing.

Anyway, that's a sampling of what `awk` can do. To try to teach more would be trying to create a five-page guide to automobile repair: I'd get you changing your oil by page 3. Maybe.

6 Shell Programming

There are fairies at the bottom of our garden!

Rose Fyleman
The Fairies

I learn by example. Throughout my school years, it gave all my teachers the willies, because they were used to "good" students who read the textbooks and regurgitated whatever was in there. I never had much patience for reading (ironic that I should be writing a book, isn't it?), so I couldn't get my examples from textbooks. Instead, I'd start by pretending I knew everything and making suggestive comments until something somebody else said gave me some clue about what was going on.

As I've gained some perspective on my youth (he says, rocking in his rocking chair and puffing on his pipe), I've come to realize that this is a good method for learning. Getting a bunch of raw facts (whether they're dates, foreign words, or programming constructs) and having to assimilate them just *doesn't work* for most people. It's much easier to take a few good examples and work from them into a general understanding of something.

That's why this chapter starts at the end: with a working shell script. I'll explain everything in it, then go on to explain why these things are the way they are. Then we'll begin working on more general stuff—but we'll have a context, an example, to go back to. Once you grab hold of a few simple constructs (there's that programmer-ese), you'll be able to use just about any UNIX command you like in a script.

A SIMPLE SAMPLE

Come, Watson, come! The game is afoot.

Sir Arthur Conan Doyle
The Return of Sherlock Holmes, 1904

All shell scripts (at least every one I've seen) start as a problem. Necessity is the mother of invention, you know. (With UNIX, it's probably better to say that efficiency is the mother of invention.) Anyway, I had a problem—writing this book, actually—that spawned the shell script I'm about to show you. More specifically, I had a problem with the screens in the book. Long before learning my editor's (rather peculiar) screen shot naming convention, I had collected about forty screens that I wanted to include. I had named them with names that made sense, like `awk-sorting-script.rs`. To me, this made perfect sense: That particular file contained a Sun Raster Image (which is why it ends `.rs`) of an `awk` script running. My editor wanted files named differently. *Way* differently.

Automating mv   This was a job for a shell script. I could have used the UNIX `mv` command to rename them one by one, but I'm so lazy that I'd rather spend an hour writing a shell script to get my job done than actually do it manually. Fortunately, this wasn't one of those times: It's an eight-liner:

```
#!/bin/sh
# Usage: rename file(s)
for badname
do
  echo "$badname: Rename it to: \c"
  read goodname
  mv "$badname" "$goodname"
done
```

What could be simpler? I think every person who uses UNIX has a script like this somewhere. Now all I had to do was type `rename *` and my script (called `rename`) would prompt me for the new name of each file. Here's how it works.

#!/bin/sh   Every shell script should start with a line saying which shell you intend it for. This line may look like a comment (lines that start with # are generally comments), but when you run the script, your shell will read this line expecting to see a program it should call. I've actually had scripts fail because they didn't have this line. For this script (as with most others) I used the Bourne shell. The Bourne shell is not great for interactive use, but it makes a wonderful parent for shell scripts.

After making the first line of your script a shell to call, make the second line a Usage reminder. It's good practice to let anybody who picks up your scripts know how to run them. And, chances are that you'll forget the syntax one day, too.

 # Usage:

A *for* loop. Now we're into programming. In a program, a loop is something that can be executed over and over. You can have endless loops (like Rush Limbaugh), and loops that execute only once. The *for* loop is rather dogmatic: It will keep going until it's out of input. In this case, it's reading its input from the command line, because you're going to be feeding *for* a filename. The filename you give *for* on the command line gets stored in the variable *badname*. (If your filename is a wildcard, the Bourne shell will **expand** the wildcard, changing it from a simple * into each and every filename in the directory, for example. Wildcard expansion is one of the hallmarks of UNIX shells, and we'll be making use of it a lot in our scripts.) The *for* loop will then execute whatever is between the *do* and *done* statements once for each argument (in this case an argument is a file).

for badname

When the script executes, *for* reads your filename(s) (expanding it if it's a variable), then takes each one, one by one, and feeds them to the stuff between *do* and *done*. In this case, we're just echoing back the current argument. The \c at the end of the line tells my UNIX's System V *echo* not to advance the screen one line. If you have a BSD system, you'll want to say *echo –n* and not put the \c at the end of the line. In either case, your response will appear on the same line as the question.

echo $badname

The *read* command is one way to get a shell script to accept your input. *read* needs a variable to put whatever you type into, so we called it *goodname* and wind up with the command *read goodname*.

read goodname

Just a regular, old *mv* command, using the *badname* and *goodname* variables. This is actually the guts of the script—everything else is just setting up for this one line, if you can believe it. The quotes protect the variables from literal interpretation by the shell.

mv...

Done with the *for* loop.

done

Programming Basics

> No person who is enthusiastic about his work has anything
> to fear from life.
>
> Samuel Goldwyn

Don't be intimidated by those shell scripts down the hall—you know, the really long ones that do really clever things. Most scripts are under ten lines long and accomplish a fairly simple task. So let's get writing. But where to start? Hmm. We need a checklist. Try this one:

1. Identify the problem to be solved. Try to write it down in five or ten words. For our *rename* script, the problem was, "To rename every file in a directory,

one by one." Ten words on the nose. This may seem silly, but, particularly with longer scripts, I get lost all the time—I'm so involved in solving one small problem that I've forgotten what the heck I'm doing.

2. Figure out which commands form the heart of your script. For `rename`, it was the `mv` command, and I knew it had to be in a loop. This is a good time to figure out what order the commands need to be executed in, too. Make a list of the commands in a text file.

3. Figure out a name for your script. You're about to save this text file—the one with your heart commands. You need a name. It must be two things: unique and easy to remember. When you think you have a name, figure out if it's unique by running the commands `which`, `whereis`, `alias`, and `whence` on it (Korn shell only).

4. Add the basic layout to the script: the `#!/bin/sh` line, the `#Usage` line, and any comments you think it should have.

5. Write the script. Easy to say. We'll get into just *how* to write the script in a bit. For now, hold on. When you're done, save and quit.

6. Make the script executable. You can do this with the command `chmod +x script`.

7. Test the script. Run it. If it's not in your path, you'll have to give an explicit path to it, like `/usr/people/john/script`. You'll probably want to make a `bin` or `scripts` directory in your home directory. You're going to have a lot of scripts by the time we're done.

8. Debug the script. Of course, it'll work the first time. But we're just being thorough here, and others may not be as proficient as you at shell programming.

By the way, these rules are pretty general to any type of programming, so if you want to develop a database or something like that, keep 'em handy.

Which Shell?

> Democracy is supposed to give you the feeling of choice, like Painkiller X and Painkiller Y. But they're both just aspirin.
>
> Gore Vidal, 1982

The ancient question, asked of all gurus by all initiates—"Which shell should I use?"—It's not an easy question, I assure you. I'm not going to try to pressure you into choosing one shell over the others—you must decide, my son. However, I'm not going to be writing any C shell script examples in this book, either.

Don't get me wrong. I love *using* the C shell because it's so easy (the aliases, history, command-line editing, and such). But for some reason, I don't use it for shell programming. I don't really know why—I just don't. There have been people who have done very careful studies of the C shell and have come up with really good reasons for not using it (mainly concerning its poor handling of writing to and reading from files). Most of the scripts I write don't have that problem. But I still don't use it. Maybe it's genetic: I bat lefty but catch righty, too.

My choice

So I have the choice between the Bourne and Korn shells (and about a billion other shells, but I'm simplifying the picture to the major players). Well, the Bourne is more widely used than the Korn. But the Korn is a lot more flexible. And it's a superset of the Bourne. But it's not on every system. And . . . And . . .

I think I have a headache. Lowest common denominator: The Bourne shell is on every system, and you can interpret its scripts from the Korn shell. Therefore I'll use Bourne.

Here are the keys to each kingdom: the lines you need to put at the top of your script to invoke any one of these shells. Without one of these lines, your script will be interpreted by whatever shell you're running at the time. Table 6.1 holds the keys.

No matter which you choose

Table 6.1 First lines for shell scripts.

Shell	Line
Bourne	`#!/bin/sh`
C	`#!/bin/csh`
Korn	`#!/bin/ksh`

Okay, okay. So you tried putting this line at the top of your script and it didn't work. Why? Because some of the newer systems are hiding their shells in different directories. On my Sun, for example, the shells are in `/sbin`. You can find your shells by typing `which sh`, `which csh`, and `which ksh`.

Using Variables

In our `rename` shell script, we used two variables: `badname` and `goodname`. Variables are simply places where your shell script can stick information until they need to use it.

You can set a variable in a couple of ways. From a command prompt, you can use an equals sign, like this:

Setting and unsetting variables

```
# badname=file1
```

To see what's in it, echo it:

```
# echo $badname
file1
```

Well, maybe don't *just* echo it. In all three shells, you need to let your shell know that what it's about to echo is a variable, otherwise you'd get a result like this:

```
# echo badname
badname
```

That's a pretty darn useless result. So you precede the name of your variable with a dollar sign to tell the shell that it's a variable.

An odd trick that you may want to know comes from using braces during your echo. Rather than just echoing a variable, you can add letters to it during the echo process by surrounding the original variable's name with braces and adding on your letters. Like this:

```
# echo ${badname}isntsobad
file1isntsobad
```

It's odd, but it works.

Once you've set a variable you may want to unset it. Oddly, there's an unset command for just this purpose, so unset badname makes anything in badname go away.

Environment variables vs. other variables

So far in this book, we've talked mainly about environment variables. Right now, we're just talking about regular variables. In case you're wondering, there's a difference. First off, the standard UNIX naming convention for environment variables is all uppercase letters (remember UNIX is case-sensitive). Regular variables are lowercase. Second off, your shell uses environment variables (like PATH and PROMPT). It doesn't use regular variables. So here's the rule: When you create your own variables (and they aren't environment variables), keep them lowercase.

Built-in variables

And a last note on variables: Your shell script can make use of some built-in variables. These variables stand for things you put on the command line, the exit status of commands (whether they worked or failed), and so on. We used an implied one in rename to read the command line argument. Table 6.2 lists some others.

Table 6.2 Built-in shell variables.

Variable	What it stands for
$*	List the value of all command-line parameters (Bourne and Korn shells)
$argv	The C shell's version of $*
$?	Return the exit status of a command (Bourne and Korn shells—in the C shell you need to set a variable to get it to work)
$n	Read command parameter *n* (Bourne and Korn shells—the Bourne shell can't go higher than 9)
$#	How many command-line parameters are there? (Bourne and Korn shells—C shell doesn't have an equivalent)
$$	What's the process ID of this shell?
$!	What's the process ID of the last process run in the background (Bourne and Korn shells)?

In case you're wondering how you can use most of these, you probably won't. The $* variable is really common, as is $?, but the others are once-a-year things unless you're into really serious shell programming. Here's an example of rename, rewritten to use $# and $* (although the $# is kind of gratuitous):

```
#!/bin/sh
# Usage: rename file(s)
echo $#
for badname in $*
do
  echo "$badname: Rename it to: \c"
  read goodname
  mv "$badname" "$goodname"
done
```

The new third line will print out how many files you're going to be dealing with. As for the rest, it does *exactly* the same thing with and without the $*. That's because your shell will assume you mean $* if it needs a variable for a for statement. Generally, I'm a proponent of clear scripting, so I actually prefer leaving it in (as I have here), rather than making you know that there's an implied variable there.

Now that we've got variables, we can talk about input (from files and—more interestingly—from you) and output. In Chapter 1, we talked a bit about standard input and standard output. We're about to add to that a little. To refresh your memory quickly, standard input is where a program expects to get its input. By default, that's the keyboard. Standard output is where your program expects to

I/O, I/O, it's off to work I go

send its output, and, as you probably guessed, the default is the screen. There's also standard error, which is where your program will send any error messages if something goes wrong. By default, that's your screen, too.

Each of these standards (in, out, and error) is assigned a number called a **file descriptor**. I'll admit that the concept of a file descriptor escapes me a bit, particularly because in this case none of the things being described is a file. These numbers are, however, the shorthand by which your shell keeps track of things. Standard input is always 0, standard output 1, and standard error 2.

Redirection

Knowing this will make some of the redirection symbols make sense. Like, did you wonder why you used 2> to redirect standard error to a file? Now it makes sense a bit, doesn't it? I mean standard error having a file descriptor of 2 and all.

Table 6.3 shows what all the redirectors do.

Table 6.3 Misdirected redirection.

Symbol	What it does
>	Standard output to a file (could be 1>, too)
<	Standard input from a file (could be 0<, too)
<>	Standard input and output to/from same file
>>	Appends standard output to a file
2>	Standard error to a file
2>&1	Standard error goes to standard output

As you probably remember, there's also the pipe (|) for sending one command's standard output to another's standard input.

The while loop

Back on track now, it's time to learn how to use standard input a little more. Let's take our `rename` script and make it so you can enter the command you want it to execute. This command would go in place of mv. We'll have to do some fairly serious rewriting to get it to work.

```
#!/bin/sh
# Usage: rename command file(s)
echo $#
command=$1
while [ $# -ne 1 ]
do
  badname=$2
  echo "$badname: perform $command with output: \c"
  read goodname
  "$command" "$badname" "$goodname"
```

```
    shift
done
```

What's changed, and why? Well:

We need to define the command we're going to be issuing right here, right now. Because the command is only issued once, we want it to be outside any loops or any odd happenings. So we set the variable command equal to the first parameter on the command line. (By the way, the zeroth parameter is the command itself, in case you're interested).   **command=$1**

Out with the `for`, in with the `while`! Our `for` loop wasn't going to let us step through all the command parameters one by one while ignoring $1 (our new command). This is also a good way to introduce `while`. The $#, as you recall, is the total number of parameters on our line. The `-ne` means "not equals." And we're using 1 because our command resides at position 1, and we want to stop before we try to treat a command as a file. Overall, this line works a lot like `for`, except that we're saying, as long as the total number of command options is not equal to 1, keep doing whatever's in the `do` loop. That wouldn't be possible without the `shift` command at the bottom, but we'll get to that. I could have done pretty much the same thing with a `for` loop, but it's time to introduce a different kind of loop.   **while [$# -ne 1]**

Defines the variable `badname` to be whatever's in the $2 spot at the moment. Thanks to the `shift` command at the bottom of the `do` loop, $2 will be changing each time we work on a file.   **badname=$2**

Before, the `mv` command was **hard-coded** into the script. Now, we need a variable to take its place. This one works just like the other two on the line.   **"$command"...**

In our script, `shift` takes whatever's in $2 and discards it, moving the value from $3 into $2 and so on up the line. In general, `shift` moves command line parameters one step to the left.   **shift**

The rest of the script stayed relatively the same. Of course, there wasn't much of the script left. Now, it's time to make our script a little more user friendly. After all, it's not particularly intuitive to type a command followed by another command and then a list of filenames, is it? So what we really need is a help screen.

```
#!/bin/sh
# Usage: rename command file(s)
# echo $#
if test $# -lt 1
then
    echo "Usage: $0 needs a command name and filenames like this"
```

```
      echo "rename cp file*"
      exit 1
fi
command=$1
while [ $# -ne 1 ]
do
   badname=$2
   echo "$badname: perform $command with output: \c"
   read goodname
   "$command" "$badname" "$goodname"
   shift
done
```

What have we done now? Well, nothing much. We made it so that if a person types rename with no options, they get a little help message and rename exits. (By the way, we commented out the echo $#—it was starting to be annoying)

if-then-fi   This is probably the most intriguing thing introduced here. It's another looping procedure. If you're familiar with loops in any programming language, the Bourne (and Korn) shell's loops work just about the same: If one thing is true, then do something. Hence, if-then. The fi is just a Bourne-shell-ism to close the if loop. By the way, we've only used part of the construction. Actually, it's if-then-elif-else-fi. It kind of reads, if A is true, then do B, otherwise if C is true do D, otherwise do E.

test   The test command is one of the most useful. You can test to see if files are there, test to see if the user supplied arguments, test to see what's in the arguments. All with this little command. It's *so* cute, isn't it?

Most often, you use tests to see if files exist. You do that with the –r or the –f switch to test. So you'd say if test –r /usr/people/john to see if /usr/people/john existed and was readable. Just to see if it is a file and exists, you'd use test –f /usr/people/john. (True pros omit the test and use a syntax more like if [–r /usr/people/john]. The spaces around the [ ] are very important.)

exit   Finally, seeing as rename doesn't have any of the parameters it needs, we exit. The command exit 1 means "exit with error status." I did it this way in case any calling program needed an exit status from rename—not that any program was calling it. It's just good programming. Otherwise, exit 0 is a normal, successful exit. You can also exit with higher numbers, and you can use a routine to test for exit status. We'll talk about that later in this chapter.

Now we have a pretty decent shell script. Except I'd love it if I could feed it different arguments and get different responses. I mean, when I feed it the rm command, for example, the syntax `"$command" "$badname" "$goodname"` really doesn't apply. I just want it to remove the files. And when I send it a –h flag, I'd love the script to print itself out. We can get it to do that using the `case` statement.

```
#!/bin/sh
# Usage: rename command file(s)
case $1 in
  -h[elp] | -? | '')
    echo "Usage: $0 needs a command name and filenames like"
    echo "this"
    echo "rename cp file*"
    exit 1;;
  rm)
    echo "Removing specified files..."
    while [ $# -ne 1 ]
    do
      rm $2
      shift
    done
    exit 0;;
  *)
    command=$1
    while [ $# -ne 1 ]
    do
      badname=$2
      echo "$badname: perform $command with output: \c"
      read goodname
      "$command" "$badname" "$goodname"
      shift
    done
    exit 0;;
esac
```

My God, we're actually creating quite a shell script here! I restructured the whole script using `case`, and it's a lot cleaner. Using `case` enabled me to get rid of the `if test` conditional at the beginning of the script. Now I can test for a –h, –help, –?, and nothing at all, all on the same line.

```
  -h[elp] | -? | '')
```

The vertical bars mean "or" and the brackets mean "what's in here is optional." So this line says, "If you see an option that looks like –h, –help, –?, or nothing, print out the help message that follows. That message includes a couple of echoes and an `exit 1`—although there wasn't really an error, just a misunderstanding.

Note that the `case` section starts with the thing you're looking for on a line ending with a right parenthesis ( )), and ends with a line that ends with a pair of semicolons. That's how `case` knows that you're ending one `case` and beginning another. You end the `case` section with `esac`—`case` spelled backwards (like `fi` is `if` spelled backwards—but `done` isn't `do` spelled backwards).

Aside from that, very little has changed in the script. Notice that I've added a lot of functions without adding a lot of lines. That's one of the wonders of shell programming—as you get better, you get briefer. Which brings me to my next point.

Up until now, there's been little need to document our shell script. After all, it's only been about a dozen lines long. Now, however, we're getting so that it's nearly a page long, and the next version will probably have to have comments.

Now it's time for one last iteration. In this one, we're making one minor change in the general section (the section of `case` that begins `*`)): We're going to check to make sure that the user enters a new filename when prompted, and if s/he doesn't, we're not going to exit, but instead we'll print an error and perform an operation called a `break`.

Breaking is a time-honored tradition, but one that you should probably avoid using if you can. See, it leads to indecipherable code—code that leaps all over the place for no apparent reason. However, what it does is to drop you out of your `while` or `for` loop and move you to the `done` command that goes with it. Go directly to jail, do not pass Go, do not collect $200.

```
#!/bin/sh
# Usage: rename command file(s)
# rename steps through files you specify and runs the
# command you tell it to on them. Usually, that's
# something like
# rename mv file?
# and rename will prompt you for new filenames for every
# file that begins file? in the current directory
#
# Created 12/25/01 by John Montgomery
#
case $1 in
  -h[elp] | -? | '')
    echo "Usage: $0 needs a command name and filenames like"
    echo "this"
```

```
    echo "rename cp file*"
    exit 1;;
rm)
    echo "Removing specified files..."
    while [ $# -ne 1 ]
    do
      rm $2
      shift
    done
    exit 0;;
*)
    com and=$1
    while [ $# -ne 1 ]
    do
      badname=$2
      echo "$badname: perform $command with output: \c"
      read goodname
      if test "$goodname" = ''
        echo "You didn't say the magic word..."
        break
      else
        "$command" "$badname" "$goodname"
        shift
    done
    echo "Exiting..."
    exit 0;;
esac
```

What we've got here is a very simple break usage. I added a few comments to the beginning, explaining basically what the script does and who wrote it (and when). This is common courtesy, so that when it gets passed around (and most shell scripts do), people will know who to ask about it.

The main changes in here come in the *) section. Now I have a test to make sure that you enter a new filename. If you don't, I give you a nasty error message (remember *Jurassic Park*?) and break. The break drops me to the done four lines up from the bottom, so the next thing you'll see is the Exiting... comment.

One thing to note here is that I'm giving a 0 exit status after the break, even though rename didn't run your command. Why? Because rename was *successful*—at least from my perspective: It caught the error and exited nicely instead of giving you a load of hard-to-understand error messages.

Debugging

> The shortest mistakes are always the best.
>
> J.B. Molière
> *L'étourde*, 1653

Now that we have this masterpiece of shell scripting, you should know how to fix all the problems that are likely to come with it. Debugging with shell scripts isn't particularly fancy. It's kind of lame, actually. You set a couple of flags in your shell script on the first line. They are **-xv**. So instead of starting out your script with

```
#!/bin/sh
```

you start with

```
#!/bin/sh -xv
```

Same for C shell and Korn shell. Simple. (You can also use these flags on a command line, like % `csh -xv`, but I use them *in* my scripts far more often.)

Graceful Exit

> We'll teach you to drink deep ere you depart.
>
> William Shakespeare
> *Hamlet*, 1600

Let's go back to exit status for a second. Every command has an exit status. Usually it's 0, for success. Sometimes it's 1 or -1, for failure. Less often there are other numbers, or these numbers are mixed up. Most commands follow these guidelines, but check the `man` pages before you go to the bank on it. You can use these values in your shell scripts, testing exit values to see what to do next. You do that with a new variable: $?. After each command runs, it leaves its exit status hanging in the air for you to check. You can `echo $?`, or use an `if test "$?" =` construct, for example.

And having said all that, it's time for me, too, to make a graceful exit. From beginning shell programming, that is. You now know enough to go out and really hurt yourself. (Big grin.) Enjoy.

PROGRAMMER'S CORNER

It is thrifty to prepare today for the wants of tomorrow.

Aesop
The Ant and the Grasshopper

After playing around with shell programming, you feel like more. I suggest you lie down until the feeling goes away. It's not that UNIX doesn't have lots of advanced programming tools. It's just that after shell programming—which is kind of like stringing commands together—the next step is something much more akin to hard-core programming than simply stringing commands together.

In particular, there are two tools you should know about (even if you don't know exactly how to use them): `make` and `perl`. Only `make` comes on nearly every UNIX system (or at least every UNIX system I've seen)—although nearly every `make` is slightly different. The other tool, `perl`, like so much that's good about UNIX, is freely available from your friends.

make

Two wrongs don't make a right, but they make a good excuse.

Thomas Szasz
Social Relations, 1973

The `make` command's job is to make programs. (I still don't know how they got the name `make` from what it does.) If you program in a high-level language, like C, you know that any one program usually consists of a whole bunch of files—libraries, headers, source code files, and other bits of miscellany. You can use `make` to put them all together.

More specifically, `make` transforms files from one form to another—for example, it causes a compiler to compile source code files, generating object files and eventually an executable. You give `make` a list of files by putting them into a file called `makefile` (or `Makefile`). More specifically, `make` transforms files from one form to another and makes sure that everything is up-to-date. For example, it compiles source code files, generating object files and eventually an executable, but only when the source code has changed since the last `make`. You give `make` a list of files and a set of commands by putting them into a file called `makefile` (or `Makefile`). When you run `make`, it reads the list from the `makefile` and checks to see if the source files are older than the destination files. If they aren't, `make` issues the command you tell it to (in the `makefile`).

A `makefile` for a typical (small) application might look like this:

```
foobar: foo.o bar.o foohead.h barhead.h
  $(LINK.c) -o $@ foo.o bar.o
foo.o: foohead.h foo.c
  cc -c foo.c
bar.o: barhead.h bar.c
  cc -c bar.c
```

So we have a program called `foobar` that needs two modules in order to function: `foo.o` and `bar.o`. To understand this example a little better, you need to know a bit about programming in general, and programming in C in particular.

C programs—executables as the programmers call them—start life as source code files (files containing gobs of the C programming language) and header files (files containing setup information for the source code files). C source code files end in `.c` and C headers end in `.h`. Once you've created a `.c` file (and maybe a `.h` file), you run a compiler (usually called `cc`) to create an object file (whose name ends in `.o`). Then (usually automatically) a program called a linker (usually run with the command `ld`) joins any files ending in `.o` together with various information it knows about the kind of computer you're on, and it shoots the executable out its other end. So the first line is saying that if `make` can find two object files called `foo.o` and `bar.o` *and* they're at least as new as `foo.c` and `bar.c`, go ahead and link them together to make `foobar`.

That's just the first line. The rest of the `makefile` deals with what happens if `foo.o` and `bar.o` aren't up-to-date. The second line says that if `foo.o` and `bar.o` are up-to-date, go ahead and link them together to create `foo`. If one or both isn't up-to-date, we skip ahead to the next four lines. The line starting `foo.o` says that `foo.o` is made up of `foohead.h` and `foo.c`. If those two files are around, you can create `foo.o` by running the command `cc -c foo.c`. The same thing could happen for `bar.o`.

So now you know how it works. You're probably wondering what *you* can do with it. Well, if you're a programmer, it should be obvious. If you're not, there's still a case or two where you can use `make`. You see, `make` doesn't really care what programming language you're using—or even if you're using a programming language at all. Its job is just to make sure everything's up-to-date. You even have to give it the commands it's to run in order to bring things up-to-date.

Let's say that once a week you have to bring together sales data from four different regions to make a weekly sales report. The sales data comes in four files, `sw.raw`, `nw.raw`, `ne.raw`, and `se.raw`. These are raw files, with lots of gobbledygook in them, and each one is different (Lord forbid all the sales regions should report data in the same way). Fortunately, you have a sophisticated `awk` script for each region that massages the data into a usable format. Here's a `makefile` that would process every raw report and generate the sales report, preceding the whole thing with a stock header that you created:

```
salesreport: header sw.reg nw.reg se.reg ne.reg
  cat header sw.reg nw.reg se.reg ne.reg >> salesreport
  lp salesreport
sw.reg: sw.raw
  awk -f sw.massage sw.raw > sw.reg
nw.reg: nw.raw
  awk -f nw.massage nw.raw > nw.reg
se.reg: se.raw
  awk -f se.massage se.raw > se.reg
ne.reg: ne.reg
  awk -f se.massage ne.raw > ne.reg
```

So you see, `awk` can be useful even to nonprogrammers.

`perl`

> On a wrinkled neck a pearl weeps.
>
> German proverb

No one has explained `perl` to me very well. I've tried it and come to the conclusion that it could be useful if only I a) knew it better and b) had the time to screw around with yet another programming language. And it is a programming language—sort of a combined C, `awk`, and `sh`. It has C-like syntax, but it's not compiled into a program like C source code is. And it's mainly designed to work on arbitrary text files.

To say that I'm going to explain `perl` in a three hundred-page book is actually reasonable. To say that I'm going to explain `perl` and anything else in those same three hundred pages isn't. If you're interested in learning `perl`, you can check out its really, really long `man` page. If you find that it isn't installed on your system, you can get it on the Internet pretty easily. You'll probably find it in a lot of places on the Net (try an anonymous `ftp` to `ftp.cis.ufl.edu` or `prep.ai.mit.edu`).

Just a little more information to entice you: `perl` can manipulate the data in files like `awk` and `sed`. It can manipulate processes. And it can just exist on its own like a real programming language. Its one problem is a somewhat high barrier to entry. (Read, it's a little intimidating at first.) But once you're past that, it's not so bad, and you'll find some really neat things to do with it.

Let's start with an example of a `perl` program—in fact, the first program that most people learn in most programming languages: Hello, world.

```
#!/usr/people/john/bin/perl
print "Hello, world\n";
```

Sheesh, what could be easier? Why the big fuss? It looks like a cross between a shell script (thanks to the first line, which tells the shell where to find `perl`) and C (the second line, with a very C-like syntax and that ending semicolon).

Okay, maybe it's not quite *that* easy. After all, what worth learning is? `perl`'s problem (from a learn-it-quick perspective) is that it can do way too much. Rather than try to give a complete, blow-by-blow of `perl`, I'm going to give you some snippets of `perl` code—parts of larger scripts—and explain what they do. It's the learn-by-example approach, and it's just about the only way I've been able to learn anything.

Here's a more powerful example, which I found on the Net. It was unattributed, but it's basically designed to figure out how much to charge users based on how much they're using the computer.

```
#!/usr/local/bin/perl
while ($line = ,.)
{
  chop;
  if ($line =~ /\s*(\S+)\s*(\s+)\s*/)
  {
    $users{$1} = $2;
  }
}
&total_summary($users);

sub total_summary {
  local($users) = @_;
  $date=`/bin/date`;
  print("Usage Report for All Users \n");
  print("Date: ",$date);
  $~ = 'SUMMARY';
  foreach $user (sort keys %users)
  {
    if ($users{$user} <= 10)
    {
      $cost = 20;
    } else
```

```
    {
       $cost = $users{$user}*2;
    }
    @passwd = getpwnam($user);
    $name = $passwd[6];
    $name =~ s/,.*//;
    write ;
  }
}

format SUMMARY =
@<<<<<<< @<<<<<<<<<<<<<<<        @##.##      @##.##
$user, $name, $users{$user}, $cost
.
```

Here's basically what it does: It reads a formatted data file line by line (the data file has two columns—users in the first, connect time in the second), then it reads each user's name and sees if they have fewer than 20 hours of connect time. If they do, they're charged $20. (I guess whoever wrote the script decided that charging $2/hour on a computer was reasonable. I'd be broke.) Otherwise, their connect time is multiplied by 2, and we print a fancy report.

I'm less interested in what this script does than in what it shows us about `perl`. Like, statements end in semicolons, just like they do in C. And there's this great `chop` command for stripping newline characters from the ends of lines. And it supports `while` and `if` constructs like the Bourne shell, but uses C-like syntax (with braces).

Rather than boring you with further vagaries of this language, I've included two of the best-commented `perl` scripts I've ever found, from Abe Singer and Jim Jacobs (both of UCSD), in Appendix A. This isn't really a programming book. Anyway, if you have `perl` installed on your system, you have an excellent `man` page.

If you want a book on programming `perl`, I suggest *Programming Perl*, by Larry Wall and Randal Schwartz. Larry Wall wrote `perl`, so he knows it better than I ever will (although at times his book assumes you already know as much as Larry Wall, which can be a problem). I won't even pretend. I also won't pretend that you're going to dive into `perl` and come out ten minutes later an expert. It just won't happen. The language is too complex, and most of the books on it aren't very well written—at least not for me (sorry guys). It's a general problem with programming books and me, I think.

A final note: `perl` is worth learning when you think that your shell has run out of steam. People who should know say that once you learn it, you'll never want to program with anything else.

7 E-mail and Networking

I am convinced that it is of primordial importance to learn more every year than the year before. After all, what is education but a process by which a person begins to learn how to learn?

Peter Ustinov
Dear Me, 1977

Do you remember when you asked someone out for the first time? I mean the first time *ever*. Remember feeling kind of awkward? Not really knowing what to say, where to put your hands, what to do with your feet, whether you had spinach stuck to your teeth? Using electronic mail (E-mail) or a network is kind of like that: awkward the first time, then gradually easier, until you find yourself married to your computer. Uh. No. Maybe not. But it does get easier.

In this chapter, we'll work on sending E-mail using two of the most common E-mail programs. We'll also play around with your network—copying files, logging into different computers, and generally wreaking havoc wherever we can.

This chapter is also a kind of a preface to the next—the Internet chapter. It should give you the tools you need to step into the next chapter so you can deal with the really fun stuff: The Internet.

But first, could you tell me what you're doing on Sat . . . uh . . . Never mind.

E-MAIL

A little inaccuracy sometimes saves tons of explanation.

Saki
The Square Egg, 1924

I love getting mail. I hate writing it. Why do I hate writing it? Well, it takes too long to get where it's going. It costs too darn much (sorry, but spending more than a quarter to send my mom a note saying the cat's sick is a bit much). I hate having to write something, print it, put it into an envelope, find a stamp, and walk to the corner to mail it. Did I mention it's slow? Basically, I want immediate gratification.

That's where E-mail comes in *really* handy. I can send my dad an E-mail (mom won't touch computers) and get a response in minutes. It costs me next to nothing. It costs him nothing at all. I can send files, favorite programs, just about anything, fast. It's so fast that I'm surprised Federal Express doesn't have some kind of electronic mail service.

Before you write . . .

Like writing a letter, there are some bits and pieces you need to know before you send E-mail. Things like how to write the address so the electronic post office will understand it and how to use the E-mail software. Mostly, this stuff is pretty simple: Addresses usually look something like `president@whitehouse.gov`, and E-mail packages usually have pretty standard commands for reading and sending mail.

But things aren't always simple. Take E-mail addresses. Please.

Addressing Your E-mail

> Progress celebrates Pyrrhic victories over nature. Progress makes purses out of human skin. When people were traveling in mail coaches, the world got ahead better than it does now that salesmen fly through the air. What good is speed if the brain has oozed out on the way?
>
> Karl Kraus
> *Die Fackel*, 1909

UNIX's E-mail addresses are actually very clever things. They're arranged hierarchically, for example, so that computers know how to pass messages along so that they get from point A to point B. But, unlike some E-mail addresses, UNIX's addresses are fairly easy to decipher. I mean, the CompuServe on-line service gives you a meaningless trillion-digit number that they expect you to remember. It bears no relation to anything. UNIX, at least, lets you have nice, clear names.

Let's take an office, for example. Say you work at a company that uses UNIX systems to deliver mail. Say you have an E-mail address like `john` or `johnm` or `john.montgomery`. (Basically, some variant on your name.) That's kind of mnemonic—it makes sense from just looking at it that `john.montgomery` is probably John Montgomery. Everybody in my office can figure that out—even my *boss* gets it, for crying out loud. People send mail to you using your username. You send mail to the others using their usernames. I send mail to `boss`, and he sends it back to `john.montgomery`. Everybody's happy.

Mailing outside your office

Until somebody wants to send mail outside the office. Or, better yet, outside the company. I mean, there are lots of `john.montgomery`s out there—my dad, for one—who probably wouldn't appreciate getting all my E-mail. It looks like a little more information is needed. Just a touch. How about adding a company name? Then I'd be `john.montgomery@pcc`. That would be unique, wouldn't it? Well, maybe, but who knows how many companies there are that could abbreviate their names down to `pcc`? Hmmm. More information is needed. Well, how about adding on the parent company? Okay: `john.montgomery@pcc.ziff`. Now that looks pretty unique. And that's pretty much what UNIX does, too, except UNIX (actually, the Internet, a worldwide network of computers) adds one more bit of information: a master domain. Ziff is a commercial enterprise, so my address would be `john.montgomery@pcc.ziff.com`. It just make sense like that, doesn't it?

Let's take this address and break it back down to see how it got like it is. First the name: Why `john.montgomery`? No good reason—there are really few rules about usernames (an example of one rule is that they can't contain certain nonalphabetic characters). It's just easy to remember.

Generally, your username will be lowercase (although UNIX doesn't really care—in this case it's case-insensitive). It's traditional to do so. You can have uppercase letters, but the UNIX mailers will lowercase them. (Increasingly these days, usernames have periods or underscores in them, like `john.montgomery`. I suppose that's supposed to make E-mail addresses easier to remember. For years, I went by an E-mail address that in no way resembled my username and somehow everybody found me. Ah, well, so much for nostalgia.)

After the username comes an @ sign. That, too makes sense: It separates the username from what's to come. Everything after the @ is called your **domain**. A domain is basically a bunch of computers that work together. A company, like `ziff` for example, can be a domain. Within that domain come subdomains, like `pcc`, the division I work in.

Domains

Well, that explains the first part of the domain. What about this `com` thing? Well, that's just a different kind of domain. An *uberdomain*, if you will. See, the Internet—the global network from which virtually all UNIX networking conventions spring—needed a way to group the different sites that were connected to it. The idea was to be able to tell at a glance what *kind* of site you were dealing with. Like `.com`—that's a commercial site. Or `.edu`—that'd be an educational site. There's also `.mil` (military), `.gov` (government), and `.net` (Internet-related). But that's the old way of grouping sites.

The Internet

Recently, the Internet has grown so much that these function-related domains have become less useful. Now the Internet honchos want to start using addresses that end in a two-letter abbreviation for the country you're in. I would be in `.us`. Someone in England would be `.uk`, and New Zealand is `.nz`. Neat, huh?

So you can see that my E-mail address can be generalized to this:

```
username@[subdomain.]domain.bigdomain
```

The subdomain in brackets is optional. There can be none, one, two, five, eleven— there's really no limit. It's usually the job of `domain` to know how to get E-mail to all the people in it, so `john.montgomery@ziff.com` should be as good as `john.montgomery@pcc.ziff.com`. I say "should" because some organizations are so large that one computer (the domain name server, it's called) can't quickly track everybody. So if you give it a little more information (like, "look for this person in the marketing subdomain") it will find people faster. Usually, though, you'll see addresses with just two dots in them.

Now let's make sure you can read your E-mail addresses out loud like a pro. First of all, pronounce the @ sign "at." Second, pronounce a period as "dot." So my address would be read aloud as "john dot montgomery at pee-see-see dot ziff dot com." You spell out only what you have to (in this case, `pcc`). So you pronounce `.mil` as "dot mill" and `.net` as "dot net." The one exception to this is `.edu`. For some reason (even though it's perfectly easy to pronounce), you spell this one out: "dot eee-dee-you." Go figure.

Odd addresses

Okay, that's a standard Internet address. Nearly every Internet address you're likely to see looks something like this. But not all. How about some of the odd ones? I used to have a particularly nasty address:

`drlabs!monty@mips.com`

And if you forgot that, you could send it to

`monty%drlabs@mips.com`

So what's going on? Well, I had a computer that was piggybacking its E-mail through a much larger domain, a company called mips. But I wasn't an employee of mips, so I didn't get a mips-style username. In fact, I had my own computer lab about fifteen miles down the road and was connecting in through modem. My mail computer in that lab was called `drlabs` (a kind of domain—at least for me), and my username was `monty`. Normally, you'd think that I'd have a name like `monty@drlabs@mips.com`. But the Internet doesn't support two @ signs in the same address. Instead, it substitutes `!`s or `%`s. Which brings us to a discussion of some non-Internet-style addressing conventions.

!-style, UUCP addressing

The !-style (pronounced "bang style") addressing is more common than that `%` thing. It's actually pretty interesting, too. It comes about thanks to a type of networking peculiar to UNIX called UUCP (originally, that stood for UNIX-to-UNIX Copy Program, but it's far more than that nowadays). UUCP enables you to hook UNIX systems together into a network, using modems. Now, this may not seem like a big thing, but imagine connecting ten thousand computers with modems—then multiply that by a hundred. That's roughly the number of computers that all talk to each other using UUCP. Impressed?

Anyway, unlike the Internet (which is pretty stable, and has computers dedicated to keeping track of other computers) UUCP has no way to track all the computers it links. So, to get from point A to point B, you need to be very explicit about the path to take. Like, "go to mips, then bounce to uunet, then drop by ibm, then you'll find a system called ddt. Send your message to john there." UUCP addresses do that with the ! (bang): `mips!uunet!ibm!ddt!john`.

The ! works kind of like the . in a regular Internet address, arranging things in a hierarchical manner, with the largest domain at the left and the username at the right.

The %-style notation is a little rarer, and as near as I can tell, it's only good for one separation: `username%machine`. After that, you need an @ and a full domain name to get anywhere.

%-style addressing

Nearly every major commercial mail service (like MCImail and CompuServe) has a method for getting to the Internet's mail (a **gateway**, in the parlance). Table 7.1 lists some sample addressing conventions for getting from the Internet to users on those networks.

Table 7.1 From the Internet to . . .

Address	How to get there
MCImail address 123-4567	`123-4567@mcimail.com` (if you have a number)
MCImail user John Montgomery	`John_Montgomery@mcimail.com` (if you have a name)
CompuServe 88888,1234	`88888.1234@compuserve.com`

Mostly, they're pretty simple (although please note that the CompuServe address has a comma, that you change to a period in the Internet style). Getting *from* these services out is more difficult. If you're on one of them, call your service provider (or drop an E-mail to one of the system operators) and ask for instructions.

Mail Front Ends

> He pasted a sheet of postage stamps
> from snout clear down to tail,
> Put on a quick delivery stamp,
> and sent the cod by mail.
>
> Holman Francis Day
> *Cure for Homesickness*, 1920

Now you know how to address your letters. Let's create some. Sending mail under UNIX is a kind of cooperative effort, with different programs passing information off to each other, each doing its own little part in the greater scheme of things. Mostly, you'll use your E-mail front end (a program that probably has a name like `mail`, `mailx`, or `elm`). Two of these programs, `mail` and `mailx`, ship with every version of UNIX I've ever seen, so I'll talk about them and ignore the far superior, infinitely better `elm`. (Sigh.) Well, maybe I won't *completely* ignore it, but there's not much to comment on, it's so easy to use.

After I'm done with the front ends, I'll talk a bit about some of the files you can change to make them behave differently.

One thing: On some systems, the administrator has aliased another program to the mail command, so when you type `mail`, you may not be getting the mail I'm thinking of. Here's a simple way to tell if mail is really mail. First, read all your mail and exit from `mail`. Now, type `mail`. If the response you get is "No mail," you're probably using the `mail` I'm thinking of. If it's "No mail for *user*," then you're using `mailx`. If it's anything else, you're not using either one. Glad to hear it.

System V's `mail`: A Must Miss

> A *tsedoodelter* said that if he found a million dollars in the street he would keep it — unless, of course, he discovered that it belonged to some poor man, in which case he would return it at once.
>
> Leo Rosten
> *The Joys of Yinglish*, 1990

The `mail` program is one of the greatest examples of why the people who created the System V UNIX system shouldn't be allowed out in public. Just kidding. Kind of. It's just a little too brief in how it does things—it doesn't have a nice interface, for example. Unless you call Figure 7.1 nice.

```
solaris# mail pricilla
Hi Priss,
          I'm just dropping you a note.
jm
.
solaris#
```

Figure 7.1 Talk about hard to use . . .

So the syntax is pretty simple: `mail user`. Nothing easier. But once you're in the body of the message, there's one question: How does `mail` know when you're done? It won't—you can create as long a message as you want, spanning as many lines as you want (although you can't fix typos in previous lines), and `mail` knows no end. To finally cut your message off, you can either type `Ctrl+d` or put a lone period on a line. That's right, a period, with nothing else.

If you have the choice between `mail` and `mailx` (or a variant called `Mail`), choose `mailx`. It's easier to use and far more powerful. I'm talking here about `mail` only because there are probably two systems out there that don't have `mailx`.

With our example, Priss will get a message that has no subject. Why? Because `mail` can't put one onto your messages. Now *that's* primitive. Cro-Magnon. Like it was written by Fred Flintstone. I would be dead if my mail messages had no subject (well, maybe just greatly inconvenienced—same thing). I'd never know what to read. And another thing: What happens if you make a mistake when you're composing a message using `mail`? You live with it: Once you press `Return`, your only choice is to dump what you've done and start over.

mail has no subjects

That's why the pros create their mail in a program like `vi`, save their messages as separate files, and use the input redirector (<) to mail the files to people. Like I do in Figure 7.2.

```
                           xterm
 solaris# cat mailfile
 Hi Priss,
          How are things?
 John
 .
 solaris# mail pricilla < mailfile
 solaris#
```

Figure 7.2 Sending someone a file.

Dan Watts recalls the old days (which you may still be experiencing): If you're planning on using a dash on a line by itself, watch out! Some older mail programs expect you to use a pair of hyphens (`--`) to separate the main body of a letter from the signature—and they gobble, chomp, snarf, and munch everything after the `--`. (Yum.) Probably best to avoid it.

Once you've sent some E-mail, you'll probably start getting some (you've got to write 'em to get 'em). At least `mail` is slightly better about reading E-mail than it is about sending it. Lots of emphasis on *slightly*. Most of its commands are one-letter deals that really don't shed a lot of light on what the heck is happening. Hopefully Table 7.2 will help out.

Reading E-mail

Table 7.2 `mail`'s commands.

Command	What it does
?	Gets help
Return	Displays current message
d	Deletes current message
u	Undeletes current message
h	Displays headers of all messages
n	Displays message number n
s	Saves current message
r	Replies to current message
q	Quits

In addition to their working on the message you're currently reading, you can make these commands work on another message by supplying a message number. For example, if you wanted to delete message 5, but you're reading message 10, just type `d 5`. However, if you want to delete messages 5 through 10, you can't—you can with `mailx`, but not with `mail`. Yet another reason to use `mailx` or to complain until somebody puts a better mail front end onto your system.

Setting a forwarding address

There are other `mail` commands, but you can see what they do by running `mail` and typing `?` just as easily as I can explain them here.

There is one really neat thing that `mail` *can* do—set a forwarding address. I'll talk about manually creating a `.forward` file in your home directory a little later, but let's deal with `mail` right now. (Is there an advantage to creating a forwarding address with `mail`? No, not really. Again, UNIX has lots of ways to do the same thing: Pick the one you like.)

Say you get a new account on a new machine and you want to keep receiving all your mail from your old account on your old machine. Well—you've moved, and just like you should let the post office know that you've moved, you should let your E-mail know, too. Say you just got an account on a machine called `tarzan` and your new user name is `johnsh`. That makes you `johnsh@tarzan`, right? Well, go back to your old machine and run the command

```
% mail -F johnsh@tarzan
```

and `mail` will start forwarding your mail to the new account.

BSD's `mailx`: Better Mail

Keep a store of sarcasms, and know how to use them.

Baltasar Gracián
The Art of Worldly Wisdom, 1647

I hope I've made it abundantly clear that I don't particularly like System V's `mail`. If you feel I haven't, either you're not reading very closely, or you're immune to irony, sarcasm, and outright insults. Wanna grab a beer sometime?

One alternative is `mailx`, the Berkeley mail front end. It's a little nicer to use than plain-Jane `mail`, but it's still not as nice as some of the other front ends like `elm`. Unfortunately, it's the best mail front end that comes on your system by default, so unless you have a better one that some kind soul installed, you're stuck.

The `mailx` program also masquerades around as `Mail` (one of the few UNIX commands to start with a capital letter) and `/usr/ucb/mail` (on a very few systems), so if you have one of those commands, you have `mailx`. Remember, a rose by any other name, etc., etc.

Other names for `mailx`

Anyway, some of the advantages of `mailx` are that it displays a nice list of messages, showing which you've read, which you haven't, and which are marked for deletion. It enables you to run commands on bunches of messages, rather than dealing with them one at a time. And, finally, it enables you to attach subjects to your messages, as Figure 7.3 illustrates.

```
solaris# Mail
mailx version 5.0 Sat Apr 24 04:23:11 1993  Type ? for help.
"/var/mail/root": 10 messages 10 unread
>U  1 root           Thu Aug 18 10:10   29/832   Returned mail: unknown ma
 U  2 root           Thu Aug 18 10:10   41/863   Returned mail: unknown ma
 U  3 root           Thu Aug 18 10:21   28/756   Returned mail: User unkno
 U  4 root           Thu Aug 18 10:21   32/784   Returned mail: User unkno
 U  5 root           Thu Aug 18 10:24   23/344
 U  6 root           Thu Aug 18 10:24   15/353
 U  7 root           Thu Aug 18 10:27   15/321
 U  8 root           Thu Aug 18 10:27   15/322
 U  9 john           Thu Aug 18 10:28   15/339
 U 10 john           Thu Aug 18 10:29   15/361   This is a test message
& d 1-10
& q
solaris#
```

Figure 7.3 `mailx` (`Mail`) beats the pants off simple `mail`.

With `mailx`, when you send somebody a message, you'll get prompted for a subject line. Just type in your subject and press **Return**. After that, you're back to the same lousy "editor" that `mail` uses. In a nutshell, you're better off creating any lengthy message in a text editor, then E-mailing the file to the person, like this:

King `mailx` *has* subjects

```
% mailx -s "That report you requested" boss < report.doc
```

The `-s` switch is that subject switch that I'm so hot on. Just enclose your subject in quotes as I did, and you'll send a great message. Aside from that, you mail files just like you did with `mail`—using the input redirector (`<`).

It's better at reading, too

When it comes to reading mail, `mailx` is again considerably more flexible than `mail`. Table 7.3 gives you a quick look at the commands.

Table 7.3 A few `mailx` commands.

Command	What it does
Return	Reads next message
d[elete]	Deletes a message
r[eply]	Replies to the message author and other recipients
R[eply]	Replies only to author of message
f[ollowup]	Replies to message and saves a copy
q[uit]	Quits from `mailx`
unde[lete]	Undeletes a message
v[i]	Edits the message in `vi`
s[ave]	Saves message to default mailbox (`~/mbox`, usually)
s[ave]	Saves message to a file named after message author

(You can type either the one-letter version, or the whole name.) And these are just a few commands. I think you get the picture about why I prefer `mailx` to `mail`. What's really neat is that you can invoke these commands on not just *one* message, but whole ranges. Say I wanted to reply to the authors of messages 10–15—I can just say that at one of `mailx`'s lovely ? prompts:

```
? reply 10-15
```

What does this do? Well, it doesn't reply to the messages one after another. It gives one reply to all the *authors* of these messages. I was a little let down when it didn't step me through a multiple-reply process, but this certainly beats the pants off `mail`'s one message per command limit.

Tilde escape sequences

But wait, it gets better. Say you want to reply to someone and include their message in your response. Well, you're in luck, because `mailx` makes it easy: Press ~m—that's right, press the tilde, then type m. Figure 7.4 shows what happens next.

Why would you want to incorporate a message into your reply? To give context, usually. In Figure 7.4, root is replying to a technical question, but the subject line doesn't say enough to give it context. Rather than retyping unnecessarily, just press ~m to pull in the message that you were sent and reply at the bottom. You can also ~m other messages—if you wanted to forward one with some more notes, for example.

There are several tilde escapes. The ones I use most are listed in Table 7.4. There are lots of others. Look in the `man` page for them under Tilde Escapes (`man mailx`).

```
┌─────────────────────────────────────────────────────────────────┐
│ ▽                            xterm                                │
├─────────────────────────────────────────────────────────────────┤
│ ? h                                                               │
│ >R  4 John I. Montgomery Thu Aug 18 11:19   14/339   Re: away from my mail │
│  R  5 John I. Montgomery Thu Aug 18 11:26   18/371   What's cookin'?       │
│  N  6 John I. Montgomery Thu Aug 18 11:28   16/375   Is there any way      │
│ ? 6                                                               │
│ Message  6:                                                       │
│ From john Thu Aug 18 11:28 PDT 1994                               │
│ Date: Thu, 18 Aug 94 11:28:10 PDT                                 │
│ From: john (John I. Montgomery -- csh)                            │
│ To: root                                                          │
│ Subject: Is there any way                                         │
│                                                                   │
│ to modify the aliases file so I get my mail?                      │
│                                                                   │
│ John                                                              │
│                                                                   │
│ ? r                                                               │
│ To: john                                                          │
│ Subject: Re: Is there any way                                     │
│                                                                   │
│ ~m                                                                │
│ Interpolating: 6                                                  │
│ (continue)                                                        │
│ Done.                                                             │
│ Sysop                                                             │
│ ·                                                                 │
└─────────────────────────────────────────────────────────────────┘
```

Figure 7.4 Incorporating messages into your replies.

Table 7.4 Tilling `mailx`'s tildes.

Sequence	What it does
`~c names`	Adds names to the carbon copy list (people who receive the message on an FYI basis)
`~m message#s`	Inserts the listed messages
`~M message#s`	Inserts the listed messages, including all header information
`~r file`	Reads file into the message
`~s string`	Sets the subject line to string
`~v`	Invokes `vi` on the message
`~!`	Invokes a shell command (`spell` is a good one)

Notification of New Mail

> I talk to myself because I like dealing with a better class of people.
>
> Jackie Mason

Figuring out that you have new mail isn't exactly easy. UNIX isn't very forthcoming. It's kind of a drag to get a phone call from your boss asking if you've completed the project he sent you mail about this morning, only to realize that you haven't checked because nobody told you to.

There are a couple of ways around that. First, when you run `mail` or `mailx` with no arguments, they'll let you know if you have mail. `mail` will say something like, "`No mail.`" `mail` is very terse. `mailx` isn't much better: It'll say, "`No mail for username.`" But if you have mail, they'll open it up so you can read it. That's one way to check for mail. It's probably not the best.

There's a program called `biff` that controls whether you'll be notified when you get mail. It has two settings, y and n. You set `biff` to y by typing `biff y`, and set it to n by typing (you guessed it) `biff n`. When `biff` is in n (which is how it starts out), you won't get notification of new mail until you run your `mail` command. When `biff` is in y, you should get not only notification of new mail, you should also see the header and first few lines of the mail message on your screen. I say "should" because, for some reason, `biff` doesn't work right on my Solaris for x86 computer. It may not work right for you, either. But it probably will. The one problem with `biff` is that it kind of interrupts your work and distracts you (just like the dog it was named after, I imagine).

Biff Trivia: According to well-informed sources, the `biff` program, which checks to see if you have new mail, is named after a dog. See, the dog barked whenever the mailman came to the door of the programmer's house. Hence, `biff`.

If you're using the X Window System, you have access to a program called `xbiff`. Basically, it's `biff` for X. Clever name, clever description. It paints a mailbox. When the arm is down, you have no mail. When it's raised, you do. Figure 7.5 shows how cute it is.

Figure 7.5 Another silent day.

Other Mailers

> The buyer needs a hundred eyes; the seller but one.
>
> Italian Proverb

The `mail` and `mailx` programs are not by any means the only two mailers you're going to run into. They're just the ones that nearly every system has. As with most UNIX utility programs, however, somebody went and did it better. In this case, a lot of somebodies. Particular kudos should go to `elm`, the best mail front end I've seen for UNIX. Not only is it easy to use, it's free. That's right, you can download it off the Internet from a number of locations—source code and all. Hunt around a bit and you'll probably find a compiled version for your computer. You can download it just for yourself, or you can install it on your system and make it the default mailer (create a master alias so that when people type `mail` they invoke `elm`). It's so easy to use that I'm not going to bother even discussing it.

There are other mailers, too. Programs such as cc:Mail from Lotus and zMail from zCode software. These are commercial products—in other words, you pay real money for them. I'm not a big fan of spending money. In fact, I think that the Free Software Foundation has the right idea—distribute software freely, including the source code, make sure the people who wrote it get proper credit, and never claim that it's your work. (The actual agreement is a bit longer.)

I'm not saying that these aren't excellent programs (both are superior mail packages with many features `elm` doesn't have). I'm just a cheapskate.

What You Can and Can't Send through E-mail

> Clarity is so clearly one of the attributes of truth that very often it passes for truth.
>
> Joseph Joubert
> *Pensées*, 1842

The one problem with E-mail is that it lives its life in only seven bits. For those of you who have no idea what I'm talking about, I'll give you a hint: You need eight bits in order to send a binary file. With seven bits, UNIX mailers can send text files wonderfully (until they get too big). But `sendmail`, the most widely used mail sorting and sending daemon, can't deal with binary files. Why should it? After all, the standard rules for sending mail that UNIX implements (called the Simple Mail Transfer Protocol) say nothing about binary files. True, recent advances in mail protocols will allow you to send binary files (look for a standard called MIME), but they aren't completely widespread yet.

Until they are, we have to use a kludge (a kind of workaround) in order to send binary files over E-mail. That kludge is a program called `uuencode` (there are two *u*'s because it's one of the UUCP programs). Anyway, `uuencode` takes binary files—even programs—and turns them into text files. You then mail them. On the other end, you receive your mail message and run `uudecode` to change the file back into a binary.

Before I give an example, here's another piece of information: uuencode is most often used on files that have been compressed with UNIX's `compress` program. So, let's make a really common example. Say you have a bunch of files that you want to send to a friend. Some are binary, some are text. You could uuencode the binary ones and send them all off one by one, but that's a drag.

Figure 7.6 shows what a typical uuencode session looks like.

```
# ls
directory.listing  jar1       script      testfile
exscript           jar2       sedscript   tmp.sh
file1              jar3       sukdjf      trouble
files              mailfile   suket       weird.awk
files.tar.Z        numbers    test.file
fire.montgomery    ping.test  test2
gopher             rolodex    test3
# tar cf /tmp/files.tar *
# compress /tmp/files.tar
# uuencode /tmp/files.tar.Z files.tar.Z > files
# mail jmontgom@pcc.ziff.com < files
#
```

Figure 7.6 Sending a lot of files through the mail.

What did I do? First, I created an archive of all the files in that directory with the `tar` command. The `c` option tells `tar` to create the archive, and the `f` option tells it to send its output to a specific file.

Note that I stuck the `tar` archive off in `/tmp`. Why? Because some ill-behaved `tar` commands will actually try to stick the archive you're creating into themselves—just imagine that you're `tarring` `*`. Well, `tar` starts by creating its archive (call it `files.tar`), and it puts a few files into there, then it sees this `files.tar` thing and tries to put it into there, too, and . . . Well, it gets problematic. Worse, when you extract the archive, `tar` will read this imposter-archive out of the original archive and blow away the original! All this is to say, don't create an archive in the directory you're taking your files from if you're using a wildcard.

Next, I used the `compress` program to compress the archive. By default, `compress` takes the original filename and just appends a `.Z` to it after it's finished crunching it together. Next, I uuencoded the file. The syntax for uuencode is not pleasant—I have the filename in there twice, for instance.

The generic syntax for uuencoding a file is:

```
% uuencode filename label
```

So you're probably wondering what a `label` is. Well, uudecode needs some information in order to create a file from this stream of text. The `label` gives uudecode the information it needs. That label is not optional, but, oddly, nearly everybody uses the filename.

But the real kicker about `uuencode` is that, by default, it prints its output to the screen. If you let it do that, you'll get a few thousand screens full of gibberish. Always remember to put a > after your `uuencode` commands.

Finally, I mailed the uuencoded file off. Now, when I receive the message, I can just save it as a file and run `uudecode file`. Fortunately, `uudecode`'s smart enough to figure out where the uuencoded part begins, ignoring header information and the like.

The Man behind the Curtain: `sendmail`

> An amateur thinks it's funny if you dress a man up as an old lady, put him in a wheelchair, and give the wheelchair a push that sends it spinning down a slope towards a stone wall.
>
> For a pro, it's got to be a real old lady.
>
> Groucho Marx

The `mail` and `mailx` programs don't work alone—not by a long shot—just like your mailbox on the corner doesn't go out and deliver all the mail by itself. There's a complicated, arcane, and downright ornery program called `sendmail` that handles the mail on most UNIX computers. It gets started when you boot your computer, and it keeps running until you either a) shut down the computer or b) kill it with an explicit command. And `sendmail` is pretty hard to kill.

For administrators only

As a normal end user, you won't have very much to do with `sendmail`. You can be thankful. There are grown men and women who have been brought to tears by it and its configuration file (a little . . . well, a very large beastie called `sendmail.cf`). If you *are* running a system (say you have a workstation on your desk), there are a few things you should know about it so that you can troubleshoot problems and generally play around. The one catch is that you must have superuser access in order to do most anything that changes the way `sendmail` behaves.

`sendmail.cf`

Actually, I've been a tad unfair to `sendmail`. In and of itself, `sendmail` is a fairly innocuous program (albeit one with about a trillion command-line options). It's that configuration file that's really terrible. Even if you're used to `.mwmrc`, the heretofore world-champion nasty configuration file, `sendmail.cf` will rot your teeth. Why? Well, not only is it long, but it appears to make absolutely no sense. The rules for writing entries in `sendmail.cf` are incredibly difficult. Editing `sendmail.cf` is a kind of voodoo ritual because you never know if what you do is going to do what you think it's going to do.

My strongest word of advice about dealing with `sendmail.cf` is *don't*. Fortunately, you won't have to very often—the file is so complex that it's nearly complete. This is not a customization file—you don't want to play with it.

But `aliases` is. That's where you set up mailing lists: You can create a group called, say, `managers`, and put `john`, `bob`, `elmer`, and `buggs` into it. The `aliases` file usually lives in a directory like `/etc` or `/etc/mail`. If it's not there, check the man page (`man aliases`). Aliases can look like those in Figure 7.7.

```
# Alias for mailer daemon; returned messages from our MAILER-DAEMON
# should be routed to our local Postmaster.
MAILER-DAEMON: postmaster

# Aliases to handle mail to programs or files, eg news or vacation
# decode: "|/usr/bin/uudecode"
nobody: /dev/null

# Sample aliases:

# Alias for distribution list, members specified here:
#staff:wnj,mosher,sam,ecc,mckusick,sklower,olson,rwh@ernie

managers:john,bob,elmer,buggs

# Alias for distribution list, members specified elsewhere:
#keyboards: :include:/usr/jfarrell/keyboards.list

# Alias for a person, so they can receive mail by several names:
#epa:eric

#######################
# Local aliases below #
```

Figure 7.7 Gaze into `sendmail`'s eyes, add an alias, turn to stone.

Also, `aliases` is really well documented, so when you open it up, you'll have no problems figuring out what to do. (Hey, *I* didn't, and you're at least as smart as I am.)

Once you've edited your `aliases` file, you'll have to create a new alias database. That's right: `sendmail` doesn't read the aliases straight out of the `aliases` file, it reads them out of a compiled database. There's a special command to compile that database (`newaliases`), but don't bother with it. Nobody else does. Instead, run `sendmail` with the **–bi** flag to initialize the new `aliases` file.

```
# /usr/lib/sendmail -bi
7 aliases, longest 21 bytes, 121 bytes total
#
```

And that's done. There are some other flags to `sendmail`, like the **–bz** flag that you run after you've meddled with `sendmail.cf`, but mostly, you'll probably be running **–bi** if you do anything at all.

`.forward`

> The Moving Finger writes; and, having writ,
> Moves on
>
> Edward Fitzgerald
> *Rubáiyát of Omar Khayyám,* 1859

We've already talked about the `.forward` file in Chapter 2, but now is a great time to go over what we already said (thereby lowering the wear-and-tear on this book so that it will stay on your shelf longer . . . Hmm . . . Maybe I shouldn't—that way the book will wear out and you'll buy another copy. Maybe not.).

A change of venue

Back to reality. If you have a `.forward` file in your home directory (`$HOME`), your E-mail will be sent to whatever address it contains. It's just like you sent the Post Office a change of address form—magically your mail starts to be forwarded to your new address.

The simplest way to create a `.forward` file is with a command like

```
% echo newaddress@newcompany.com > ~/.forward
```

This lengthy command will place one line into your `.forward` file: `newaddress@newcompany.com`. If I suddenly changed companies and started working at `mti.com`, I'd put a line like `jmontgomery@mti.com` into my `.forward` file at my old company. You can also use `.forward` to forward mail to different users on the same system—you really don't need that `@newcompany.com` stuff if it's going to somebody in the same organization.

Auto-answering your mail

This is just the simple stuff you can do in `.forward`. You can also make `.forward` forward your E-mail through a program using the pipe (`|`) character. The most common practice is to pipe your E-mail through a program called `vacation` (if you have it). The `vacation` program automatically replies to your E-mail, even if you're on vacation (hence the name). There are a couple of ways to use it. The simplest is to edit your `.forward` file and add a line like this:

```
"|/usr/bin/vacation john"
```

Your mail will be automagically answered with the message stored in `~/.vacation.msg`. On my system, you can even run the `vacation` program interactively to set it up—you don't have to know about how to edit any files or anything. See Figure 7.8 for a vacation party.

`vacation` is one of the two programs I couldn't live without. I'm out of the office as much as I'm in, and I need people to get automated responses. My system didn't have it, so I found a copy on the Internet, downloaded it, and got it to run. It's worth the effort.

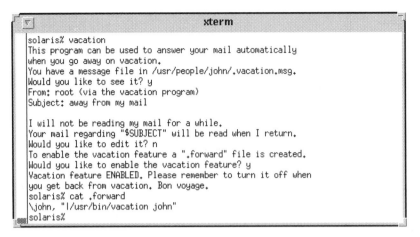

```
solaris% vacation
This program can be used to answer your mail automatically
when you go away on vacation.
You have a message file in /usr/people/john/.vacation.msg.
Would you like to see it? y
From: root (via the vacation program)
Subject: away from my mail

I will not be reading my mail for a while.
Your mail regarding "$SUBJECT" will be read when I return.
Would you like to edit it? n
To enable the vacation feature a ".forward" file is created.
Would you like to enable the vacation feature? y
Vacation feature ENABLED. Please remember to turn it off when
you get back from vacation. Bon voyage.
solaris% cat .forward
\john, "|/usr/bin/vacation john"
solaris%
```

Figure 7.8 Gone fishin'.

But there's something different about the way `vacation` set up my `.forward` file. It put a `\john,` at the front of the file. Why? To avoid what are called **forwarding loops**. Imagine what would happen if you told your office to forward all your mail to your home, and when it got to your home, you forwarded it back to your office. Not only would you never get any mail, the post office would soon take you off their route. The `\john,` says exactly the same thing to the UNIX mail programs: "Give it one try, but if you're just going to send the mail back to me here, forget it."

Dan Watts, my esteemed technical editor, chimes in with a `.forward`–looking tale. Says he: Some braindead sendmails (IBM AIX 3.x used to and may still) read only the *last* line of the `.forward` file and ignore the others. So if you had a `.forward` file like:

```
\john
"| vacation john"
```

the sender of the message would get an "I'm not here" message, and it would drop the actual incoming E-mail into the bit bucket (UNIX's nether regions) instead of forwarding a copy to `john`. Of course, you'll have a lot less E-mail to read when you get back from your trip . . .

The solution is to put everything on one line:

```
\john, "| vacation john"
```

Sending to multiple people   The last note about `.forward` is that you can put several names into it, each on its own line. This is pretty useful if you want to set up a generic account (called, say, `info`) and have people mail to it. You then just create a `.forward` file in `info`'s home directory and put in a list of everyone who should receive requests for information. Creating an account and setting a `.forward` file like this isn't the best way to handle the process of sending mail to one address and having it broadcast to multiple people—that's the job of the `aliases` file, which a system administrator keeps current. See the section in this chapter on `sendmail` for more information.

.signature

> So many signatures for such a small heart.
>
> Mother Teresa, on paperwork in a California hospital

There's another clever file that some mailers read. It's `.signature`. The basic idea is that you usually want to sign your messages with a common ending, like

```
John Montgomery
The Underground Guide to UNIX
"Buy it or you're in trouble"
```

Well, all you have to do is create `.signature` and put your unique signature into it. Most mailers will automatically append this message to your regular outgoing E-mail.

.mailrc

> I am not in the roll of common men.
>
> Shakespeare
> *King Henry IV*, 1598

If you want to customize the way your mailer behaves, there's a dot file for you: `.mailrc`. When you run your mailer, it reads a global customization file (an oxymoron if ever there was one) with a name like `Mail.rc`. Usually the defaults in this file are for the lowest common denominator. You are neither low, nor common, so you want to add some of your own customizations.

Since I don't want you using the generic System V `mail` program, I'm going to deal only with `mailx`. If you open the `man` page on `mailx`, you'll see a huge list of variables that you can set—variables that control whether `mailx` asks you for `cc:` and `bcc:` lines, what character precedes a message that you included with ~m, and so on. See Table 7.5 for a quick rundown of ones you're likely to change.

Customizing `mailx`

You can also unset any of these variables with the `unset` command, so if something that you don't like is turned on by default, you can just turn it off. Figure 7.9 shows how it works, at least with my own `.mailrc` file.

Table 7.5 Changing `mailx`'s variables.

How to set the variable	What it does
set askcc	Tells `mailx` to prompt you for a cc: line
set askbcc	Tells `mailx` to prompt you for a bcc: line
set asksub	How `mailx` asks you for a subject
set autoinc	If you get new mail while you're in `mailx`, includes it
set bsdcompat	If you invoke `mailx` as `Mail`, reads `/etc/mail/Mail.rc` and makes `more` your default pager
set EDITOR=cmd	Sets your default editor (invoked with `~e`) to `cmd`
set escape=c	Replaces the `~` with `c` for escaping commands
set indentprefix=xyz	Sets the string that will precede lines of files you include with `~m`
set sign=xyz	If you include a signature with `~a`, `xyz` is what will be included
set VISUAL=cmd	Changes the editor invoked when you press `~v` to `cmd`

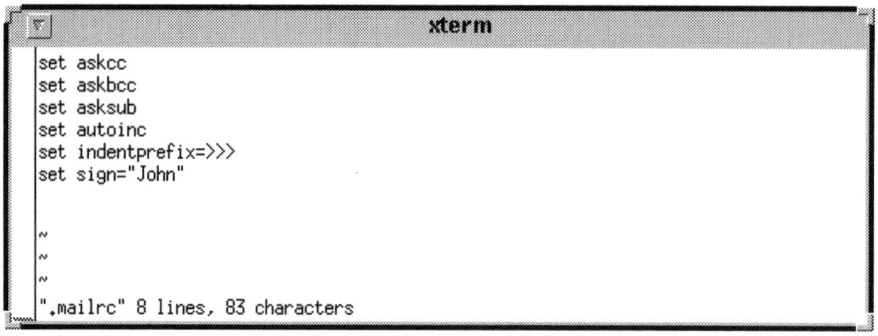

```
xterm
set askcc
set askbcc
set asksub
set autoinc
set indentprefix=>>>
set sign="John"


~
~
~
".mailrc" 8 lines, 83 characters
```

Figure 7.9 My `.mailrc` file (with `vi`'s tildes).

NETWORKS

> There must be, not a balance of power, but a community of power; not organized rivalries, but an organized common peace.
>
> Woodrow Wilson
> *Address to Senate*, 1917

When you connect one computer to another, you've created a network. It doesn't matter whether you've connected them with Ethernet, ARCnet, DECnet, or tennis net. Heck, if two tin cans and some string can be a telephone, two PCs connected by a parallel cable can be a network. So there.

There are some obvious questions that need to be asked about networking two computers. Like, what do you connect them with (assuming that you're out of string and tin cans)? Once they're physically connected, how do you get them talking? And the biggie—once they're physically talking, what the h-e-doublechopsticks do you do now?

Let's see how many of those questions we can answer before hopelessly obscuring a pretty simple subject.

Layers upon Layers

> Well, if I called the wrong number, why did you answer the phone?
>
> James Thurber
> Cartoon in the *New Yorker*

Let's go back to the can phone for a second, and think of it in a slightly different way. Well, a *really* different way.

Okay, you have two soup cans and some string. In networking parlance, we'd call the string the physical connection or **physical layer** between the two cans. Unless you want to network your office with Campbell's soup cans (I can imagine a nice Warhol decorating the lobby), this information is pretty useless. Real networks use physical layers with names such as Ethernet, Token Ring, ARCnet, and (pretty infrequently) Fiber Distributed Data Interface (known more by its acronym, FDDI).

Physical layer

The world of networking is a horrible place for people used to English. It's a world that uses a language composed largely of capital letters strung together, like FDDI, TCP/IP, MAU, and such. I'll define as many of these terms as are relevant, but unless networking is your *thing*, don't pay too much attention.

Most of these odd names correspond to the actual physical layer (the wire and that kind of stuff) and some of the rules for talking to and over that wire. Maybe an analogy is in order. Let's take our soup can telephone system and go up to a slightly larger version—from Mama Campbell to Ma Bell.

Let's get physical—layer, that is

You pick up your phone and dial a number. Somebody on the other end picks up his or her phone and answers. You talk, then you hang up. Networks work kind of exactly like that. (Kind of.) Your computer needs to know who to call (that's called an address in network terms), it needs a way to make the call (the physical connection), and it needs to speak the same language as the person who picks up the other end (in network-speak, that's called a protocol). There, that should make sense.

Making a connection

Moving along to some of the terms you're likely to encounter, most networks (unlike the phone system) are made up of layers of different ways to talk. For example, you could be running a protocol called the Transmission Control Protocol/Internet Protocol over a physical layer called Ethernet. That's a very common combination. Let's talk hardware for a second.

How Ethernet works   An Ethernet network connects all its systems together into one party line (to use the phone analogy some more). Only one computer can talk at a time, or you get what's called a collision. When a collision occurs, everybody has to stop talking for a while, and then try again. All the computers on your Ethernet network are always listening to see if their address is called. Ethernet, like so many other really neat things, came out of the Xerox Palo Alto Research Center (PARC).

How Token Ring works   Probably the next most common type of network physical layer is called Token Ring, and it comes from IBM. As you can probably guess, very few UNIX systems use Token Ring. Anyway, in a Token Ring network, rather than everybody listening all the time and having a risk of talking at once, there's a special electrical impulse that travels around and around the network. It's called a token. You can only talk to somebody else if you have the token. No collisions, guaranteed speed. In theory, it's a great system.

ARCnet is another type of network. It used to be very common because it was easy to wire an office for ARCnet—the adage is that "ARCnet will run over barbed wire." It probably would. There's not much of it around anymore, so I'm not going to bother with it.

TCP/IP's Applications

> Regard all men as equal, since God's light is contained in the heart of each.
>
> Arjan (a Sikh mystic), ca. 1600 AD

Once you've got a physical connection, you need to agree on the language you're going to speak. That's the protocol we were talking about earlier. Your computer can run a whole lot of different types of software that will enable it to speak different protocols. Most likely (since it's UNIX), it's running software that enables it to speak the Transmission Control Protocol/Internet Protocol or TCP/IP. TCP/IP is a pretty typical network protocol, with mechanisms for sending and receiving **packets** of information (little . . . uh . . . bite-sized chunks) and passing them along to you, the user, an intelligible form. TCP/IP is actually a bunch of network protocols. At the bottom of most of them is IP itself. IP is basically a trailblazer, handling the lowest-level grunt work that it can. It sets up a connection and hangs out to see when it terminates. Above that there are a bizillion protocols that all behave completely differently.

Don't worry about them. It's not worth it. They're incredibly complicated when it comes to talking to each other, but when it comes to talking to you, they're only moderately complicated. Instead of worrying about those protocols, let's worry about the applications you're likely to see that talk to IP.

ping

> Poetry is not the proper antithesis to prose, but to science. Poetry is
> opposed to science, and prose to metre. The proper and immediate object
> of science is the acquirement, or communication, of truth; the proper and
> immediate object of poetry is the communication of immediate pleasure.

> Samuel Taylor Coleridge
> *Definitions of Poetry*, 1811

The `ping` command is one of the simplest commands there is. At its simplest, you
tell it to ping a host, like this:

```
% ping solaris
solaris is alive
```

This means that the host called `solaris` is up and functioning on the network. I
use `ping` as a kind of diagnostic command, because I usually expect all the
computers, or **nodes**, on my network to be up and functioning. But `ping` gets
more useful when you deal with larger networks.

By the way, this is the System V version of `ping`—it prints out only a brief
output. Yours may give more detail, like the output in Figure 7.10.

**BSD vs.
System V
pings**

```
xterm

tarzan# ping -s solaris
PING solaris: 56 data bytes
64 bytes from solaris (1.0.0.2): icmp_seq=0. time=64. ms
64 bytes from solaris (1.0.0.2): icmp_seq=1. time=64. ms
64 bytes from solaris (1.0.0.2): icmp_seq=2. time=64. ms
64 bytes from solaris (1.0.0.2): icmp_seq=3. time=64. ms
64 bytes from solaris (1.0.0.2): icmp_seq=4. time=64. ms
64 bytes from solaris (1.0.0.2): icmp_seq=5. time=64. ms
64 bytes from solaris (1.0.0.2): icmp_seq=6. time=64. ms
64 bytes from solaris (1.0.0.2): icmp_seq=7. time=64. ms
64 bytes from solaris (1.0.0.2): icmp_seq=8. time=64. ms
64 bytes from solaris (1.0.0.2): icmp_seq=9. time=64. ms
^C
----solaris PING Statistics----
9 packets transmitted, 9 packets received, 0% packet loss
round-trip (ms) /min/avg/max = (64/64/64)
tarzan#
```

Figure 7.10 Hello? Anybody home?

By adding the **-s** switch, I told `ping` that I wanted to see statistics about what
it's doing? So what *is* it doing? Well, it's sending very small packets (they only
have 56 bytes of data in them) to a host called `solaris`. This host is responding,
sending 64-byte acknowledgment packets (as they're called). We also get to see
`solaris`'s IP address—the address that other systems on the network use to talk

to it. All IP addresses look at least something like this one, with groups of numbers divided by periods. Next, ping tells us what ping packet number we're getting (starting with 0 for some odd reason), and how long the system took to respond. Sixty-four milliseconds is pretty fast.

 For some reason, BSD ping commands don't provide a continuous output. They'll just tell you if the remote host is alive. This is one case where I side with System V: I prefer to see the scrolling output that I have to kill with a Ctrl+c. If you're on a BSD system, I suggest you alias ping to ping -s. This is the one case where I feel it's okay to alias a command to itself.

telnet

> Pure truth cannot be assimilated by the crowd; it must be communicated by contagion.
>
> Henri-Frédéric Amiel
> *Journal,* 1883

The telnet command is kind of fun and kind of simple. You remember when you logged in this morning? Well, telnet does it again—but this time it logs you in to another system. Basically, telnet is a way to start a terminal session on another computer (or **host**—yet another term for "another computer") on your network. At its simplest, to use telnet you type:

% telnet *host*

And telnet sends a message to the remote system asking it to send a good, old login: prompt back your way. See Figure 7.11 for an example.

```
shelltool – /sbin/sh
tarzan% telnet solaris
Trying 127.0.0.1 ...
Connected to solaris.
Escape character is '^]'.


UNIX(r) System V Release 4.0 (solaris)

login: john
Password:
Last login: Wed Aug 17 11:46:36 from localhost
Sun Microsystems Inc.   SunOS 5.1       Generic April 1993
solaris%
```

Figure 7.11 telnet is as telnet does.

Now that you're logged in to a remote system, I'm willing to bet that your `Backspace` key doesn't work anymore. At least, it never does for me. So, the first two commands I issue nearly every time I log in to a remote system are

```
% setenv TERM xterm
```

and

```
% stty erase ^h
```

Remember them? The first one sets my `TERM` variable correctly so that applications like `vi` will work. The second one maps my `Backspace` key so that it'll erase characters (remember to press the `Backspace` key after you type `erase`, don't just type the caret and a lowercase `h`).

But if that were all `telnet` did, it would be a very simple utility, indeed. In fact, `telnet` is much more powerful than that, thanks to its command-line mode. Rather than typing

```
% telnet host
```

try typing just

```
% telnet
```

and see what happens. You should get a prompt like this:

```
telnet>
```

It's awaiting instructions. What instructions do you give it? Well, here're two. You've got the `open` command, which opens a connection to the host you specify, like saying `telnet host` at the shell prompt. Then you have the `close` command, which closes a connection to a host if one is open. Those are the two biggies.

Simple `telnet` commands

Once you're in a `telnet` session, you have the capability of dropping back to the `telnet>` prompt by using the `telnet` escape sequence. By default, this sequence is `Ctrl+]` (hold the `Ctrl` key and press the right bracket). Why would you want to do this? One reason is that your session is "hung," as the term goes. What's a hung session? Basically, it's a session that don't do nothin': You type, it's silent; you scream, it's silent. So press `Ctrl+]`, get to the `telnet>` prompt, and type `close`. That will terminate your session. It's not the nicest way to do things, but it works.

If you ever have questions about a `telnet` command, try typing a `?` at the `telnet>` prompt.

ftp

> Travel only with your equals or your betters.
> If there are none, travel alone.
>
> Dhammapada, ca. 100 AD

Doing file transfers Although `telnet`'s fine if what you want to do is work on a different system, if you want to get a file from a remote system (or send a file to one), you need the file transfer program, `ftp`. Unfortunately for all of us, `ftp` bites the big banana. It's oddly hard to use, and more than once I've had file transfers mysteriously abort and cores dump when running `ftp`. Watch out for this piece of junk.

It works very much like `telnet`, in that you just type

```
% ftp host
```

to get to the remote host. After that, things get a lot different with `ftp`. It will open a connection to the remote host using the username and password you provide, and it will put you in the default directory for that username. (By default, `ftp` thinks that you're going to try to log in with the username you're using on your own machine.) If you log in as `john`, and `john`'s home directory is `/usr/people/john`, you'll wind up in `/usr/people/john`. Figure 7.12 illustrates the process.

```
shelltool - /sbin/sh
tarzan% ftp solaris
Connected to solaris.
220 solaris FTP server (UNIX(r) System V Release 4.0) ready.
Name (solaris:root): john
331 Password required for john.
Password:
230 User john logged in.
ftp> pwd
257 "/usr/people/john" is current directory.
ftp>
```

Figure 7.12 A simple `ftp` session.

Some of ftp's commands So what commands can you use? Well, you've seen one—the `pwd` command. That goes along with the `cd` and the `ls` commands very nicely. These function on the remote system just as they do on the local system: The `pwd` command lets you know what directory you're in, the `cd` command enables you to change to a different one on the remote system, and the `ls` command prints out a listing of the files in the remote directory.

When the time comes to actually send and receive files, there are two commands you need to know (at least, for starters): `put` and `get`. The first sends a file to the current directory on the remote system, the second retrieves one. See Figure 7.13 for an example of how they work.

```
┌─────────────────────────────────────────────────────────────┐
│ ▼                     shelltool – /sbin/sh                   │
├─────────────────────────────────────────────────────────────┤
│ ftp> put theCatOut                                           │
│ 200 PORT command successful.                                 │
│ 150 ASCII data connection for theCatOut (127.0.0.1,-32734).  │
│ 226 Transfer complete.                                       │
│ ftp> get whatsComingToYou                                    │
│ 200 PORT command successful.                                 │
│ 150 ASCII data connection for whatsComingToYou (127.0.0.1,-32732) (47 bytes). │
│ 226 ASCII Transfer complete.                                 │
│ local: whatsComingToYou remote: whatsComingToYou             │
│ 50 bytes received in 0.57 seconds (0.086 Kbytes/s)           │
│ ftp>                                                         │
└─────────────────────────────────────────────────────────────┘
```

Figure 7.13 `put` the cat out and `get` what's coming to you.

So these two commands work pretty much as you'd expect them to. No surprises. Until you go to transfer multiple files using a wildcard. For some reason known only to whomever wrote `ftp`, `put` and `get` won't *do* more than one file at once. Instead, you need to use `mput` and `mget`—short for multiple `put` and multiple `get`. Figure 7.14 shows you how to do this.

```
┌─────────────────────────────────────────────────────────────┐
│ ▼                     shelltool – /sbin/sh                   │
├─────────────────────────────────────────────────────────────┤
│ ftp> mput *                                                  │
│ mput testscript.sh? y                                        │
│ 200 PORT command successful.                                 │
│ 150 ASCII data connection for testscript.sh (127.0.0.1,-32730). │
│ 226 Transfer complete.                                       │
│ mput theCatOut? y                                            │
│ 200 PORT command successful.                                 │
│ 150 ASCII data connection for theCatOut (127.0.0.1,-32728).  │
│ 226 Transfer complete.                                       │
│ mput whatsComingToYou? y                                     │
│ 200 PORT command successful.                                 │
│ 150 ASCII data connection for whatsComingToYou (127.0.0.1,-32726). │
│ 226 Transfer complete.                                       │
│ ftp>                                                         │
└─────────────────────────────────────────────────────────────┘
```

Figure 7.14 Wildcards need different commands.

Wildcards in `mput` and `mget` (both `*` and `?`) work just as they do at a regular shell prompt.

The problem with `mput` and `mget` is that they both stop with each file and ask, "Are you really sure you want to do this?" If you're transferring 150 files, you're probably pretty sure, yes. There is a way to turn off this prompting: Type `prompt`. All of a sudden, `mput` and `mget` will just assume that you know what you're doing (always dangerous). You could also invoke `ftp` from the command line with the `-i` option:

```
% ftp -i solaris
```

As a summary, Table 7.6 lists the basics of `ftp`.

Table 7.6 `ftp`'s simpler commands.

Command	What it does
pwd	Prints the directory you're in on the remote machine
cd	Changes the directory you're in on the remote machine
put	Sends a file to the remote machine
prompt	Tells `ftp` not to prompt when you're doing something that involves lots of yes/no questions
get	Retrieves a file from the remote machine
mput	Sends multiple files to the remote machine
mget	Retrieves multiple files from the remote machine

There are some other, very important `ftp` capabilities that we haven't touched. For example, so far all we've sent are text files. Normally, UNIX doesn't take too much notice of what kind of files you're pushing around its file systems, but when it comes to `ftp`, things get hairy. Hirsute, actually. Or maybe fuzzy is a better word.

UNIX has two file types

There are two basic types of files in UNIX—text files and everything else (called binary files). Text files are straightforward: They contain text. Duh. Things like documents you create in `vi` and shell scripts are just text files. Things like programs and directories are binary files. If you're not sure what kind of file you're dealing with, UNIX provides a nifty way to find out—the `file` command. (See Figure 7.15.)

```
# file whatsComingToYou
whatsComingToYou:        commands text
# file /etc/shutdown
/etc/shutdown:  executable /sbin/sh script
# file /bin/ls
/bin/ls:        ELF 32-bit LSB executable 80386 Version 1, dynamically linked, n
ot stripped
#
```

Figure 7.15 What kind of file am I?

You probably won't use the `file` command very often, except for when you're about to do something like an `ftp`, but it's useful to know about it then. In this example, I've run it on three different types of files: a straight text file, a shell script, and a program. (That's the one that says it's an ELF 32-bit LSB executable. Oooph.)

ftp accommodates them

So, back to `ftp`. What can you do about all this? Well, `ftp` has two file types: `ascii` (for text files) and `binary`. By default, it comes up in `ascii` mode. Figure 7.16 shows how you can change it.

```
┌─────────────────────────────────────────────────────────┐
│ ▽              shelltool - /sbin/sh                      │
├─────────────────────────────────────────────────────────┤
│ ftp>                                                     │
│ ftp>                                                     │
│ ftp>                                                     │
│ ftp> ascii                                               │
│ 200 Type set to A.                                       │
│ ftp> binary                                              │
│ 200 Type set to I.                                       │
│ ftp>                                                     │
│ ftp>                                                     │
└─────────────────────────────────────────────────────────┘
```

Figure 7.16 Type, type, type.

Many is the time I've pulled a program from somewhere only to find that I had my file type set wrong. It's so annoying I can't even begin to fume about it here. Okay, maybe I'll just fume a little. Fume, fume, fume, fume. Okay, that's enough. Anyway: Always remember to set your file type correctly before you start to transfer files.

It's odd, don't you think, that I've gotten this far into talking about `ftp`, and I haven't mentioned how to find out the names of files on a remote system? I mean, how many of us connect up with a remote computer and already know exactly what file we're going to download? Not very many, I'd venture. That's okay, because `ftp` has tools for that. Two tools, in fact.

As you probably guessed, you can issue an `ls` command to see the contents of   **`ls` and `dir`** the entire directory. You can also give `ls` one file name to look for. If you don't want to use the `ls` command, or are a true DOSaholic (or VMSaholic), there's a `dir` command that basically does the work of an `ls -l` command (which you can issue just as easily). It's yet another of those cases where UNIX provides a billion ways to do everything. Figure 7.17 shows their different outputs.

There are also a pair of commands (`mls` and `mdir`) for capturing the output of a directory listing. You specify the file(s) you want listed and the file you want it to save the listing in, and one of these commands will dump all its vital statistics into that file. Be careful using `mls * outputfile`—it will do a recursive listing of all directories starting from where you are, which can be very long.

So, let's see, we have `cd`, `ls`, `pwd`, what more do we need? Of course, `mv`! Here   **No `mv`!** `mv`. Here boy. Where are you, boy? Oh. There is no `mv` command in `ftp`. Instead, we get a DOS (or VMS) lookalike: `rename`. Heck, there's no `rm` command, either. Instead, we get `delete`. As one of my past bosses used to say (all the time, actually), "WTF!?" He never explained what it meant, and I'd been working for him for about three years before I figured it out. Let's see how long it takes you.

Anyway, I'm not going to waste time on `rename` or `delete`: They work just as you'd expect, except that they're named wrong.

Actually, if you type `rm` at an `ftp>` prompt, you can cause quite a stir. It's an abbreviation for `ftp`'s `rmdir` command—a command for destroying entire directories. This is *not* intelligent.

```
 ▽                    shelltool – /sbin/sh
ftp>
ftp> ls
200 PORT command successful.
150 ASCII data connection for /bin/ls (127.0.0.1,-32686) (0 bytes).
directory.listing
exscript
file1
fire.montgomery
jar1
jar2
jar3
numbers
ping.test
rolodex
script
sedscript
test.file
test2
test3
testfile
trouble
weird.awk
226 ASCII Transfer complete.
174 bytes received in 0.03 seconds (5.7 Kbytes/s)
ftp> dir
200 PORT command successful.
150 ASCII data connection for /bin/ls (127.0.0.1,-32684) (0 bytes).
total 38
-rw-r--r--   1 root     other         1340 Aug 15 15:10 directory.listing
-rwxr-xr-x   1 root     other           16 Aug 14 10:50 exscript
-rw-r--r--   1 root     other           43 Aug 15 09:30 file1
-rw-r--r--   1 root     other          314 Aug 11 18:45 fire.montgomery
-rw-r--r--   1 root     other           43 Aug 14 10:50 jar1
-rw-r--r--   1 root     other           41 Aug 13 19:23 jar2
-rw-r--r--   1 root     other           36 Aug 13 19:32 jar3
-rw-r--r--   1 root     other           34 Aug 13 16:15 numbers
-rw-r--r--   1 root     other          757 Aug 17 10:43 ping.test
-rw-r--r--   1 root     other          207 Aug 11 19:46 rolodex
-rw-r--r--   1 root     other           17 Aug 13 19:29 script
-rw-r--r--   1 root     other           52 Aug 14 23:48 sedscript
-rwxr-xr-x   1 root     other           43 Aug 15 14:52 test.file
-rw-r--r--   1 root     other           60 Aug 13 16:44 test2
-rw-r--r--   1 root     other           26 Aug 13 16:44 test3
-rw-r--r--   1 root     other           83 Aug 13 16:38 testfile
-rw-r--r--   1 root     other           52 Aug 13 10:34 trouble
-rw-r--r--   1 root     other           29 Aug 11 23:11 weird.awk
226 ASCII Transfer complete.
1156 bytes received in 0.02 seconds (56 Kbytes/s)
ftp>
```

Figure 7.17 ls versus dir: Is there a difference?

As long as we're talking about directories, ftp has both the mkdir and rmdir commands. Again, no time wasted, just a notification that, if you want to create a directory before stuffing a file into it, there's a way.

Running local commands
Next, let's talk about something a lot more interesting—issuing commands for the *local* machine to do something with. See, when you issue a command, by default ftp thinks that the remote machine (the one you're ftp'd into) should take a whack at making it run. But lots of times what you really want to do is do something locally, like get a listing of your local directory. To make a command run on your local system, precede it with a !. It's that simple.

Well, mostly that simple. The one exception is the one command you'll probably be making the most: `!cd`. It won't change the current directory on the local machine. I'm not sure why they did it this way, but instead of `!cd`, you'll use a command called `lcd`, for local cd.

Now that we've covered the basics, it's time to do the advanced stuff—define **Macros** some `ftp` macros. There's an `ftp` command, `macdef`, that enables you to define up to sixteen macros, each up to 4,096 characters long. Not many people use it, because most file transfers are very straightforward. Let's create a very simple macro, one that prints out the directory on the remote system, then the one on the local system. It would look something like the one in Figure 7.18.

```
shelltool - /sbin/sh
ftp> macdef ls-ls
Enter macro line by line, terminating it with a null line
ls
!ls

ftp>
```

Figure 7.18 Okay, so it's a stupid macro.

When you press `Return` to create the blank line, `macdef` terminates. To run your new macro, type

```
ftp> $ls-ls
```

That's right—precede it with a dollar sign to let `ftp` know it's a macro you're calling. Now here's a more useful macro—one that checks (roughly) to see if a remote file and a local file are the same:

```
ftp> macdef a
mdir $1 difffile1
!ls -l $2 > difffile2
!cmp difffile1 difffile2

ftp>
```

First of all, keep your macro names short and make sure they all have unique first letters. When I tried to create a series of macros that all started with the word `test`, I found out that `ftp` doesn't like commands with similar names: It kept trying to run the first macro I defined. That's because it saw the letter `t` and assumed I meant a macro called `test1`. I didn't, and this slowed me down for about ten minutes (Considering that I was writing a three-line macro, this was a long time.) This might be an anomaly on my system, but it's still good practice.

So anyway, here we've created a three-line macro called a. On the first line, we invoke the `ftp` command `mdir` and tell it to take a directory of argument 1 from the command line (that's what `$1` is), then dump its output to a file called `difffile1`. We then invoke the local command `ls -l`, tell it to take a directory of the second element on the command line, and stuff its output into `difffile2`. We then use the nearly-useless `cmp` command to compare the two files. If there's a difference, `cmp` will let us know. If not, it remains silent.

Turn prompting off
Oh, and before you run this macro, turn prompting off so that `mdir` won't ask you for a filename. I could have made that the first line, but if I already had prompting off, it would have turned it on, so I left it to manual purposes.

```
ftp> prompt
Interactive mode off.
ftp> $a file1 file2
difffile1 difffile2 differ: char 1, line 1
ftp> $a file1 file3
ftp>
```

Now it's time to say goodbye. There are three commands in `ftp` for closing down your connection: `quit`, which closes the connection and exits `ftp`; `close`, which just closes the connection; and close's synonym, `bye`. Use whichever you want.

There's one last thing to know about `ftp`: Use `.netrc` .to set up your `ftp` for you so you don't have to set your machine name, login name, password, define macros, or anything. Here's mine:

```
machine tarzan login john macdef init
!ls
```

Some things to notice: I don't put my password in here. That would be suicide—anyone could get at it. And notice two things about the macro definition (`macdef`): First, I called the macro `init`, which means that it will be automatically executed when I log in; second, there's a blank line in my `.netrc` right after `!ls`. The macro definition needs that in order to know that the macro is over.

Vince, one of my tech editors, says: "One gripe about `ftp` is you can't get entire directory trees. Some sites archive up their directory trees, so it's not too bad, but every once in a while I need to get an entire tree. Some special sites will now automatically `tar` and compress a tree if you "get" a directory. Pretty neat. You just type the name of the directory, and append `.tar.Z` or `.tar.gz` to the directory name, and the server will do the rest! I've only seen this at two or three sites so far."

`rlogin`

Dr. Livingston, I presume?

H.M. Stanley
Ujiji, Lake Tanganyika, 1871

If you ever get tired of `telnet`, you can try `rlogin`. It does much the same job (logs you into a remote system), only it's faster. You typically use it when you want to make a quick pop over to a remote system to check on something. It works like this: You type `rlogin host`, and `rlogin` prompts you for a password and logs you in.

A better `telnet`

If this doesn't sound much faster than `telnet`, that's because it isn't. However, by adding a file to your home directory on the remote machine, you can *make* it faster. That file's called `.rhosts`. I talked about it some in Chapter 2, when I was talking about customizing your shell. Anyway, you just create `.rhosts` and add the names of any hosts that you'll be logging in from to it. You could do something like

Make sure `.rhosts` works

```
% echo tarzan >> ~/.rhosts
% chmod 600 ~/.rhosts
```

if you're planning on logging in from `tarzan` a lot. Now `rlogin` won't prompt you for a password. (The second command is for security reasons: It sets the file so that you and only you have read and write access to this file. You don't want *anyone* to be able to get into a `.rhosts` file—it's just too darn dangerous.)

You can do even more with `rlogin`, like making it think you're somebody else with the `-l` switch, using syntax like `rlogin tarzan -l john`. I use `rlogin` a lot more than I ever touch `telnet`. I guess `telnet` is the last refuge of a scoundrel.

If you find that your `rlogin` session is jammed, press `~.` (tilde followed by a period). That will terminate your session immediately. If you've done an `rlogin` from `hosta` to `hostb`, then from `hostb` to `hostc`, typing `~.` will put you back to `hosta`. But if you type `~~.`, you'll go back one host—to `hostb` in this case.

Unhang `rlogin`

`rsh`

Best Wishes for a Happy and Successful First Marriage

Marc Rosen
"Unconventional Greeting Card Competition," *New York Magazine*, 1976

The `rsh` command is a relative of `rlogin`—it uses the same `.rhosts` file. Except, `rsh` is like a "one-time only" login. While `rlogin` gives you an interactive session just like `telnet` does, `rsh` only enables you to send one command line to a remote system and get a response. If that sounds like `rsh` has no use, think again—it's probably the most wonderful command in your repertoire, because all of a sudden devices on remote systems can be *yours—all yours*. Get greedy. Let's look at Figure 7.19 for an example.

```
                    shelltool – /sbin/sh
solaris% rsh solaris ls
file1
file2
testscript.sh
theCatOut
whatsComingToYou
solaris%
```

Figure 7.19 Using `rsh` for a quick-and-dirty question.

The `rsh` command *demands* that the username you're trying to log in under has a `.rhosts` file and that it's set up correctly. If it ain't, you don't get it. Follow the instructions in the previous section to get your `.rhosts` working. It's not that hard (just remember `chmod 600`).

An example   I used to have one system (my favorite) with a bum tape drive. Since I was lazy (I still am) I never got it fixed. Instead, I used the tape drive on a neighboring system to `tar` off my tapes directly onto the local system. How? Like this:

```
% rsh solaris 'dd if=/dev/rmt8' | tar xvf -
```

I think this is probably the neatest command I ever saw. The `rsh` command tells `solaris` to issue a data dump and pull all the data right off the device `/dev/rmt8` (the QIC tape drive). I then pipe that command into `tar`—a `tar` that's running on my local system—and tell `tar` to extract verbosely from the standard input (`-`). Geez, I'm a genius sometimes. [Editor's note: Do not disillusion author at this point—it could be hazardous to your health. In particular, don't tell him that we just found a variant of this command in the `man` page for `rsh`.]

You should keep this string of commands in your toolchest. Memorize it. There will be a day, probably not too far off, when you need to get data from a tape, and the machine you're on doesn't have one. UNIX networks can save the day in this respect, because there is not another operating system that I know of that is more flexible about sharing resources over a network than UNIX (and I have passing familiarity with *a lot* of operating systems).

rcp

> They copied all they could follow, but
> they couldn't copy my mind.
>
> Rudyard Kipling
> *The "Mary Gloster,"* 1894

In case you haven't already guessed, `rcp` is short for remote copy. It's the last **Better than ftp**
relative of `rlogin`. Again, it uses the `.rhosts` file, so you don't have to supply a
password. Blah. Blah, blah, blah. Oh, and it beats the *pants* off `ftp`. I mean, when
you just have one file to transfer, or even a bunch, who needs to go into an
interactive `ftp` session, set your file types, turn prompting off, turn left at the
third oak tree, lay down a bundle of newspaper, and pray to the nearest rosebush?
Ugh!

**Like `rsh`, `rcp` *needs* `.rhosts`. If it isn't there and set up properly (mode of 600,
owned by the person trying to log in, etc.) your `rcp` will fail.**

There's nothing particularly interesting about `rcp`. It must be wonderful to **Easy to use**
hear that, huh? It works just like regular `cp`, only on one side of the command,
you specify a remote host name:

```
% rcp doesntWork solaris:/usr/testfiles
```

This command would copy a file called `doesntWork` to the host `solaris` and
put it into the directory `/usr/testfiles`. The only interesting thing is the colon
that separates the hostname from the directory—it's how `rcp` knows the host
name from the directory name or filename.

Unlike both `rsh` and `rlogin`, `rcp` doesn't have a `-l` option to specify a
different username. Instead, you use an E-mail–like notation:

```
% rcp doesntWork bob@solaris:/usr/testfiles
```

Notice that everything else is the same, except I've added `bob@` before `solaris`.

**The `rcp` command isn't just for remote systems—you can use it just like `cp`,
too. That may sound odd, but if your system doesn't have a `-R` option for your
`cp` command, you'll love it: You can use `rcp -r` locally and get the same
results.**

Superusing a Network

> I teach you the superman. Man is something to be surpassed.

> F.W. Nietzsche
> *Also Sprach Zarathustra*, 1885

Administrators only

Sorry to say this, because a lot of you probably don't, but . . . if you don't have root (superuser) access to your system, you probably don't need to read this section. It's all about how to configure network cards. Why am I putting administration stuff into a book for users? Well, I figure that you might be a power user or a power user wannabe. And power users know this stuff. Heck, they breathe it. All that said, I'll try to be brief. There's no reason to belabor commands that are documented (so-so).

Starting and stopping a network

Let's start your network and stop it again, just to see what happens. Normally, this kind of operation is handled by a bunch of complicated shell scripts when you boot your computer. Never let it be said that there was a subject I couldn't oversimplify.

Your network's on/off switch is a command called `ifconfig`, for interface configuration. It's a fairly hostile command, but you can boil it down to a very simple syntax:

```
% ifconfig interface address up
```

This will turn your network on. Except . . . what are those things in italics? Interface? Address?

Discovering your network's name

Your interface is the device driver that talks to your network card. It probably has a name like `/dev/le0`, or `/dev/en0`. Or something like that. To find out, you can use a command like this:

```
% netstat -i
```

You'll see a brief listing of information on your interfaces. You'll have at least one, even if you're not on a network: `lo0`. The loopback. Put very simply, `lo0` makes every UNIX computer a network unto itself. It's pretty neat in theory, but you'll probably not have a lot of use for it.

The on/off switch

Check out the line after `lo0`. The first thing on that line is your interface. Mine's called `le0`. Let's play with it.

```
% ifconfig le0 down
```

Judging by the screams coming from down the hall, I just turned my network off. Oops. (Heh, heh. Sly smile.)

```
% ifconfig le0 1.0.0.2 up
```

It's baaaack. And this is the key command for fixing problems. If your system isn't working—for example, you configured your system for use off a network and now you want it on a network—this command, or one like it, will bring your system up on the network at a network address of 1.0.0.2.

IP addresses

Remember that I said IP addresses tend to come as four numbers separated by periods? This is one of those. Don't try to bring a system up on your network before you get an address (called an IP address). If you *are* the system administrator and are just setting up a network for your own use, use simple addresses like 1.0.0.1, 1.0.0.2, and so on.

What do all those numbers mean? Well, IP addresses read from left to right, getting ever-more specific. So 1 is kind of the global network. The first 0 is a subnetwork of that, the second is a subnetwork of the first 0, and the 2 is the address for the actual machine you're on. IP addresses are kind of like ZIP codes, getting gradually more specific, until (with ZIP+4) you have one number for everybody.

Fiddling with /etc/hosts

So now your network is up and running. Let's play. Most of the information about the other systems on your network is stored in a file called /etc/hosts. Open it, and you'll see that all the lines have a very similar format:

```
1.0.0.2          solaris          sunsolaris, backupsystem
```

The first column is the IP address we're talking about. Next comes the primary name of the host at that address. Finally, we get the nicknames of that host. Every line should read just like that (except the names will change to protect the innocent).

Add the names and addresses of the other systems on the network, and save the file. Now your network is really ready to go.

8 The Internet

Every day, in every way, I'm getting better and better.

Émile Coué

No idea is so antiquated that it was not once modern. No idea is so modern that it will not someday be antiquated.

Ellen Glasgow, 1936

The Internet is a big place. Its data repository size is measured in Sagans (remember "beellions and beellions" from "Cosmos"?). There are tens of millions of users, and millions of computers—all talking to each other thanks to this wondrous thing. Count me *in!* The electro-surf is *up!* Let's *party hearty!* God, this is starting to read like a Zippy the Pinhead cartoon. (Did I mention that he's on the Internet, too?) There's almost nothing in the way of information that you can't get on the Internet.

So much for the sales pitch. In this chapter, we're going to be talking about what the Internet is and what's on it, and looking at some ways to get at what's on it. It's not comprehensive. It couldn't be, and even if it were comprehensive when I wrote it, it would be sadly out of date by the time you read it. That's the problem with a target moving as fast as the Internet. The problem and the power.

PHILOSOPHY AND HISTORY

These lands are ours. No one has a right to remove us, because we were the first owners. The Great Spirit above has appointed this place for us, on which to light our fires and here we will remain. As to boundaries, the Great Spirit knows no boundaries.

Tecumseh, 1810

"The Information Superhighway." "The InfoBahn." You know, for a technology that's been around for a quarter of a century, there sure are a whole lot of trite, hackneyed expressions. It's the Internet. Feel proud: The Internet is historically a UNIX thing.

Where It Came From

> Colonel Cathcart had courage and never hesitated to volunteer his men for any target available.
>
> Joseph Heller
> *Catch-22*, 1961

The DoD   In the late 1960s and early 1970s, the US Defense Department decided that, in the event of a nuclear attack, it needed a secure, reliable way to keep sending data to and from its various centers of activity. The DoD created ARPAnet to test its theories. ARPAnet was redundant. Built upon repetition, and the duplication of effort, and repetition and repeating things. Basically, if a Bomb ever went off, electronic communications would be disrupted (gee, how inconvenient), so this network had to have multiple ways of getting information to and fro. The DoD then linked some of its major research centers (universities, government offices, some commercial ventures, some military sites) together with ARPAnet. The foundation was laid.

But ARPAnet is not the Internet. That takes a slightly different turn. See, as network technologies advanced, everybody started installing them. Smaller networks, called local area networks or LANs, started sprouting up like weeds in Mom's garden. Since bigger is better, the people who owned the LANs (companies and other universities, mainly) wanted to join their LANs to their neighbors' LANs, creating wide area networks (WANs).

The NSF   One of the largest of these WANs was the National Science Foundation's NSFnet. The NSF wanted to use ARPAnet to link its computers, but couldn't (remember, we're talking about two government agencies here—if you don't have form NE88375823-M8+1.4e1000 filled out in quintuplicate, nothing gets done). So The NSF took the ARPAnet's underlying technology—a networking system called the Transmission Control Protocol/Internet Protocol—and did it itself.

Lots of other LANs—companies, universities, whoever—quickly joined the NSFnet's project. And the Internet was born. At last count, there were several million sites on the Internet and several tens of millions of users. Pretty successful, huh?

Naming conventions   The Internet still shows some signs of its ARPAnet heritage. Take the naming convention for sites for example. Remember those four types of research centers that ARPAnet used (universities, government offices, some commercial ventures, some military sites)? Well, up until very recently, you were classified as one of those when you joined the Internet—you were .edu (for educational), .gov (for government), .com (commercial), or .mil (military). (Recently, a new naming convention has come into being, using country codes. Seems the Internet is so big it's more important *where* you are than *what* you are now.)

The Internet is so big that no one really manages it like they do commercial services such as CompuServe or America OnLine. There's a central registry that makes sure you don't choose a name or TCP/IP address that conflicts with anyone else's, but aside from that, it's up to the members of the Internet to police themselves. And this is a major philosophical difference between the Internet and the commercial services. The Internet has a kind of motto: "Leave it a better place than when you came." And many have done just that. Far from dying of effete technology, the Internet has proven to have a life of its own, and if there's a problem, the Internet's users fix it themselves. **It's self-managed**

If a problem is too big to be fixed by the ad hoc style of management that the Internet favors, there's a pair of somethings called the Internet Architecture Board (IAB) and the more popular Internet Engineering Task Force, or IETF. Neither of these really governs the Internet, but they make policy decisions about how the Internet should be engineered. Network addresses, for example, must be approved by the IAB.

New Internet networking technologies (for example, network protocols) go before the IETF for debate. Eventually these proposals (called RFPs, or request for proposal) can be either shot down or made into "Internet law"—an RFC (request for comment). RFC is one of those innocuous names ("gee, you mean *my* input matters?"), but usually by the time an RFC is issued, it's gotten to the point that it's acceptable to a majority of the IETF members. So who gets to be an IETF member? Just about anyone. If you're interested in how this works, send E-mail to `isoc@nri.reston.va.us`. **The IETF**

Where It's Going

> Fame is but wind.
>
> Thomas Coryate
> *Crudities*, 1611

So the Internet is sitting on a stool in the malt shop when suddenly it's discovered. Who discovered it? About fifteen million people at once, it seems. After years of being a great network that technical people knew about, suddenly *everybody* wants access to it, and *everybody* has an opinion about what it should be. As far as the Internet philosophy goes, that's just fine: It's meant to be a place where lots of people exchange ideas, argue, and generally exchange information. In fact, exchanging information is what the Internet is all about. But the Internet technology isn't as wholeheartedly behind the new demand as its philosophy is.

We're running out of Internet addresses, for one. Each Internet address looks a bit like this: 128.44.32.59. Four numbers separated by periods. There are some **The address problem** limitations on how high the numbers can go: Each must be below 256. That means, in theory, a *lot* of numbers. In practice, however, many of these numbers get allocated and not used. So there aren't as many numbers as you'd think. So we're running out. One of the IETF's jobs is to figure out how to fix that. The project is called "IP, the next generation," or IPng for short.

Increasing commercialism
You'll also see more commercialism on the Internet. When the NSF started it, the rule was, "Don't advertise, don't even hint at it. The Internet is not commercial, and if you do anything vaguely commercial, we'll beat you with a stick." Or something like that. Anyway, things loosened up a bit recently and though we still can't have advertisements per se (although some people have tried), you can set up some commercial ventures (like offering information about your products).

Finally, you're going to see a lot of people using the Internet for personal use. Ever since Vice President Al Gore mumbled something about an "Information Superhighway," everybody and their ninety-year-old parents have wanted Internet accounts. Mainly, these accounts get used for a little E-mail, but as the Internet reaches more and more people who are less and less technical, there will probably be some changes in the types of content you can get, how you get on, and such. Be a pioneer and get on today—that way you can tell your children, "I remember when you had to use a *computer* to get onto the Internet." And they'll ooh and aah and say, "What an old fart" when you're not listening.

What Did You Say Your Name Was?

> Well is him that hath a good name.
>
> *Proverbs of Wisdom*, ca. 1450

"Can I buy you a drink?" Okay. "So, what's your name?" `vsat.tcm.rlfe.com`. "Oh. See ya." Yeah, Internet naming can be discouraging. The way the Internet Protocol (IP for short) works, each computer gets a number (like that 128.44.32.59 thing I mentioned earlier). Now, remembering a bunch of numbers like that can be a birch (ask anyone who uses CompuServe). So IP has the capability to associate a name with that address. Computer names, like the numbers, use dots to figure out where they are. Let's take a look at my (fictitious) example, in Table 8.1.

`vsat` could be a single computer or a group of computers—you don't know and you don't particularly need to know. That's one of the joys of the Internet: Domains are expected to take care of themselves to a large extent. `vsat`'s in a

Table 8.1 I'm having a breakdown!

sub-sub-subdomain	sub-subdomain	subdomain	domain
vsat.	tcm.	rlfe.	com

larger group called `tcm`, `tcm`'s a member of `rlfe`, and, over the whole thing is the commercial `com` domain.

You can pretty much choose your subdomain names (as with all things, all the good ones are already taken), but your main domain is assigned by the Internet Architecture Board. Here in the US, there are a few main domains you could be assigned to. They're listed in Table 8.2.

Domain naming conventions

Table 8.2 The rain in Spain stays mainly on domain.

Domain	Who'll get it
com	Commercial ventures (businesses)
edu	Universities, schools, and that ilk
mil	Military sites
gov	The government
net	Network-related sites (people who make changes to the Internet)
org	Anything else

Now, this is the *old* style addressing. More recently, we've started to see geographic distributions. There are over three hundred of these, so I won't list them, but you can see names ending in `.uk` (England), or `.ca.us` (for California). Don't be surprised.

After the main domain type, you choose your subdomain name (like `att` for AT&T or `ibm` for IBM), and then further subdomains under you will pretty much create themselves. At each step along the subdomain trail, the subdomains get smaller. Eventually you're down to one computer. After that, there's the person. Addressing people is done by preceding this dotted name with an @ sign and the person's name. Like bob@vsat.tcm.rlfe.com.

There's a system, called the Domain Name Services, (DNS) that translates all these names into the numbers necessary for the Internet to work. You really don't have to know very much in order to get it to do your dirty work. Say I know that there's somebody with a username of bobw who works at Microsoft. Well, there are thousands of computers at Microsoft—how the heck do I figure out which machine he's on? I don't: I can probably address my E-mail to bobw@microsoft.com. It's the responsibility of the nearest DNS server to get my message to `microsoft.com`, and the responsibility of `microsoft.com` to get the message to bobw, wherever he is. DNS servers usually either know or know how to find out where somebody or something is. If they don't, you'll get a message like "host unknown," or "user unknown." That's what the phone is for: Call and ask for a better address.

The magical DNS

What's Out There?

> Everything unknown is taken to be magnificent.
>
> Tacitus
> *Life of Agricola*, ca. 98 AD

So enough with the hype and hoopla. What's the Internet good for? There are four basic things you can do: Send and read E-mail, enter discussions in news groups, upload and download files, and browse something called "The Web."

- **E-mail**. We've already talked about this at some length in the previous chapter, but here's a quick summary: You can send and receive electronic mail through the Internet. It has the largest coverage of any E-mail system, with tens of millions of people on it.

- **Network news**. Usually just called net news or netnews, this system isn't really news in the sense of the *New York Times* or the Associated Press, nor is it (technically speaking, anyway) part of the Internet. But let's suspend disbelief for a sec here: Net news usually comes in through the same pipe that brings you other Internet services. It provides a forum for exchanging ideas, thoughts, and comments. It's really a kind of on-line conversation forum, where you can ask questions ("I can't get `telnet` to work right—what's wrong?") and get answers ("Have you tried turning your computer on?").

- **Files**. There are billions of files scattered all across the Internet—all waiting for you to read them, download them, and use them. People from all around the world upload everything from the latest versions of shareware and freeware software to great literature. From reading the last chapter, you already know one tool that's used to get at these files: `ftp`. Recently, some very clever people have figured out that, gee, with a few billion files out there, it's pretty hard to find anything. Anyway, they've succeeded in indexing a lot of them. There are a few results, including a program called `gopher` and one called `WAIS` (for Wide Area Information Servers).

- **The Web**. This creation is kind of hard to explain. Basically, somebody took the Internet and made it more usable. By using **hypertext** (you know, where certain words on your screen turn up blue or green or something and you click on them and are whisked off to a definition of that word or a different screen?), the World-Wide Web (that's its full name) enables you to leap from topic to related topic, file to file, without knowing any arcane addresses or anything.

The Internet also allows you to do some other things, like `telnet` to sites that are off your own local network, but you already know how to use `telnet` (if you don't, read the previous chapter), so I'm going to concentrate on some of these newer technologies.

CONNECTING UP

Little drops of water,
Little grains of sand,
Make the mighty ocean,
And the pleasant land.

> Julia Fletcher Carney
> *Little Things*, 1845

The horror! The horror!

> Joseph Conrad
> *Heart of Darkness*, 1902

There are two basic ways to get onto the Internet: a direct connection and a dial-up connection. The advantages of the first are (1) speed (2) you don't have to deal with modems. The advantage of the second is that it's cheap.

With a direct connection, somebody will come to your site with a box—a gateway to the Internet. One side will plug into your network, the other into a line you leased from the phone company. These lines carry names like T1, Switched 56, and ISDN. You'll then get Internet numbers assigned to you, you'll choose a unique domain name, and you're a full-fledged Internet site. Simple, no? **Direct connection**

Well, not really. Actually it involves many more phone calls and probably a bit of system reconfiguration on your part. Oh, and a *lot* of money. A leased line can cost tens of thousands of dollars a month. Probably not the best thing to be spending your personal money on, but if your company wants to get on the Net (as we call it), try calling UUNET at (800) 4UU-NET3, Performance Systems International at (703) 620-6651, or Advanced Networks and Services at (313) 663-7610. These are three of the many companies that offer dedicated connections to the Internet all over the world. You can also do a roll-it-yourself version, but you'll probably find that calling a service provider takes less time and winds up costing about the same. At least, it was about a break-even when I did it several years ago.

If you're not into dedicated phone lines, you can also use some of UNIX's built-in networking utilities to get onto the Internet. There are three basic systems: UUCP (the UNIX-to-UNIX Copy Program), the Serial Line Internet Protocol (SLIP), and the Point to Point Protocol (PPP). **Dial-up connections**

UUCP is different from SLIP and PPP in a few ways that are important (and a whole lot that aren't). First off, it's a lot more limited than the other two. It was originally designed to enable computers to copy files over phone lines (hence the name). Since then, it's capabilities have expanded somewhat (a lot, actually), so that you can send mail and read network news, too (both of which are just specialized file copying, so they're really no great shakes).

UUCP   Here's basically how UUCP works: Let's say you want to exchange files and E-mail with another site. You'll edit a bunch of files (they probably live in a directory called `/etc/uucp`), connect a modem to your system, swear and cuss for a week while trying to get the modem to work right, and then finally you'll be able to exchange mail and files with this site. You'll use the "bang-style" addressing (your E-mail addresses will have `!`'s in them rather than `@`'s).

This system works well, enables very efficient ad-hoc networks, and only ties up your phone lines when it has something to say. You can run a UUCP connection with virtually any other UNIX computer in the world, because all the UUCP software is distributed for free with UNIX. Figure that it will hang about once a week and you'll have to (at best) run a program to clear things up or (at worst) reboot your computer and turn your modem off and on.

The problem with UUCP is that it doesn't actually put you *on* the Internet. You won't have to get an address from the Internet Architecture Board, you won't have a "real" Internet site name, you won't be able to do an `ftp` (see below) to retrieve files from all the neat servers on the Net, and so on. It's very good at getting you E-mail connectivity quickly, but not very good for much after that.

SLIP and PPP   Enter SLIP and PPP. When you want a full-fledged, domain-style Internet address, when you can't stand not being able to use `ftp` and Mosaic like all your friends, you'll need one of these two. The basic idea of both is to establish a dial-up connection with a site that has a direct connection to the Internet, then to pretend that the dial-up connection is really just like any other network link (like an Ethernet card, for example). SLIP and PPP then enable you to run IP, the Internet's networking lingua franca, over that dial-up line. Very clever.

SLIP is the older of the two, and a bit more widely distributed (it comes with IBM's AIX, Novell's UnixWare, and Silicon Graphics' Irix, for example), but it's gradually disappearing as the more robust PPP takes over. SunSoft, for one, bundles PPP with its UNIX systems (Solaris 2.3 for SPARC). Given the choice, you're probably better off choosing PPP if you're starting from scratch. If you or a friend is already on the Net, you should be able to find a free SLIP or PPP implementation for your system. Table 8.3 has some places you can find SLIP and PPP.

And if you have questions, there's help on the Net (the newsgroup **comp.protocols.ppp**, for example, has lots of info on PPP).

Table 8.3 Finding SLIP and PPP.

`ftp` to:	Look at:	And you'll get
`ftp.ee.lbl.gov`	`/cslip3.7.tar.Z`	SLIP for older SunOS
`ftp.uu.net`	`/networking/ip/slip`	Lots of different SLIPs
`ftp.uu.net`	`/networking/ip/ppp`	Lots of different PPPs
`merit.edu`	`/pub/ppp/*`	Lots of different PPPs

That's one thing I really hate about the Internet: You've got to be on in order to get on. I mean, if you don't have an Internet hookup, how the *heck* could anyone expect you to be doing anonymous `ftps`? Get serious. Fortunately, there are many nice people around who will help by doing things like putting PPP or SLIP software onto a tape for you and mailing it to you. Your best bet is to corral somebody with Internet access, ply them with fine wine, then ask if they'll do you a little favor.

NETWORK NEWS

Impropriety is the soul of wit.

> William Somerset Maugham
> *The Moon and Sixpence*, 1919

The masses feel that it is easy to flee from reality, when it is the most difficult thing in the world.

> José Ortega y Gasset
> *The Dehumanization of Art*, 1948

Network news (netnews) is really just a bunch of people talking to each other—a couple million of them at once. Long before the Internet came into being, people were exchanging electronic conversations using netnews. Here's how it works (the big picture). Say you want information on how to wax a surfboard. You could post a message to netnews. A day or so later, check netnews again, and you should find some responses to your question from other people who regularly scan the news. If you're familiar with CompuServe's forum discussions (or any bulletin board, for that matter), you're probably going to understand netnews really easily.

Okay, so it's not that simple. I mean, imagine a couple of million people just dumping their questions into a giant ether—confusion would preclude anybody getting anything answered. So there's a basic organization: You post your questions to the particular news group that is best suited to answer them. There are about three thousand news groups, but all share some common features. Mostly, they look like this:

News group names

```
comp.unix.wizards
```

or

```
rec.folk-dancing
```

or

```
alt.sex.bondage
```

(I'll bet that last one got your attention.) Unlike Internet addresses (which get more general as you head farther to the right), netnews groups start with the most general topic and work themselves into more specific topics.

There are seven main news groups (they come from an organization called USENET) and a whole bunch of alternate news group hierarchies. The seven main ones are

- **comp** For topics relating to computer science (software, hardware, operating systems, and so on).

- **news** Stuff related to netnews.

- **rec** Recreational activities (hobbies, music, food, and so on).

- **sci** Scientific topics.

- **soc** Social topics, sociology, socialization, socialism, and that ilk.

- **talk** Pretty much what the name implies. This is where Rush Limbaugh would hang out.

- **misc** Whatever doesn't fit elsewhere.

Of the alternate hierarchies, my favorite is `alt`, for alternative ways of looking at things. Some of these are weird, but most are a lot of fun.

When you create a netnews message, it's replicated to everybody that subscribes to that news group—they all get your posting. That means there are certain rules of decorum you might want to follow (like, try not to make a fool of yourself). Or maybe not.

Popular news readers

There are a couple of popular news readers. The oldest is probably `rn` (read news). It's so hard to use and so outdated that I'm not going to talk very much about it. More recent is `nn` (net news). It's a little younger and a lot easier to deal with. Best of all is `xrn`, a news reader for the X Window System. It's easy to use and very pretty. I'll give a bit of information on both of the latter.

The instructions for setting up `nn` are pretty simple, because its behavior is governed by two files: `~/.newsrc` and `~/.nn/init`. The first of these files tells `nn` all the news groups you're subscribed to (by default, you're subscribed to *all* of them). The second, `init`, file controls `nn`'s choice of pager and editor, for example.

To set up `nn`, the easiest thing to do is to start it, then quit immediately (hit Q). This will create `.newsrc`. Then, you just edit `.newsrc` and remove those news groups you don't want to subscribe to. You do that by changing the last character on each line from `:` to `!`. You can do this in `vi` using this command:

```
:1,$ s/:/!/
```

Now you can wander around the newsgroups and change ! back to : for those you want to subscribe to.

There are two modes in nn: selection mode and reading mode. You start off in selection mode—presumably, you're going to select the groups and threads you want to read. To get into reading mode, select something and type X.

After that, you can start nn and issue ? for help. You'll see a lengthy list of commands. Tables 8.4 and 8.5 list the ones I use most.

Table 8.4 nn's Selection Mode Commands.

Command	What it does
Space	Goes to the next item
?	Gets help (I use this daily)
Q	Quits
N	Skips to the next news group
P	Goes back to the previous news group
U	Unsubscribes to a news group
D	Decrypts something encrypted with rot13

Table 8.5 nn's Reading-Mode Commands.

Command	What it does
n	Skips to the next item
k	Skips the rest of this thread
s	Saves an item to disk
f	Responds to a posting

A note on the D option. When somebody posts something that could potentially offend someone, it's standard practice to "encrypt" it using a scheme called rot13. This is not a serious encryption (it just shifts all the letters of the alphabet 13 letters higher so a becomes n and so on), but it keeps stray eyes from reading something that might offend them. Yes, it's a kind of self-censorship, but it's mainly just courteous.

The xrn news reader is very easy to use. To start it, just type xrn at your shell prompt. You'll be confronted with a screen that looks something like Figure 8.1.

You can pretty quickly see that there are no arcane commands to remember (aren't graphical interfaces *wonderful?*)—all you do is click on buttons. I don't like

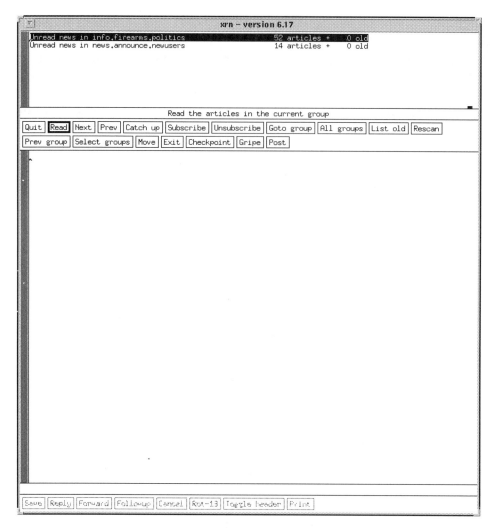

Figure 8.1 A first look at `xrn`.

to belabor the obvious (at least not *too* much), so I'll just show one or two instances of what I'm talking about. First, let's read some news. Hit the `Read` button, and you'll see something like Figure 8.2.

Anyway, I'm not going to walk through every possible button—you can figure them out by reading them. There are (as far as *I* know, anyway) no secrets hiding inside `xrn`, although it does crash on occasion for no apparent reason.

```
┌─────────────────────────────────────────────────────────────────────────┐
│                          xrn - version 6.17                               │
├─────────────────────────────────────────────────────────────────────────┤
│+  5706 Web users:  http://english-server.hss.cmu.e  [198] client surfer   │
│   5707 NRA/Black supporters?                          [8] rats@ihlpm.att.com│
│   5708 Re: Gov. Edgar Signs Anti-Gun Bill            [10] Jim De Arras     │
│   5709 Gov. Edgar Signs Anti-Gun Bill                 [2] rats@ihlpm.att.com│
│   5710 Re: NRA/Black supporters?                     [50] rats@ihlpm.att.com│
│   5711 response for nuclear weapon analogy           [18] client surfer  17-Au│
│   5712 Gun Ban Blitz                                  [7] Woody Henderson  │
│   5713 Re:  LETTER: To Congress opposing bans: no    [36] Jeff Chan        │
│   5714 FW: The Crime Bill                            [137] John Clifford   │
├─────────────────────────────────────────────────────────────────────────┤
│            Questions apply to current selection or cursor position         │
│ [Quit][Next unread][Next][Scroll forward][Scroll backward][Scroll line forward][Scroll line backward]│
│ [Scroll to end][Scroll to beginning][Prev][Last][Next group][Catch up][Fed up][Goto article][Mark read]│
│ [Mark unread][Unsubscribe][Subject next][Subject prev][Session kill][Local kill][Global kill][Author kill]│
│ [Subject search][Continue][Post][Exit][Checkpoint][Gripe][List old]        │
├─────────────────────────────────────────────────────────────────────────┤
│Path: nntp2.Stanford.EDU!headwall.Stanford.EDU!agate!howland.reston.ans.net!vixen.cso.uiuc.edu!gateway│
│From: nancyb@ranger.enet.dec.com (client surfer)                            │
│Newsgroups: info.firearms.politics                                         │
│Subject: Web users:  http://english-server.hss.cmu.edu/BS/BadSubjects.html │
│Date: 15 Aug 94 16:59:05 GMT                                               │
│Organization: University of Illinois at Urbana                             │
│Lines: 198                                                                 │
│Approved: Usenet@ux1.cso.uiuc.edu                                          │
│Message-ID: <9408151654.AA28409@us2rmc.zko.dec.com>                        │
│NNTP-Posting-Host: ux1.cso.uiuc.edu                                        │
│Originator: daemon@ux1.cso.uiuc.edu                                        │
│                                                                           │
│                                                                           │
│        A CMU grad student publication --                                  │
│                                                                           │
│a publication of the Bad Subjects Collective                               │
│Welcome to our world-wide web server, devoted to anything and everything   │
│remotely related to the journal Bad Subjects: Political Education for      │
│Everyday Life. Bad Subjects was first published in September 1992 by       │
│editors Annalee Newitz and Joe Sartelle, with the assistance of Charlie    │
│Bertsch. It has completed its second year with a new collective            │
│production team and an expanded online presence. We look forward to your   │
│participation.                                                             │
│Bad Subjects is published monthly, to the extent our limited resources     │
│make possible. It is intended to promote radical thinking and public       │
│education about the political implications of everyday life. We offer a     │
│forum for rethinking American "progressive" or "leftist" politics. We      │
│invite you to join us and participate in all aspects of our work.          │
│Bad Subjects can be contacted in two ways: 1) our mailboxes in 322         │
│Wheeler Hall, University of California, Berkeley, CA 94720, or 2)          │
│through e-mail at our address on the Internet:                             │
│badsubjects-request@uclink.berkeley.edu                                    │
│                                                                           │
│SUBMISSIONS: We welcome bth articles and letters, either on original       │
│topics or as responses to what you have read here. We are looking for      │
│short (no more than 15 double-spaced pages) non-academic articles,         │
│accessible to a broad audience. Submissions may be sent in two ways: 1)    │
├─────────────────────────────────────────────────────────────────────────┤
│Article 5706 in info.firearms.politics (51 remaining) (Next group: news.announce.newusers, with 14 articles)│
│ [Save][Reply][Forward][Followup][Cancel][Rot-13][Toggle header][Print]    │
└─────────────────────────────────────────────────────────────────────────┘
```

Figure 8.2 A little light reading.

ANONYMOUS `ftp`

> Friends share all things.
>
> Pythagoras
> *Diogenes Laertius, Lives of Eminent Philosophers*

There's one guy in every office who has everything everybody needs. "Hey Bob, you got a razor knife?" Sure. "Say Bobby, do you have a dozen postage stamps?" Yup. "Oh Bob-o, you have a copy of *Mildred Kneutwarst: Her Life and Times*, don't you?" Check shelf three. Yup, ol' Bob (not his real name) is a pretty popular kind of guy. He's so popular that he never gets any work done. He's going to be fired pretty soon unless he figures out how to get out of his role as provider of all things interesting. Well, Bob is in luck: He can set up an anonymous borrowing program. People just come in and take what they want. (Presumably they return it when they're done. Okay, so it's not the best metaphor.)

File library   The Internet has an anonymous borrowing program, too, only it's called anonymous `ftp`. Most sites on the Internet have something interesting to share, but they need a way to distribute their stuff without inconveniencing their workers. So most of them enable you to `ftp` to a particular machine on their networks and log in as `anonymous`. Once you're in, you can take what you want and leave. It might work like this:

```
% ftp ftp.nota.bene.com

Welcome to Nota Bene's Anonymous FTP Server

login: anonymous
password:
```

Ooops. At this point you're stuck, right? I mean, it's asking you for a password. Who do you call? How are you going to answer this question?? I wouldn't be building up all this suspense if I didn't have an answer. Just use your full username (including the full domain) as the password. For me, that would be `john@solaris.tugunix.com`. Most of these password programs look for the @ sign and some dots. Some are even clever enough to check for a final `.com` or `.edu` or other recognized extension.

Now that you're logged in, what do you do? Well, it's probably a UNIX system (`ftp` servers don't have to be UNIX, but they usually are), so you can look around. If it's properly administered, the server won't let you do anything dangerous. If you know which directory your files live in, just `cd` to that directory and get them as you would running any other `ftp` session (see the previous chapter).

Where to look   If you don't know, here are some guidelines. Most servers have a `/pub` directory. That's the directory for public consumption, and you're likely to find subdirectories in there that will eventually lead you to the files you want. Also check for files with names like `readme` or `index`. These will contain information about the machine and what files are available on it. They're very useful. When you're done transferring your files, just quit as you normally would.

Two points are left to cover: compression and common server names. Sometimes you'll see files on a server whose name ends in `.Z` or `.ZIP`. The first type have been compressed with the UNIX `compress` utility, the latter with the DOS `PKZIP` (or `GZIP`) utility. You'll have to uncompress them before you can use them.

Now for that note on `ftp` server names. Mostly, `ftp` servers have as their top-level domain name `ftp`. So, instead of being `microsoft.com`, it's `ftp.microsoft.com`. Remember this when you want to try to get files from someplace, but you don't know what the `ftp` server is called: Chances are it's the site's main domain name with an `ftp` first. Not always, but often.

ARCHIE

Life is one long struggle in the dark.

Lucretius
On the Nature of Things

`archie` is one of those occasionally useful tools for searching the Internet. Specifically, it searches a couple of thousand `ftp` servers and gets the names of a few million files. This may sound like it's incredibly useful, but . . . Well, it *can* be useful, but . . . Well, it just *isn't* useful all that often. The problem is that unless you know a file's name, you just aren't likely to find it.

With that caveat up front, `archie` is a good, fast way to find something you **Searching `ftp`** otherwise have no hope of finding. It works like this: You attach to an `archie` server (if you can get on to one), run your query, find out where your file is, then `ftp` it. There, you're done. Except for that bit about "if you can get on to one." There are currently about a dozen `archie` servers in the world. They all have names that start with `archie`: `archie.au` (for Australia), `archie.rutgers.edu`, `archie.unl.edu`, `archie.sura.net`, and `archie.mcgill.ca` (in Canada). With so few `archie` servers and so many Internet users, it's easy to see that you may not get on.

Basically, what `archie` does is to run an anonymous `ftp` to all the sites it knows about, log in, run an `ls -lR` (find all the files on the system), and dump that information into a giant database. It does that once a day.

`archie` isn't itself a command, it's a site you `telnet` into (see the previous chapter for instructions on using `telnet`):

```
# telnet archie.sura.net
Trying 128.167.254.179...
connected to nic.sura.net.
Escape character is '^]'.

SunOS UNIX (nic.sura.net)

login: archie
...
archie>
```

So you just log in as `archie`. If you were to tell `archie` to search right now, unless you knew the exact filename you were looking for (case and all), `archie` wouldn't find it. So I suggest that the first command you issue be

```
archie> set search sub
```

This will cause `archie` to ignore case and look for your search string, even if it's inside a word. Now let's see some other `archie` commands, in Table 8.6.

Table 8.6 `archie`'s malt-shop commands.

Command	What it does
`prog word`	Searches for word
`whatis word`	Gives you more information on word
`help`	Help!
`list`	Lists the `ftp` servers `archie` indexes

As with all things great and wonderful, there's a graphical version of `archie`, called `xarchie`. With it, you don't have to `telnet` anywhere—your `xarchie` client takes care of everything behind the scenes. Plus it's easy to use. Type `xarchie` and see what happens. If it's installed, you should see a nice screen, just waiting for you to search. Type something in under `Search Term:` and select the `Query>` menu, then `Query Item`. (See Figure 8.3.)

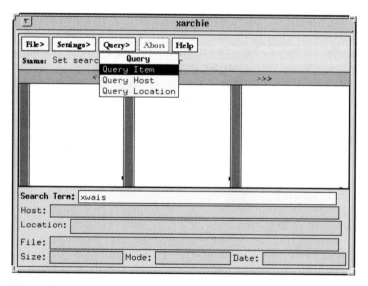

Figure 8.3 I'm feeling a little bit query today.

Pretty, isn't it? After you run your query, `xarchie` will probably turn up something. You can get to it by clicking on it, then selecting `File>`, then `Get...` (See Figure 8.4.)

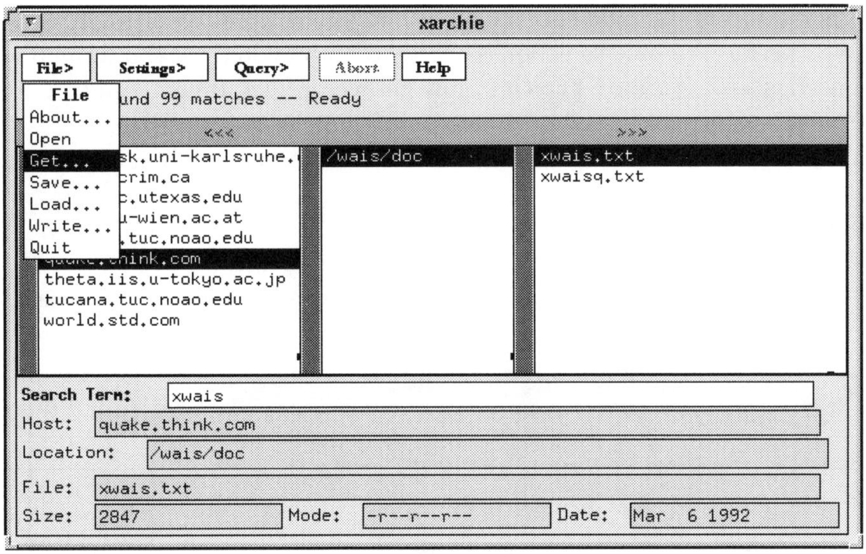

Figure 8.4 Gimme!

`xarchie` will retrieve the file, just like `archie`. Only easier. If `xarchie` were a movie, it'd be a must-see, just because it's *so* much easier to use than `archie`.

GOPHER

> Beauty is in the eye of the beholder.
>
> Margaret Hungerford
> *Molly Bawn*, 1878

`gopher` is the product of some of the warped (in the best sense of the word) minds at the University of Minnesota (the Golden Gophers). They needed a way to organize their campus information—class schedules, syllabi, office hours, paperwork, campus information, that kind of stuff. It all already lived on computers, but finding what you wanted wasn't as easy as it should be. Imagine being a freshman and getting a note that says, "For all the information about the campus, find the `campus.information` file and read it." Talk about intimidation—where the heck is this file anyway?

They decided that they could create a system that appears to a user like a bunch of menus. Behind the pretty face, however, is a network of servers, each of which holds some information. Without the knowledge of the user, the `gopher` **client** (the software) could pop all over that network, getting dribs and drabs of information from different servers. Once you've answered your final question, `gopher` performs whatever action is necessary to get you what you want. If what you need is a file, `gopher ftps` it from wherever it lives. If you need to `telnet` into some site, `gopher` can do that, too.

If `gopher` is installed on your system, you can probably run it by typing

```
% gopher
```

Try it and see what happens. You should get a screen like the one in Figure 8.5.

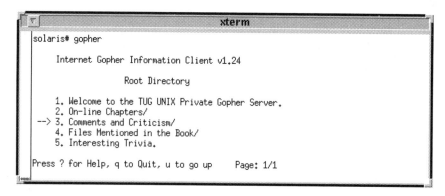

Figure 8.5 A look at my ugly, text-only `gopher` server.

The great thing about `gopher` is that it's pretty easy to use: Just keep pressing `Return` on the options that lead to the answer you want.

You use the arrow keys on your keyboard to move the pointer (`-->`) up and down your choices. If a choice ends in a slash, there are more choices behind it. If it ends in a period, when you select it you're at the end of the road and the next thing you'll see is a document. There are two other common endings to `gopher` entries: `<TEL>`, which means the next thing you'll be doing is `telnetting` to a remote site, and `<CSO>` which brings up a kind of phone book that you can use to look people up (mostly at universities).

`gopher` has six basic capabilities: viewing text files, going to another `gopher` server, performing an indexed search, doing an `ftp`, running a `telnet` session, and searching a white pages. Here's each one really quickly:

- **Viewing text files**. You'll be doing a lot of this. There are text files scattered all across the `gopher` network. They answer many frequently asked questions (FAQs) and generally form a big part of the backbone of `gopher`'s services.

- **Going to another `gopher` server**. While you're maneuvering around all those `gopher` menus, you have no idea where you really are—`gopher` handles all of it—but you could be on any `gopher` server around.

- **Performing an indexed search**. If you ever see a `gopher` entry that ends <?>, the next menu you get will be something like this:

```
Index word(s) to search for:
```

Usually this happens when you're near the end of the line in your search.

- **ftp**. On many `gopher` menus, you'll see an option to peruse FTP sites. Unlike a straight anonymous `ftp`, where you have to know the address (and frequently the file) you're looking for, `gopher` can just list some `ftp` sites that it knows about. You just keep pressing your `Return` key as you've been doing, and eventually you'll find yourself transferring files.

- **telnet**. Some `gopher` choices end in a `telnet` session. They're usually not too interesting, though.

- **Searching a white pages**. Universities and colleges put a phone, address, and general information service on-line. White pages options enable you to find out more about your professors and sometimes even other students.

Now on to the nice stuff: the X version of `gopher`. No more of this ugly stuff. Type `xgopher` and see what happens. If it's installed, you'll see something like Figure 8.6. Then you just point and click your way through the menus.

VERONICA

Appearances are often deceiving.

Aesop
The Wolf in Sheep's Clothing

As you probably noticed, `gopher` has a *lot* of information at its fingertips. Now wouldn't it be great if somebody indexed all that and . . . Oh, somebody already did? Well, fancy that. Keeping with the Jughead theme (and yes, there is a `jughead` command), it's called `veronica`.

`veronica` is `archie` for `gopher`. How's that for a sentence? All those lovely `gopher` servers out there will, every once in a while, index their contents and

Searching gopher

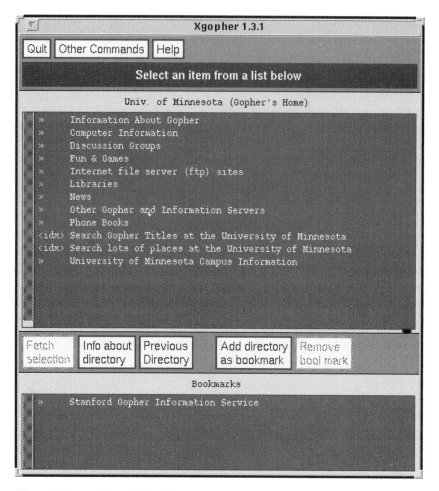

Figure 8.6 xgopher finds a home.

send that index to `veronica`, a giant database with tons of information on how to get anything from any gopher server on the Net.

On many `gopher` menus you'll see an option like, `Search titles in Gopherspace using Veronica <?>`. All you have to do is say yes, then type in the word you want to search for: `veronica` will run the search for you and return a list (numbered) from which you choose the topic you really want. When you choose your document, `veronica` won't just display *where* the document is (that would be too useless)—`veronica` will take you there. Whisk, plunk. You're there. `veronica` is at one with `gopher`.

Normally, you have to choose a `veronica` server to use, but recently there's an "experimental" `veronica` that will choose your `veronica` server for you (based on the nearest one, the one with the lowest load, and so on). Try that.

Back to the graphical stuff, xgopher will search veronica, just as gopher will. You just select something like Search titles in Gopherspace using veronica, and you'll see what I mean. Follow the sequence in Figures 8.7–8.9.

xgopher and **veronica**

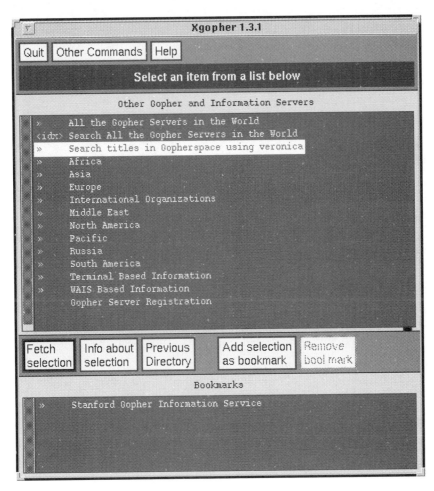

Figure 8.7 Just select "Search titles . . ."

Figure 8.8 . . . enter your search . . .

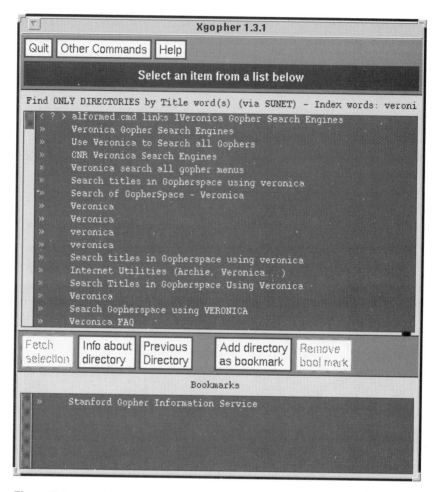

Figure 8.9 . . . and you'll get your result, all nice and pretty.

WAIS

> There is no sin except stupidity.
>
> Oscar Wilde
> *The Critic as Artist*, 1891

WAIS (Wide Area Information Server) is another index to the Internet's archives, but it's a bit easier to use than some of the others. (Even though it's an implementation of a protocol that sounds like it comes out of a science fiction movie: Z39.50.) The basic idea of WAIS is like `veronica` and `archie`: Somebody, somewhere creates an index of the contents of files and posts the index to the WAIS server.

Basically, you tell the WAIS server what you're looking for, and it comes back with a list of documents that contain the phrase you gave it. Not just that, but it knows enough to rank documents that contain more instances of the words you gave it higher than others. That's called a weighted search.

One of the things I dislike about WAIS is that it's not smart enough to know that throwaway words (like "and" and "or") shouldn't be counted. Never use common prepositions, conjunctions, or articles in a WAIS search.

You access WAIS through a client (just as you do `gopher`). If you have a system directly on the Net, see if you have one called `xwais`. (If you don't, `ftp` to `ftp.cnidr.org` and look for it there.) It provides a nice graphical user interface to WAIS. If not, you can `telnet` into one of the public WAIS sites listed in Table 8.7 and use their services (although they're awfully busy).

Table 8.7 Public WAIS sites

Name	Login
cnidr.org	demo
info.funet.fi	wais
quake.think.com	wais
sunsite.unc.edu	swais
swais.cwis.uci.edu	swais

One of the problems with WAIS is that it's relatively new, so it doesn't have many archives (it's very strong in computer science—surprise). That drawback is almost made up for by its incredibly easy-to-use interface. It's definitely one of the simplest front ends to the confusion that is the Internet.

When you load a WAIS client, you'll be asked to select a "source." These are the archives that WAIS knows about. You can scroll this list to see if there are any relevant to what you want to ask about. By default, WAIS wants to search all of them. Fine, I say, let it. Now enter your "keyword"—the word or words you want to search for. Remember to omit overly common, unneeded words like "the" and "and." Now run your search.

After you've run it, if you have a good client software version, you can keep refining it, selecting documents that are close to what you want. WAIS knows enough to find similarities between the documents you select and what's left in the WAIS index. Eventually you select the document or documents you want to view, and the WAIS client will bring them up for your perusal.

Searching the Net

Refining searches

THE WORLD-WIDE WEB

> I cannot forecast to you the action of Russia. It is a riddle wrapped in a
> mystery inside an enigma.
>
> Sir Winston Churchill, 1939

"...and welcome aboard our newest member, Ms. W. W. Web." "Thank you, thank you.
It's great to be here. I know I'm spread a little thin right now, but I hope to make
up for that by being hyper." Text that is. Hypertext.

If you think that anonymous `ftp` is for the birds, and `gopher` is just too hard
to use, and you really don't like the malt-shop crowd, then you should give the
World-Wide Web a try. (You can call it "The Web," or W3 for short.) It's a great
idea, and probably the future of the Internet. It provides all the services we've
talked about already (`gopher`, anonymous `ftp`, `telnet`, `veronica`...every-
thing) in a truly lovely interface—by using **hypertext**.

What's hypertext?
Okay, that's the second time I've used that word. Now it's time for a quick
definition. (You've probably used some kind of computer software that employs
hypertext, so once I start describing it and you recognize it, feel free to tune out.)
Hypertext works like this: Imagine a piece of paper with a few paragraphs of text
on it. Got that picture? Okay. Now imagine that this piece of paper uses all sorts of
words you don't know the definitions of (like "antidisestablishmentarianism"). If
this were a hypertext document, the odds are that those words would be boldfaced or printed in a different color, and when you came to them, a note card with
a definition would magically appear in your hands. It's what I'd call a "drill-
down" approach: You start at the macro level and, as you need more information
on particular subjects, you get it.

Hypertext pages on **computers** tend to look a bit like **this**, with words
popping off the page in different colors and **typefaces**. If you want more information on one of these words, you just **click** on it, and the hypertext **engine** will give
you more information.

The way the Web does hypertext is even better. Not only can you get definitions of words, you can move around the network, from domain to domain,
computer to computer, looking for files, people, and services, without knowing
where any of them are. The Web's hypertext is created in a special, cross-platform
language called the Hypertext Markup Language, or HTML (often seen lowercased
as `html`). (The only reason that I'm telling you this is because most addresses on
the Web start with `html`, and you'll probably be wondering why.)

Web browsers
Accessing the Web is done through a front end called a browser. There are two
types of browser, line-oriented and graphical. The line-oriented ones (like `www`)
are really ugly, and the graphical ones (particularly one called Mosaic) are really
neat. When you start your Web browser, you'll be dumped into what's called your

home page. This is really just an access point for the rest of the Web. Your home page will have all sorts of hypertext on it for you to use to get elsewhere. In addition, a graphical Web browser such as `xmosaic` will have menus that enable you to jump to new places and do new things (like `veronica` searches) relatively easily.

"How easily?" you ask. Type `xmosaic` (again, to see if it's installed). You should see the screen in Figure 8.10.

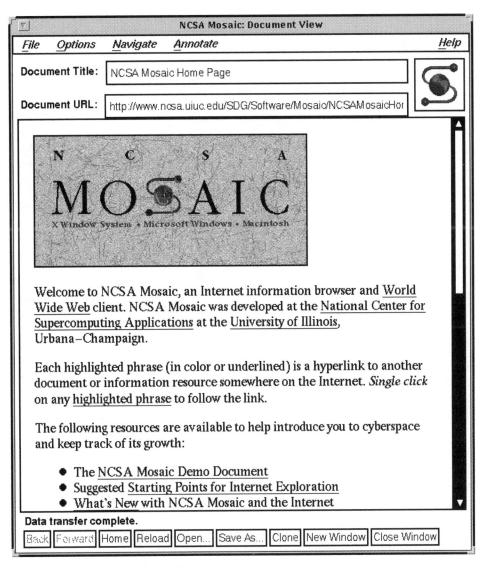

Figure 8.10 Home again—the Mosaic home page.

Then you pull a few menus, run around the Net a bit, and you can get some pretty pictures like the ones in Figure 8.11.

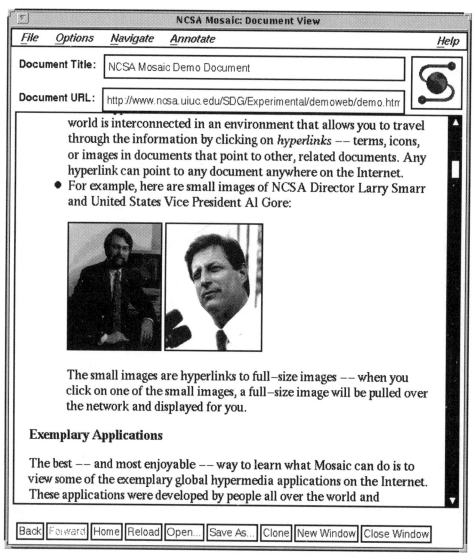

Figure 8.11 We pop over to see just what Mosaic can do.

It's not like this is all Mosaic can do, but this is a lot of it—pretty pictures, sounds, and linked documents all combining to make the information on the Internet easy to get at and understand. Look for it in stores everywhere soon.

NET ETIQUETTE

> Hello, sucker!
>
> Texas Guinan

You've probably read all this somewhere before, but I'm going to waste your time with it again. In addition to the legal rules about using the Internet (read my SLIPs: No Commercial Activity), there are some rules of etiquette that keep the Net fresh and usable.

- **Always leave the Net a better place than when you arrived**. If you download a program you really needed, upload one for others to enjoy. If you ask somebody you don't know for help and get it, give somebody else you don't know the help they need.

- **Respect bandwidth limitations**. There are thousands of `ftp` servers all across the world. Many are mirrored—the information is available on many servers. Don't download files from far-off lands unless you aboslutely must, and even then don't do it. You'll tie up precious bandwidth over expensive intercontinental lines—bandwidth that you *really aren't paying for.*

- **Be succinct**. This is a rule for netnews and E-mail, mainly. Remember, particularly with netnews, that your twelve-page exegesis on the evils of nose hair is going out to millions of computers across the world, and although a few kilobytes may not seem like a lot to you, it is when it has to go over a series of lines that measure speed in thousands of *bits* per second. Do you really need to send it?

- **Avoid unmarked sarcasm and humor**. I realize that you're a funny person (but looks aren't everything), but it's hard to tell when you're serious and when you're just playing with my mind when what you're doing is sending me a straight-laced sentence. You probably don't even notice the verbal and physical clues that let you know the person you're talking to is using irony—but they're there. They aren't on a written page. The Internet has a series of symbols to help people know you're kidding. The most common is `:-)`—a sideways smiley face. It means "just kidding." There's also a smirk `:-^` and a wink `;-)` that you should use whenever appropriate.

- **Don't flame**. On a note related to the previous two, netnews frequently sees very heady and hot-under-the-collar responses to its postings. They (the responses) are called **flames**, because they're so hot. Avoid the urge to send a flame. Drink a glass of water, cool down, and have a little understanding for the person that posted the statement. Then hire a hit man to kill them. :-)

- **Never give out your password or other personal information**. You don't know who's listening, and posting your phone number is an invitation for people to give you a call—about ten million people with modems that can keep dialing until you have to have your number changed. That's not to say that everybody on the Net is vindictive and nasty. In fact, by far the majority are good people who are there to help (and who follow these rules). However, one rotten apple, as the saying goes. Passwords deserve a particular note: NEVER GIVE OUT YOUR PASSWORD TO ANYONE EVER EVER EVER EVER. It's incredibly easy to impersonate somebody else using E-mail—some of the best jokes on the Internet come from people who know how to do this and make up replies from very odd sources (like presidents of industry and countries). If you ever get a request for your password, reply, politely but firmly, that you won't give it out. Even if the request comes from your system administrator—what the heck does s/he need with your password? I mean system administrators have superuser privileges!

NEAT PLACES

> So little done—so much to do.
>
> Cecil John Rhodes, 1902

The Internet is much too large for me to begin to catalog. I'm not going to try. Having said all that, I've probably completely undermined the following lists. These are some of the places I "hang out" when I'm on line.

Anonymous `ftp` Sites

> In our world of big names, curiously, our true heroes tend to be anonymous. In this life of illusion and quasi-illusion, the person of solid virtues who can be admired for something more substantial than his well-knownness often proves to be the unsung hero: the teacher, the nurse, the mother, the honest cop, the hard worker at lonely, underpaid, unglamorous, unpublicized jobs.
>
> Daniel J. Boorstin
> *The Image*, 1961

Connect with `ftp`, login as `anonymous`, and give your username as the password and you should be in.

Andrew User Interface System

`emsworth.andrew.cmu.edu`

Kind of hard to explain, the Andrew User Interface is a bunch of neat applications that you can use with the X Window System—a word processor, E-mail front end, etc.

Carnegie-Mellon University Networking

`ftp.net.cmu.edu`

The latest in networking technology from our friends at CMU.

Digital Equipment Corporation Archive

`gatekeeper.dec.com`

Almost everything interesting I've ever found on the Net has come from here.

GNU Software Archive

`prep.ai.mit.edu`

The Free Software Foundation's GNU project gets some of the best software for UNIX widely circulated for free. Try `emacs`, the text editor, if you haven't already. Then try `chess`.

James Cook University

`ftp.jcu.edu.au`

Freeware for the DEC Alpha/OSF systems and X11R5 distribution software make this interesting.

MIT Media Lab

`cecelia.media.mit.edu`

Papers and programs about projects at this advanced perceptual computing research site.

MIT/Athena

`athena-dist.mit.edu`

The X Window System, Kerberos security system, and other neat stuff are here.

National Center for Supercomputing Applications

`ftp.ncsa.uiuc.edu`

NCSA Telnet for the Macintosh and PC, not to mention Mosaic, and a bunch of other stuff. A good place for the latest and greatest useful software.

SunSITE

`sunsite.unc.edu`

Software for Sun Microsystems computers, and odd things like Linux (a free UNIX lookalike) and software you can play around with.

University of Michigan

`archive.umich.edu`

Everything.

gopher Sites

> Make thee an arc of gopher wood.
> *Genesis*

You can reach the following sites using your gopher client software.

The Apple Computer Higher Education Gopher Server

`info.hed.apple.com`

Information on Apple's products, public relations efforts, news, and a forum for a lot concerning Apple Computer. I'm an ex-Macintosh-head, so it's kind of fun.

Association for Computing Machinery

`gopher.acm.org`

These are the hard-core geeks—people who design lasers in their garages for fun. You'll get their conferences, publications, and a list of activities in your area. Try it, you'll . . . Well, you may not like it, but you'll probably learn something.

Boston University Gopher

`gopher.bu.edu`

I used to live in Boston, and still like to keep in touch with stuff there. Boston University's `gopher` server provides schedules of events, an electronic phone book, and access to the library catalog and circulation system. If I ever need to check out a book three thousand miles away . . .

Electronic Frontier Foundation Gopher

`gopher.eff.org`

The EFF is a watchdog for E-mail privacy and that kind of stuff (you know, those *social* issues of computer use). There's even a newsletter. See what they have to say.

InfoSlug

`scilibx.ucsc.edu`

Despite the somewhat comical name, you'll find all sorts of useful information quickly on this gopher server. In particular, there's an on-line catalog to the University of California at Santa Cruz's library, and a large selection of other gopher servers you can go to. It's a good place to start.

Lund University Electronic Library

`munin.ub2.lu.se`

It's in Sweden, and it's a phenomenal resource, with lots of gateways to other gopher servers, WAIS databases, and the like.

Minnestota Regional Network

`gopher.mr.net`

MRNet is a commercial Internet service provider, but don't hold that against it. This gopher server has a bit for anyone just starting out on the Internet.

NASA Goddard Space Flight Center

`gopher.gsfc.nasa.gov`

The most notable things here are the images. Captured from the shuttles and various flights, you can download all sorts of pretty pictures.

Ogpher

`sunsite.unc.edu`

An unprepossessing name, but a lot of Net resources, including `archie` access and a lot of useful files.

Sam Houston State University

`niord.shsu.edu`

Sheesh—I've never seen this much stuff before. There's stuff about economics and business, stuff for computer hackers, stuff for my investments. I start here about once a week just to see what's new.

Texas A&M University

`gopher.tamu.edu`

It may seem odd, but they have a neat collection of archives from the former Soviet Union that I enjoy poking around in. Slavic languages and literature was my college major (see what I'm doing with it now?).

Texas Department of Commerce

`gopher.tdoc.texas.gov`

Another good place (nearly as good as Sam Houston State) for finding business information. Who said the Internet was all fun and games?

Ulibrary

`gopher.lib.umich.edu`

An odd place where you'll find the UPI Newswire and US Census information for Michigan slammed up against the Bryn Mawr Classical Review.

University of Maryland Information Server

`inform.umd.edu`

An on-line library including *The Night Before Christmas* and *Aladdin's Magic Lamp* make this a good place to visit for a little on-line reading.

University of Minnesota

`gopher.tc.umn.edu`

Be there: It's got the listing of all the `gopher` servers in the world, plus recipes, movie reviews, and WAIS and `ftp` gateways.

World-Wide Web Sites

> Come, follow me, and leave the world to its gabble.
>
> Dante
> *Purgatorio*, 1320

Just type in these addresses at the URL: prompt in Mosaic.

City of Palo Alto

`http://www.city.palo-alto.ca.us/home.html`

Want to know what goes on in the home town of Stanford University?

CommerceNet

`http//www.commerce.net/cgi-bin/textit`

Commercial Internet—under construction.

Dead Sea Scrolls

`http://sunsite/unc/edu/expo/deadsea.scrolls.exhibit/intro.html`

Not quite so dead. See the exhibit—it's kind of fun and you may learn something.

GNN

`http://nearnet.gnn.com/gnn/GNNhome.html`

This one's the product of O'Reilly and Associates and it's brilliant. Check out Dilbert, the cartoon, on-line.

Internet Tools

`http://www.rpi.edu/Internet/Guides/decemj/internet-tools.html`

The name says it all.

KiwiClub

`http://kiwiclub.bus.utexas.edu/finance/kiwiserver/`
`  kiwiserver.html`

Lots of economic data for you business types.

NASDAQ

`http://www.law.cornell.edu/nasdaq/nasdtoc.html`

Want to know what's up with your stocks? Try this update service.

Space Telescope Science Institute

`http://stsci.edu.top.html`

I'm Hubbled by your presence on this one.

 # Most Useful Commands

This isn't a complete list. I won't pretend. But these are the commands I find myself using over and over, along with the switches I use the most.

LISTING FILES: `ls`

Table A.1 `ls` has an option or two.

Option	What it does
`-a`	Lists all files
`-l`	Gives all information
`-C`	Gives multicolumn output
`-f`	Lists files in directories, but not directories themselves
`-F`	Puts / after directory names, * after executables, and @ after symbolic links
`-r`	Lists files in reverse order
`-R`	Lists all directories recursively
`-t`	Lists files in chronological order

SEARCHING FOR A FILE: `find`

Table A.2 Help! Where's my head?

Option	What it does
`-print`	Prints what you find
`-exec`	Runs the following command(s)
`-mtime`	Searches by modification time
`-name`	Searches by name
`-user`	Searches by owner
`-size`	Searches by size

SEARCHING THROUGH STUFF:* `grep`

Table A.3 Wanna `grep` in the closet?

Option	What it does
-i	Ignores case
-v	Shows only lines that don't match
-c	Counts matching lines
-w	Searches for a pattern as a word
-l	Shows only names of files with matches

*Searching through files or the output of other commands by using the |

WHO'S ON THE SYSTEM: **who, whoami, or who am i**

Table A.4 Who am I, where am I, what does it matter?

Option	What it does
-u	Displays users currently logged on
-a	Gives lots of extra information

WHAT'S RUNNING ON THE SYSTEM: **ps**

Table A.5 System V ps.

Option	What it does
-e	Every process
-f	Full listing
-l	Long listing

Table A.6 BSD ps.

Option	What it does
a	All processes
u	User-oriented format
x	Processes not associated with this terminal
l	Long listing

TYPE OUT THAT FILE: `cat` and `more`

Table A.7 `cat`'s out of the bag.

Option	What it does
`-v`	Substitutes printing for nonprinting characters
`-e`	Puts a $ at each line end

Table A.8 The `more` the merrier!

Option	What it does
`-c`	Clears terminal before displaying
`-f`	Prevents folding of long lines
`-r`	Displays control characters
`-s`	Squeezes multiple blank lines into one

`more` is useful to halt the output of commands that generate more than a window full of text, like `ps`. When you're in a `more` session, you can type the letter q to stop it and b to scroll back a page, and you can use the / as in `vi` to search for text.

FIX FILE PERMISSIONS: `chmod, chgrp, chown`

Table A.9 Spare `ch`?

Option	What it does
`-f`	Ignores errors
`-R`	Does it recursively

COPY A FILE: `cp`

Table A.10 There's never a `cp` around when you need one

Option	What it does
`-r`	Makes a recursive copy
`-i`	Asks for confirmation before copying each file

RENAME A FILE: `mv`

Table A.11 On the `mv`.

Option	What it does
`-i`	Asks for confirmation before each file
`-f`	Blows stuff away, no matter what

DELETE A FILE: `rm`

Table A.12 Go to your bed`rm`.

Option	What it does
`-i`	Asks for confirmation
`-f`	Ignores warnings and errors
`-r`	Makes a recursive removal

COMPARE TWO FILES: `diff`

Table A.13 Don't be `difficult`.

Option	What it does
`-e`	Produces an ex script

PUT THINGS IN ORDER: `sort`

Table A.14 What sort are you, anyway?

Option	What it does
`-m`	Merges input files
`-o`	Sends output to file

MAKE YOURSELF SUPERUSER: `su`

Table A.15 `Su-oooey!`

Option	What it does
`-`	Read user's login files

READ THE BEGINNING/END OF A FILE: `head` and `tail`

Table A.16 Can't tell my `head` from my `tail`

Option	What it does
–n	Read *n* lines

MISCELLANEOUS I/O REDIRECTION: <, >, |, and >>

Table A.17 Misced me much?

Redirector	What it does
>	Outputs to file
<	Reads from file
|	Pipes to command
>>	Appends to file

COMPRESS A FILE: `compress`

Table A.18 A cold `compress`.

Option	What it does
`-v`	Shows percentage each file is shrunk by

MAKE A FILE ARCHIVE: `tar`

Table A.19 A dark, `tarry` night.

Option	What it does
`x`	Extracts from archive
`v`	Maakes output verbose
`f`	Reads from file
`c`	Creates a new archive
`t`	Reads contents of archive but doesn't extract

`x`, `c`, and `t` are mutually exclusive (which makes sense, doesn't it?).

FIND OUT WHERE AN EXECUTABLE IS LOCATED: `which`, `whereis`, and `whence`

Three commands with slightly different purposes. Use all of them to find out where a program lives (if it's in your path). Table A.20 lists the options to `whereis`.

Table A.20 Wherefore art thou?

Option	What it does
-b	Searches for binaries (programs) only
-m	Searches for manual sections
-s	Searches only for source files (usually ending in `.c` or `.f`)

FIND OUT ABOUT YOUR DISK USAGE: `du` and `df`

du tells you how much space a file takes up (usually in KB), df lists the volumes in your system and lets you know how much free space there is on them.

Table A.21 duh

Option	What it does
-a	Reports on every file (or file system if you're using `df`)

FOREGROUND AND BACKGROUND TASKS: `bg`, `fg`, and `&`

When you first run a command in the C shell, you can append a `&` so that it runs in the background. bg moves a stopped job into the background, and fg moves background jobs into the foreground.

GET MORE INFORMATION ON COMMANDS: `man`

Table A.22 Man, oh man.

Option	What it does
-k *word*	Prints out one-line descriptions of all `man` entries containing *word*

B Common Problems and Fixes

Things go wrong all the time. You can't always foresee just what's going to go—
Hey!! They're towing my car!!!

Back again. As I was (pant) saying, things go wrong all the time, and you've got to be prepared to handle them. Obviously, it'd be better if they never happened. Here's a rundown of the problems I have all the time and either the way to fix them once they've gone wrong or the way to keep them from going wrong in the first place (or both). Photocopy this list and keep it handy.

TERMINAL PROBLEMS

Have you had this experience:

```
% telnet distanthost
Trying 112.42.2.21 ...
Connected to distanthost
Escape character is '^]'.

UNIX(r) System V Release 4.0 (distanthost)

login: john
Password:
Last login: Wed Aug 17 10:21:22 from solaris
Sun Microsystems Inc.   SunOS 5.1     Generic April 1993
distanthost% gret^H^H^H^H^H^H^H
```

Annoying, isn't it? What happened to your terminal settings? If you echo $TERM, you're set up correctly. So what's wrong?

Your `stty` settings are messed up. To fix them, you'll have to do something like this:

```
% stty erase ^h
```

Note that I didn't really type a caret and an h—I pressed the **Backspace** key. A messed up **Backspace** key is probably the most common problem I find. The problem is that terminal vendors all map their keys to send different control signals, and when I log in to a remote host from my terminal, it interprets them wrong. Oh, and if you log in with your username in all capital letters, your entire session will be in capital letters—it's a function of the program that reads your username. It tries to determine if your terminal supports lowercase letters. If you type your username in with all capital letters, it assumes that your terminal doesn't. You'll have to log out and back in to fix the problem.

DELETED FILES

There's not a lot you can do once you've deleted a file. Unlike DOS, there's no undelete command. You could try reading blocks directly off the disk, but you probably wouldn't be successful—you'd have to know the inode that originally stored the file.

You're better off preparing yourself in the first place. The simplest thing is to alias your `rm` command so that it copies files into a temporary directory, then deletes them. For example,

```
% mkdir ~/.rmtrash
% alias saferm 'cp \!$ ~/.rmtrash; rm \!$'
```

Then once a day (or week or whatever), you could clean out this directory. Notice that I didn't alias the rm command itself—that isn't a great practice. What happens if you're used to having a safety net below your rm command and you work on a system or account that doesn't have it? Better to create the new command, get into the habit of using it, and get an error when you're on somebody else's account.

If you don't like the alias idea, try using a version control system such as RCS or SCCS. See Chapter 4 for more details.

ERROR IN A DOT FILE

After reading this book, you're probably going to go and make abundant changes to all your dot files: `.profile`, `.login`, `.cshrc`, `.kshrc`, and whatever others you can find. Before you do, create a backup directory for the original (working) files:

```
% mkdir ~/.backup
```

Now copy all your dot files into it:

```
% cp ~/.* ~/.backup
```

(Ignore the error message when `cp` tries to copy `.backup` into `.backup`—it's nothing to worry about.) Now it's okay to go ahead and play with your files.

Once you've made your changes, don't log out and log back in to test them. You can try a few different methods that won't leave you stranded if something doesn't work. The simplest is to reexecute the instructions in these files, which you can do with the C shell's `source` command, or by using the dot (`.`) in the Bourne and Korn shells. For example, you could test your changes to the Bourne shell's `.profile` like this:

```
# . $HOME/.profile
```

and check out the C shell's `.login` like this:

```
% source ~/.login
```

If you really do want to check out what your changes will be like and feel you need to execute a full login (although I can't think why), you can use `telnet` to test everything:

```
% telnet localhost
...
```

Then log in as yourself. If something goes wrong, you can abort your `telnet` session by typing `Ctrl+]`—the default key sequence for aborting your `telnet` session. You can then restore (or repair) your dot files. If you're interested in another way to test your dot files, try using the `su` command:

```
% su -
```

su stands for superuser (or substitute user, depending on whom you ask). When you run it, you can become another user (or, when you don't supply a username, yourself). The dash tells `su` to execute what's in your dot files.

LOST FILES

I leave files around behind me like bird droppings. Consequently, I'm constantly losing them. I use the `find` command to find them. If I know the name, I do this:

```
% find / -name "filename" -print
```

which is a relatively straightforward `find` command. If I don't know the name, I try this:

```
% find / -user john -print
```

which searches by who owns the file, rather than what its name is. In fact, I use these two commands so often that I've aliased them in my `.cshrc`.

PROCESS PROBLEMS

I had a friend—someone relatively new to UNIX—who used to log out of her sessions by pressing `Ctrl+z`, and then `Ctrl+d` until her shell gave up issuing the message `There are stopped jobs` and logged her out. Stopping jobs is kind of a common problem, and because of her, I gained a full appreciation of just how to deal with process problems.

As you knew (or now know, anyway), `Ctrl+z` will stop a job. What does this mean? Well, if you remember, `Ctrl+c` cancels a job—it's gone for good. But `Ctrl+z` just tells the job to pause. You can then kill the job or restart it (at least in the Korn or C shells—the Bourne shell don't do dat). I'll give C shell examples here.

To restart your job and make it the active job, use `fg`, the foreground command. If you want it to be in the background, use `bg`. If you want to kill it, you have to know its job number. The C shell numbers every task that you perform from the shell prompt. When you're just running one job, it's job number 1—or `%1` as the C shell thinks of it (the % tells the C shell that we're talking about a job).

If you're running more than one job, you'll want to use the C shell's `jobs` command to find out your job's number.

```
% jobs
[1] + Stopped              find / -name "testfile" -print
[2] - Stopped              vi .cshrc
[3] - Running              make
%
```

The job number is in the far left column. You can bring any of these jobs to the foreground by supplying the `fg` command with a job number:

```
% fg %1
```

Or you can use the shorthand for this, which is just to type the job number at the prompt:

```
% %1
```

Or you can resume a job in the background in the same way:

```
% bg %2
```

or

```
% %2 &
```

(Remember that the ampersand means "put this job in the background.") Or you can kill any of them with the `kill` command:

```
% kill %2
```

C Editor Summary

Dear Mom,

Enclosed please find selected shortcuts for using the `vi` and `emacs` text processing utilities.

Love,
John

VI SHORTCUTS

`vi` has two main modes: insert mode and command mode. By default you're in command mode and can use the motion letters. Use the characters in Table C.2 to start adding text.

Table C.1 Command line options.

Option	What it does
-c *command*	Executes the `vi` command *command*
-r *file*	Recovers *file* from a crash
-R	Edits in read-only mode

Table C.2 Moving the cursor.

Letter	What it does
h	Moves left one character
j	Moves down one line
k	Moves up one line
l	Moves right one character
w	Moves to the first character in the next word

Table C.2 (continued) Moving the cursor.

Letter	What it does
b	Moves to the first character in the previous word
(	Moves to the beginning of the sentence
)	Moves to the beginning of the next sentence
{	Moves to the beginning of the paragraph
}	Moves to the beginning of the next paragraph
+	Moves to the beginning of the next line
−	Moves to the beginning of the previous line
G	Moves to the last line in the buffer
nG	Moves to the beginning of line n
H	Moves to the first line in the buffer
L	Moves to the last line on the screen
fx	Moves right to character x
Fx	Moves left to character x
Ctrl-f	Scrolls forward one window
Ctrl-d	Scrolls forward one-half window
Ctrl-b	Scrolls back one window
Ctrl-u	Scrolls back one-half window

Table C.3 Commands for adding text.

Letter	What it does
i	Starts inserting text to the left of the cursor
a	Starts appending text to the right of the cursor
o	Opens a new line below the current one
O	Opens a new line above the current one
Esc	Ends insert mode
Ctrl+v	Takes the next character literally
Ctrl+w	Erases what you just typed
^Ctrl+d	Starts this line at left margin (autoindent on)
0 Ctrl+d	Cancels autoindent

Table C.4 Commands for deleting text.

Letter	What it does
x	Deletes the current character
dd	Deletes the current line
@	Deletes the current line (also)
dw	Deletes from wherever the cursor is to the next space
Backspace	Deletes the previous character
Ctrl-w	Deletes the current word

Table C.5 Commands for changing text.

Letter	What it does
r	Replaces the current character
s	Substitutes whatever you type for the current character (until you press Esc)
S	Replaces the current line
~	Switches the case of letters
cw	Replaces from the cursor to the next space with whatever you type
cc	Replaces all characters on the line
C	Replaces from the cursor to the end of the line
&	Repeats previous global replacement
@n	Executes command in buffer n
yy	Yanks the current line

emacs

emacs has a few oddities. First, the Meta key is really just your Esc key (usually). Second, you set the "mark" by pressing Ctrl+Space.

Table C.6 Command line options.

Option	What it does
+n file	Opens file and goes to line n
-q	Prevents loading of initialization file

Table C.7 Moving the cursor.

Key combo	What it does
Ctrl+f	Moves forward one character
Ctrl+b	Moves backward one character
Ctrl+n	Moves to the next line
Ctrl+p	Moves to the previous line
Ctrl+e	Moves to the end of the line
Ctrl+a	Moves to the beginning of the line
Meta+m	Moves to the first nonblank character
Meta+f	Moves forward one word
Meta+b	Moves backward one word
Meta+r	Moves to the beginning of the line
Meta+e	Moves forward to the end of the sentence
Meta+a	Moves backward to the first character of the sentence
Meta+]	Moves forward one paragraph
Meta+[	Moves backward one paragraph
Ctrl+x]	Moves forward one page
Ctrl+x [	Moves backward one page
Meta+<	Moves to the beginning of the buffer
Meta+>	Moves to the end of the buffer
Meta+x goto-line	emacs prompts you for the line number to go to

Table C.8 Erasing, Moving, and Copying Text.

Key combo	What it does
Ctrl+d	Deletes forward one character
Del	Deletes backward one character
Ctrl+w	Kills the selected text
Ctrl+k	Kills up to end of line
Meta+d	Kills next word
Meta+Del	Kills previous word
Meta+k	Kills next sentence
Ctrl+x Del	Kills previous sentence
Meta+z	Kills all characters up to the one emacs prompts you for
Meta+\	Deletes spaces and tabs around cursor
Meta+Space	Replaces multiple spaces/tabs with one space
Meta+^	Joins current line and preceding one
Ctrl+x Ctrl+o	Deletes blank lines
Ctrl+y	Copies recently killed text into buffer (yanks it back)
Meta+w	Copies text into kill ring

Table C.9 Various miscellaneous good stuff

Key combo	What it does
`Ctrl+x Ctrl+f`	Opens a file
`Ctrl+x b`	Switches to another buffer
`Ctrl+x Ctrl+b`	Gets a list of available buffers
`Ctrl+x o`	Goes to the next buffer
`Ctrl+x 0`	Closes current subwindow
`Ctrl+x 1`	Closes all windows but the one you're using
`Ctrl+x Ctrl+s`	Saves
`Ctrl+x Ctrl+c`	Exits

D Useful `perl` Scripts

Some things don't belong in the main book because they're a little too esoteric or a little too specific. Here are two `perl` scripts that fit that category.

COLUMNS AND ROWS

Abe Singer at UCSD posted this `perl` script on the Internet. It's very useful for culling specific columns and rows out of a file. It's also an excellent example of what `perl` can do. It's called `chunks`.

```
#!/usr/local/bin/perl
'di';
'ig00';
#
# $Header: chunks,v 1.9 93/03/12 15:58:30 asinger Exp $
#
# $Log: chunks,v $
# Revision 1.9  93/03/12  15:58:30  15:58:30  asinger (Abe Singer)
# Fixed footer ID
#
# Revision 1.8  93/03/12  15:52:06  15:52:06  asinger (Abe Singer)
# Jazzed up the manpage.
# Recursive format files are now caught.
# It all works!
#
# Revision 1.7  93/03/10  16:01:07  16:01:07  asinger (Abe Singer)
# Big overhaul.  Completely changed how arguments are read, both
# from command line and format file.
# Printing of chunks is a little more efficient.
# Cleaned up code a little bit.
```

```
# Added wrapman'ed manpage, change &Usage to use it.
# See manpage for more.
#

# $Source: /u/ssdb/staff/asinger/bin/RCS/chunks,v $
# $Revision: 1.9 $
# $Date: 93/03/12 15:58:30 $
# $State: Exp $
# $Author: asinger $
#-----------------------------------------------------------------
# Abe Singer (abe@ucsd.edu)
# Central University Library, Mail Code 0175-R
# Social Sciences Database Project
# University of California, San Diego
# San Diego, California 92122
# (619) 534-5758
#-----------------------------------------------------------------

# Globals...
$sleepTime = 0;
$defaultLrl = 80;
$defaultOffset = 1;
$defaultILength = $defaultLrl;
$defaultDelim = " ";
$defaultBLength = 0;
$newLine = "";
$progName = $0;
$verbose = 0;
$lrl = $defaultLrl;
$delim = "";
$test = 0;
@formatFiles = ();


#*****************************************************************
# Name            : Usage
# Purpose         : Prints out usage message and bails
# Arguments       : 1 - String containing useful error message.
# Return Value    : None
# Calls           : Exit
# Globals Accessed :
```

```perl
# Notes              :
#******************************************************************

sub Usage {
  local($pager);

  $, = ": ";
  $pager = ($ENV{'MANPAGER'} || $ENV{'PAGER'} || '/usr/bin/more');
  if (@_) {
    print STDERR $progName, @_;
    print "\n";
    print "Hit <return> for manpage, interrupt to abort...";
    $_ = <STDIN>;
  }
  exec("nroff -man $0 | $pager");
}


#******************************************************************
# Name               : ReadFormat
# Purpose            : Opens a file, reads in lines from file, and
#                      passes tokens on each line to ParseArg.  Skips
#                      anything after a '#' on each line.
# Arguments          : 1 - filename
# Return Value       : none.  Calls Usage() upon error.
# Calls              : ParseArg()
# Globals Accessed   : none.
# Notes              : Since ParseArg() calls ReadFormat(), and
#                      ReadFormat() calls ParseArg(), it is possible
#                      to nest format files.  I'm not sure why you
#                      would want to do this, but you can...
#******************************************************************
sub ReadFormat {
  local ($infile) = @_;
  local ($line, $word);
  local(@args) = ();
  local(@files) = ();
  local($_);

# Check for recursive format declaration
  die "$progName: format file $infile is declared recursively\n"
    if grep(/^$infile$/, @formatFiles);
```

```
  push(@formatFiles, $infile);
  open infile || &Usage("Can't open format file $filename: $!");
  @args = ();
  while (<infile>) {
    chop;
    while ($_) {
      if (s/^\s*'([^']*)'\s*//) {
# Check for literal string (single quotes, no backslashes)
        $x = $1;
      } elsif (s/^\s*"(((\\")|[^"])*)"\s*//) {
# Check for interpolated string, do eval to handle any escaped chars
        eval qq|\$x = "$1";|;
        &Usage('Bad String', $@) if ($@);
      } elsif (/^#/) {
# Bye-bye if comment
        last;
      } elsif (s/\s*(\S+)\s*//) {
# Got a normal word here
        $x = $1;
      } else {
# Empty string (Anything else woulda matched last regexp)
        last;
      }
      push(@args, $x);
    }
  }
  push(@files, &ParseArg(0, @args));
  close(infile);
  pop(@formatFiles);
  return(@files);
}



#************************************************************************
# Name              : ParseArg
# Purpose           : Parses options from the command line (or a
#                     file...).  Expects arguments to be as specified
#                     above.  Leading "-" is optional -- this allows
#                     reading in of arguments from a format file.
# Arguments         : 1 - argument word.
# Return Value      : non-zero if illegal flag.
```

```
# Calls             : ReadFormat (if a format-file is specified).
# Globals Accessed : All of the above globals.
# Notes              : Hmmmm.....
#*****************************************************************

sub ParseArg {
  local ($cmdline, @args) = @_;
  local ($o, $l);
  local ($b, $e);
  local ($x);
  local (@files) = ();

  PARSEARGS: while ($_ = shift @args) {

# Check for -- option, which means that all following arguments are
# filenames
    if (/^--$/) {
      push(@files, @args);
      last PARSEARGS;
    }

# If reading ARGV, check for leading hyphen, otherwise it's a filename

    if ($cmdline && !s/^-//) {
      push(@files, $_);
      next PARSEARGS;
    }

# Parse for -sleep option

    if (/^s(leep)?$/) {
      if (@args && $args[0] =~ /^\d+$/) {
        $sleepTime = shift @args;
      } else {
        $sleepTime = 1.0 unless ($sleepTime);
      }
      next PARSEARGS;
    }

# Parse for -lrl option
    if (/^l(rl)?$/) {
```

```perl
      if (@args) {
        $x = shift @args;
        &Usage("Bad $_ value (must be numeric): $x!")
          unless ($x =~ /^\d+$/);
        &Usage("Bad $_ value (Must be > 0): $x!")
          if ($x < 1)
      } else {
        &Usage("$_ must have a number after it!");
      }
      $lrl = $x;
      next PARSEARGS;
    }
# Parse for -delim option
    if (/^d(elim)?$/) {
      $delim = shift @args if @args;
      $delim = $defaultDelim unless $delim;
      next PARSEARGS;
    }
# Parse for -format option
    if (/^f(ormat)?$/) {
      &Usage("$_ must be followed by a filename!") unless
        (@args);
      push(@files, &ReadFormat(shift @args));
      next PARSEARGS;
    }

# Parse for -index option. NOTE: This can be given more than once...
# Since legal values are dependent on the LRL, legality will be
# checked after all arguments are read.

    if (/^c(ol(umn(s)?)?)?$/) {
      &Usage("$_ must be followed by a range!") unless
        (@args);
      $x = shift @args;
      ($o, $l) = &ParseRange($x, $defaultILength);
      &Usage("Illegal column value: $x") unless
        (defined $o);
      push(@offset, $o);
      push(@length, $l);
      $defaultOffset = $o;
      $defaultILength = $l;
```

```
        next PARSEARGS;
    }


# Parse for -block option. NOTE: This can be given more than once...
# pairs will first be stored in a single array so they will be sorted
# properly, and then will be split into two arrays.

    if (/^b(lock)?$/) {
        &Usage("$_ must be followed by a range!") unless
            (@args);
        $x = shift @args;
        ($b, $l) = &ParseRange($x, $defaultBLength);
        &Usage("Illegal block value: $x") unless
            (defined $b);
# And store the results...
        push(@tblock, "$b:$l") ;
        $defaultBLength = $l;
      next PARSEARGS;
    }


# Parse for -newline option.
    if (/^n(ewline)?$/) {
      $newline = "\n";
      next PARSEARGS;
    }


# Parse for -verbose option.
    if (/^v(erbose)?$/) {
      $verbose = 1;
      next PARSEARGS;
    }


# Parse for -test option.
    if (/^t(est)?$/) {
      $test = 1;
      next PARSEARGS;
    }


# Parse for -help option
    &Usage() if (/^h(elp)?$/);
```

```perl
# if we know it's a flag (has a preceding minus), generate an error
# cuz if we got to here, it's not a valid option

    if ($cmdline) {
# generate an error if it's not a valid command-line option
        &Usage("Bad Option: $_") if $cmdline;

    } else {

# assume that it's a filename, and push onto list of filenames.
        push(@files, $_);
    }
  }

  return(@files);
}


#******************************************************************
# Name               : ParseRange
# Purpose            : Takes a string containing ##, ##:## or ##-##,
#                      and a default length (for the first example),
#                      and returns a list of the start and end points.
# Arguments          : 2 - string to parse, default length
# Return Value       : 2 numbers, or undef if error.
# Calls              :
# Globals Accessed   :
# Notes              :
#******************************************************************

sub ParseRange {

  local($arg, $def) = @_;
  local($start, $len);

  $_ = $arg;

  if (/-/) {

# We gots a start-end range
```

```
# Make sure that it's a legal string
    return(undef) unless m/^(\d+)-(\d+)$/;

    $start = $1;
    $len = 1 + $2 - $1;

  } elsif (/:/) {

# We gots a start-length range

# Make sure that it's a legal string
    return(undef) unless m/^(\d+):(\d+)$/;

    $start = $1;
    $len = $2;

  } else {

# We gots only a starting position

# Make sure that it's a legal string
    return(undef) unless m/^(\d+)$/;

    $start = $1;
    $len = $def;
  }

  return($start, $len);


}

#*********************************************************************
# Name               : CheckValues
# Purpose            : Checks contents of @offset and @length to make
#                      sure they're legal.
# Arguments          : 1 - argument word.
# Return Value       : non-zero if illegal flag.
# Calls              : Usage() if there's an error.
# Globals Accessed   : @offset, @length, $lrl
# Notes              : Initializes the two arrays if nothing is
#                      in them.
#*********************************************************************
```

```
sub CheckValues {
  local ($i, $o, $l);

# Check to make sure the index arrays have matching lengths...
  &Usage("Internal error  (index) -- $#offset != $#length !")
    if ($#offset != $#length);

# No indexes specified, set up default to be entire record...

  if ($#offset < 0) {
    @offset = ($defaultOffset);
    @length = ($lrl);
  }
# Check to make sure the block arrays have matching lengths...
  &Usage("Internal error  (block) -- $#begin != $#end !")
    if ($#begin != $#end);

# Initialize block list if empty...

  if ($#begin < 0) {
    @begin = (0);
    @end = (0);
  }

# Check all the indexes for legality...

  foreach $i (0..$#offset) {
    $o = $offset[$i];
    $l = $length[$i];

# This one's too small...
    &Usage("Column start ($o) must be > 0 !") if ($o <= 0);

# This one's too big...
    &Usage("Column start ($o) must be <= LRL ($lrl) !") if ($o > $lrl);

# This one's too big too...
    &Usage("Column length ($l) must be <= LRL ($lrl) !") if ($l > $lrl);

# These two are too big together...
    &Usage("Column start ($o) + length ($l) must be <= LRL + 1 " .
      "($lrl + 1) !") if (($l+ $o) > $lrl + 1);
```

```perl
# This one must be juuuuuuust right!
  }
}


#*****************************************************************
# Name              : SortBlocks
# Purpose           : Sorts @tblock, checks for legal values, and
#                     splits @tblock entries into @begin and @end
#                     arrays.
# Arguments         : none
# Return Value      : none
# Calls             : Usage if there are illegal values...
# Globals Accessed  : @tblock, @begin, @end
# Notes             :
#*****************************************************************
sub SortBlocks {
  local ($_, $end);

  foreach (sort ByNumber @tblock ) {
    /(\d+):(\d+)/;

# This one's too small...
    &Usage("Block start ($_) must be >= 0!") if ($1 < 0);

# This one's also too small...
    &Usage("Block end ($_) must be >= 0!") if ($2 < 0);

# This one's not big enough...

# And this one's juuuuuuust right!
    @begin = (@begin, $1);
    $end = $2 ? $1 + $2 - 1 : 0;
    @end = (@end, $end);
  }
}


#*****************************************************************
# Name              : ByNumber
# Purpose           : For numeric sorting of block sizes.
# Arguments         : 2 - $a and $b
# Return Value      : -1 if $a < $b, 0 if $a = $b, 1 if $a   $b
```

```
# Calls            : none
# Globals Accessed :
# Notes            : Called by sort.
#*****************************************************************
sub ByNumber { $a <=> $b; }


#*****************************************************************
# Name             : Verbose
# Purpose          : Prints out all variables set by user.
# Arguments        : none.
# Return Value     : none.
# Calls            : none.
# Globals Accessed : All of them...
# Notes            :
#*****************************************************************
sub Verbose {
  local ($i);

  print "$progName: Settings are...\n\n";
  print "LRL = $lrl\n\n";
  print "Index list:\n";
  foreach $i (0..$#offset) {
    print "\t#$i) Offset = $offset[$i], Length = $length[$i]\n";
  }
  print "\n";
  print "Block list:\n";
  foreach $i (0..$#begin) {
    print "\t#$i) Begin = $begin[$i], End = $end[$i]\n";
  }
  print "\n";
  print "Newline is on.\n" if ($newline);
  print "Delimiter is \'$delim\'\n" if $delim;
  print "Sleep Time is $sleepTime.\n" if $sleepTime;
  $i = $,; $, = " ";
  print "Files are:", @files, "\n";
  $, = $i;
}


#*****************************************************************
# Name       : MakePrintChunks
# Purpose    : Creates a routine to print out the specified chunks
```

```perl
# Arguments          : 1 - input buffer;
# Return Value       : none.
# Calls              : none.
# Globals Accessed   : @offset, @length
# Notes              : We do this cuz it's a mite faster than a
#                      subroutine
#                    : which loops through the list of columns
#*****************************************************************
sub MakePrintChunks {
  local ($i, $x);
  local($sub);
  local(@list) = ();
  local(@o) = @offset;
  local(@l) = @length;
  local($o, $l);

  $sub = <<'EOF';
sub PrintChunks {

  local($_) = @_;
  local($,) = $delim;
  local($\) = $newline;
EOF
  while ($o = shift @o) {
    $o--;
    $l = shift(@l);
    push(@list, "substr(\$_, $o, $l)");
  }
  $sub .= "\tprint " . join(', ', @list) . ";\n";
  $sub .= "}\n";
  eval $sub;
  die "$progName: Eval error\n", $@ if $@;
}


#*****************************************************************
#
# Main() starts here...
#
#*****************************************************************
```

```
# Parse command line arguments.  Anything not beginning with a "-"
# (with the exception of "-" and "--") is taken to be a filename

@files = &ParseArg(1, @ARGV);

# If no files specified, make STDIN the input file.
@files = ("-") unless (@files);


&SortBlocks();  # Sort block list.
&CheckValues(); # Check variable values for legality.

&Verbose if ($verbose); # Print out stats if requested.

&MakePrintChunks;

exit(0) if ($test); # Go bye bye if in test-mode

$, = $delim;
$b = shift(@begin);
$e = shift(@end);
$blockCount = 0;

$linesRead = 0;
$linesPrinted = 0;

print "Block #$blockCount ($b:$e).\n"
  if ($verbose);

  READFILES: foreach $infile (@files) {
  $recnum = 0;
  open(INFILE, $infile) || die "$progName: Can't open input file
    $infile: $!\n";
  while ($bytes = read(INFILE, $buf, $lrl)) {

# Check for read errors...

    die "$progName: System read error $!, file $infile, " .
      "record $recnum\n" if ($!);
```

```
# Check to make sure enough bytes are read, and pad if not...

    $recnum++;
    $linesRead++;
    if ($bytes != $lrl) {
      $l = length($buf);
      warn "$progName: Incomplete record, file $infile, " .
        "record $recnum, length $l.\n" ;
      $buf .= " " x ($lrl - $l);
    }

# Check to see if record should be parsed and printed...

    if (($linesRead >= $b) && (($e == 0) || ($linesRead <= $e))) {
      &PrintChunks($buf);
      $linesPrinted++;

# Check for end of block
      if ($linesRead == $e) {
# Go to next block if there are more...
        if (@end) {
          $b = shift(@begin);
          $e = shift(@end);
          $blockCount++;
          print "Block #$blockCount ($b:$e).\n"
            if ($verbose);
# Otherwise, quit.
        } else {
          last READFILES;
        }
      }


    }
# Sleep, if requested...
    select(undef, undef, undef, $sleepTime) if ($sleepTime);


  }
} continue {
  close(INFILE);
}
```

```
print "$progName: $linesRead records in, $linesPrinted records
    out.\n"
    if ($verbose);

exit(0);


###############################################################

    # These next few lines are legal in both Perl and nroff.

.00;                          # finish .ig

'di            \" finish diversion--previous line must be blank
.nr nl 0-1     \" fake up transition to first page again
.nr % 0           \" start at page 1
'; __END__ ##### From here on it's a standard manual page #####
.TH CHUNKS 1 "March 12, 1993"
.ds )H U. of C.A. at San Diego
.ds ]W $Revision: 1.9 $


.AT 3
.SH NAME
\fBchunks\fR \- print out sections of Logical-Record-Length (LRL)
datafiles.
.SH SYNOPSIS
.ta 1.5i
.B chunks
.IR \t[-b[lock] <range>]
.RS 0.75i
.br
.IR [-c[olumns] <range>]
.br
.IR [-l[rl] <LRL>]
.br
.IR [-f[ormat] <format-file>]
.br
.IR [-d[elimiter] <delimiter>]
.br
.IR [-n[ewline]]
.br
.IR [-s[leep] [<sleep-time>]]
```

```
.br
.IR [-t[est]]
.br
.IR [file]...
.RE

.SH DESCRIPTION
.I Chunks
reads records from fixed-line-length
.I
(Logical-Record-Length)
```

files and prints specified chunks of the
file to stdout. You can specify for printing particular
records or ranges of records, or columns or ranges of
columns, or both. A newline can be added to the end of
each output record if you desire. A delimiting character
can be placed between each column-range you specify. A
time delay can be specified between each record printed.
All options can be placed in a format file instead of on
the command line.

```
.SS OPTIONS

.TP 1.25i
.I
-columns
```

specifies which columns of each record to print.
It can be in one of 3 formats: NN-NN, NN:NN, or
NN, where NN is an integer number. The first
example specifies a range of columns, where the
first number is the starting column, and the
second is the ending column (e.g. 5-10 would
print columns 5 through 10 inclusive). The
second example specifies a starting column and a
number of columns to print (e.g. 5:10 would
print columns 5 through 14 inclusive). The last
example takes the number as the starting
column, and supplies a default length, which is
either the last length specified, or the LRL if
no previous length has been given. If no column
specifications are supplied, a default of 1:LRL
is created.

```
.TP 1.25i
.I
-block
```
specifies which records to print. The format of
the argument is the same as for columns (above).
The block specs are sorted prior to printing,
preserving the original order in the file.
Overlapping blocks are reduced to one single
block. Default is entire file. And ending record
of 0
means "to the end of the file" (e.g. 50:0 will
print from record 50 to the end of the file).

```
.TP 1.25i
.I
-lrl
```
specifies the Logical Record Length of the
file(s). Default is 80. If \fI-lrl\fR is specified
more than once, the last one is used. Note
that chunks doesn't know anything about
newline characters as delimiters in an input
file; if your input file has a newline
character at the end of each record, simply
tell chunks that the logical record length
of the file is the length of the record plus
the number of byte used by the newline
character. Note also that the DOS convention
for a newline is 2 bytes (CR/LF) and the UNIX
convetion is 1 bytes (LF). Example: if you
have a card-image file (by definition: record
length of 80) that has newlines at the end
of each card and the file is on a CD-ROM
intended for use in a DOS environment, you
would tell chunks the lrl is 82 (\fI-l\fR 82). If
this same file with newlines had been created
in a UNIX environment, you would tell chunks
the lrl is 81 (\fI-l\fR 81). If this same file
had no newlines at then end of records, you
would tell chunks the lrl is 80 (\fI-l\fR 80).
Unfortunately, you cannot (yet!) specify
different lrl's for different files. You'll

just have to use separate iterations of
chunks.

.TP 1.25i
.I
-format
specifies a format file which contains all
of the same stuff that you might put on the
command line. The '-' is not necessary in
the format file. Line breaks in the format
file are okay. You can specify more than
one format file if you wish. You can even
nest format files it you want (although I'm
not sure why you would...).

Within a format file, parameters with spaces or
special characters can be enclosed in quotes.
If double-quotes (") are used, escaped
characters such as \\t, \\n, \\ddd (where 'd' is a
digit) will be interpolated (in the usual Unix
way) into tab, newline, and the octal-value ddd,
respectively. A double-quote can be escaped,
e.g., "\\"" will result in one double-quote. If
single quotes are used, no interpolation is
done, e.g. '"' will get you the same as \"\"",
but '\\n' will get you the same as "\\n"
(escaping a backslash will get you a single
backslash). A string (something in quotes)
cannot be split across a line, not even if you
try to escape the newline.

.B
NOTE:
Attempting to declare recursive format files (a format file nested
inside itself), either directly or indirectly, is not allowed (you
wouldn't want to do it anyway).

.TP 1.25i
.I
-delimiter

allows you to specify a delimiting character
between each chunk (range of columns in a
record) printed. The default delimiter is
no delimiter. Don't forget to put quotes
around the entire argument if you are trying
to delimit with a <space> on the command
line! \fI-delimiter\fR with no value given defaults
to a space. (Examples: \fI-d\fR " " will delimit
each chunk of columns with a space. \fI-d\fR will
do the same thing. \fI-d\fR "\\t" will delimit each
chunk with a tab.)

.TP 1.25i
.I
-newline
prints a newline at the end of each record printed.

.TP 1.25i
.I
-sleep
specifies an amount to sleep (in seconds) between reading
each record. non-integer values are okay, but the resolution is
dependent on the system implementation (the select(2) call is used
for the
timing). Default is 0 (no sleep).
If no value is given (just \fI-sleep\fR), default is 1.

.TP 1.25i
.I
-verbose
causes chunks to print (to stderr) all the
options that have been set after the entire
command line is parsed. This may be useful
for debugging particularly when used with
\fI-test\fR (see below).

.TP 1.25i
.I
-test
evaluates the command line, but does not
actually read the input files. This is for

debugging purposes (e.g., testing your format file).

.TP 1.25i
.I
-help
prints out the usage message and exits the
program.

.TP 1.25i
.I
Files
Anything not preceded with a minus ('-') or which
doesn't look like an argument to chunks is considered to
be a file name. If no files are specified, STDIN is used. A "-" by
itself will cause chunks to read from STDIN (like cat(1)). A "--"
on the command line will cause all arguments following to be
interpreted as file names.

.SH ENVIRONMENT
MANPAGER or PAGER are used for the pager used with the -help option
/usr/bin/more is used by default.

.SH FILES
\fI/usr/bin/more\fR (default pager), \fInroff\fR (formatter for
manpage)

.SH AUTHOR
Abe Singer (abe@ucsd.edu)

.SH DIAGNOSTICS
Hopefully the diagnostics are self-explanatory (I've tried... I
really have!).

.SH BUGS
I'm sure there are a few...

SUMMARIZE FILE CONTENTS

This perl script is from Jim Jacobs, also of UCSD. Its job in life is to summarize a file by printing the first seventy characters of its first twenty-five lines. It's called cio (for check it out).

```perl
#!/usr/local/bin/perl
'di';
'ig00';
#
# $Header$
#
# $Log$
$using_wrapman = 1;

# "cio" (Check It Out)
# Date: 94/01/16
# Author: jajacobs
#-------------------------------------------------------------------
# Jim Jacobs
# Central University Library, Mail Code 0175-R
# Social Sciences Database Project
# University of California, San Diego
# San Diego, California 92122
# (619) 534-1262
#-------------------------------------------------------------------
# this is the version that uses "read" and an lrecl for files
# that do *not* have newlines!

require "getopts.pl";

&Getopts('n:l:hqm') ;


##################################################################
# print help and program description if -h flag used:
# see end of this script for text.
##################################################################

if ($opt_h) {
  &help;
}
```

```perl
if ($opt_m) {
  &Usage();
}

$width = 75;
$rec = 0; $maxrec = 0; $minrec = 9999;

#################################################################
# set up STUFF as output format for write.
# print top ruler.
#################################################################

$~ = "STUFF";

print "                 10        20        30        40        50
60 \n";
print "------ +----*----+----*----+----*----+----*----+----*----+--
--*----+----*----+\n";

#################################################################
# begin reading stdin
#################################################################
if ($opt_l) {
  while (read(STDIN, $tmp, $opt_l)) {
    $rec++;
    &main_loop;
  }
} else {
  while ($tmp = <STDIN>) {
    chop $tmp;
    $rec++;
    &main_loop;
  }
}

sub main_loop {

#################################################################
# check for 'n' value and if on first 25 records.
# (if the record number is not a multiple of opt_n, don't write
# the line.)
```

```
# (if the record number is in first 25 or if it is a multiple of
# opt_n, write the line.)
# create a short record $line for writing.
# check for length of original line and choose appropriate end of
# line character.
###################################################################

    if ($opt_n) {
      unless ( $rec % $opt_n) {
        $line = substr($tmp, 0, ($width - 5));
        if (length $tmp > ($width - 5)) {
          $cont = '>';
        } else {
          $cont = '|';
        }
          write;


      } elsif  ($rec <= 25) {
        $line = substr($tmp, 0, ($width - 5));
        if (length($tmp) > ($width - 5)) {
          $cont = '>';
        } else {
          $cont = '|';
        }
          write;
      }
    } else {
      if  ($rec <= 25) {
        $line = substr($tmp, 0, ($width - 5));
        if (length($tmp) > ($width - 5)) {
          $cont = '>';
        } else {
          $cont = '|';
        }
          write;
      }
    }
```

```
###################################################################
# get lenght of current record
###################################################################

    $len = length($tmp);

###################################################################
# check for minimum and maximum record lengths
###################################################################

    $minrec = $len < $minrec ? $len : $minrec;
    $maxrec = $len > $maxrec ? $len : $maxrec;

###################################################################
#   count ($length) the number of records of this length ($len)
#   note: associative array.
###################################################################
    $length{$len}++;

###################################################################
# if this is the first record of this length, keep track of the
# record number of this record as $onerec[$len]
# Increment $a to keep track of how many unique record lengths
# there are in this file.
###################################################################
    if ($length{$len} == 1) {
  $onerec[$len] = $rec ;
  $a++;
  }

###################################################################
# keep a count of the records
###################################################################
$reccnt = $rec;

###################################################################
# if 'q' (quick) option is used, end after 25 records + 1 'n'
###################################################################

  if ($opt_q) {
    if ($reccnt == (25 + $opt_n) ) {
```

```
        $reccnt = (25 + $opt_n);
        last;
    }
  }

  } # end of main_loop

################################################################
#   print ending ruler.
#   print max and min recs and total recs.
################################################################

$~ = 'STDOUT';

print "------- +----*----+----*----+----*----+----*----+----*----+--
   --*----+----*----+\n";
print "                 10        20        30        40        50
   60 \n";

print "\nMax rec len: ", $maxrec, "\n";
print "Min rec len: ", $minrec, "\n";
if ($opt_q) {
  print "Total number of records checked: ", $reccnt, "\n";
} else {
  print "Total number of records: ", $reccnt, "\n" ;
}
print "\n";

################################################################
# make a new array $l to store both the length of records and
# the number of records of each length.
################################################################

$i = 0;
foreach $x (keys %length) {
  $l[$i++] = "$x:$length{$x}";
  print $l "\n";
}
################################################################
# subroutine for sorting.
################################################################
```

```perl
sub sortlengths {
  local ($x1, $y1) = split(/:/, $a);
  local ($x2, $y2) = split(/:/, $b);
  $y1 <=> $y2;
}


###################################################################
# sort the records/length array @l  to array @sorted
# use reverse sort so that final array will print with most
# frequent record size first, least frequent record size last.
###################################################################

@sorted = reverse sort sortlengths @l ;

###################################################################
# split the @sorted array to get its separate values for the
# record size and numbers of records of that size.
#
# write the records-sizes and count of record-sizes.
# use stdout format to print  counts of recs of each size
# use ONE format to write if $s_count == 1.
###################################################################

$i = 0;

while ( $i < $a) {

  ($s_length, $s_count) = split(/:/,$sorted[$i]);
  if ($s_count == 1) {
    $~ = ONE ;
    write ;
    $i++;
  } else {
    $~ = STDOUT;
    write STDOUT;
    $i++;
  }
}

print "\n";
```

```
###############################################################
# formats for writes:
###############################################################

format STDOUT =
There are @>>>>>>>>>> records of length @>>>>>>>>>
$s_count, $s_length
.

format ONE =
There is  @>>>>>>>>>> record  of length @>>>>>>>>> rec. number:
  @<<<<<<<<<
$s_count, $s_length, $onerec[$s_length]
.

format STUFF =
@>>>>>
|@<<<<<<<<<<<<<<<<<<<<<<<<<<<<<<<<<<<<<<<<<<<<<<<<<<<<<<<<<<<<<<<<@
$rec, $line, $cont
.


sub help {
  print <<EOF;
This /usr/bin/perl script ($basename$0) checks data files.  Reads
from stdin,
writes to stdout.  Prints part of file for examination. Assumes
datafile has
newlines, unless -l flag used.
Reports:  - minimum and maximum record lengths,
          - number of records of each record length,
          - for records of unique record length reports the record
            number.

By default, prints first 70 columns of first 25 records.  (Inserts
a "|" at the end of lines 70 or shorter and a ">" at the end of
lines or record length 71 and longer.
Flags:  -h   prints this help screen.
  -m   print man page.
  -n#  prints 1st 25 lines and every nth record.
  -q   quick mode: prints only 25 lines, (opt.: first nth record)
       and rpt.
```

```
      -l#   give lrecl for files with no newlines.
    Examples:
      $basename$0 < datafile
      $basename$0 < datafile -q
      $basename$0 < datafile -q -n 500
      $basename$0 < datafile -l80 -n 500
      $basename$0 < datafile > reportfile
      zcat compressed_datafile.Z | $basename$0
      zcat compressed_datafile.Z | $basename$0 -n 1000 | more
      cat datafile | $basename$0
EOF
exit(1);


} #end of help.



#***************************************************************
# Name             : Usage
# Purpose          : Prints out usage message and bails
# Arguments        : 1 - String containing useful error message.
# Return Value     : None
# Calls            : Exit
# Globals Accessed :
# Notes            :
#***************************************************************

sub Usage {
  local($pager);

  $, = ": ";
  $pager = ($ENV{'MANPAGER'} || $ENV{'PAGER'} || '/usr/bin/more');
  if (@_) {
    print STDERR $progName, @_;
    print "\n";
    print "Hit <return> for manpage, interrupt to abort...";
    $_ = <STDIN>;
  }
  exec("nroff -man $0 | $pager");
}
###############################################################
```

```
       # These next few lines are legal in both Perl and nroff.

.00;                            # finish .ig

'di             \" finish diversion--previous line must be blank
.nr nl 0-1      \" fake up transition to first page again
.nr % 0         \" start at page 1
'; __END__ ##### From here on it's a standard manual page #####
.TH cio 1 "January 17, 1994"
.AT 3
.SH NAME
cio \- "Check It Out" -- examines datafiles and reports on contents.
.SH SYNOPSIS
.B cio [-hqln]
.SH DESCRIPTION
.I cio
```

This /usr/bin/perl script checks a datafile and creates a report on
the contents of the datafile (see below).

Cio assumes datafile has newlines, unless -l flag is used (see below).
The terms "record" and "line" are used synonymously in this
description of cio.

Cio reads from stdin.

Cio creates a report on the datafile it examines and writes this
report to stdout. The report includes: the minimum and maximum
record lengths in a datafile, the number of records of each length,
and, for records that have a unique length, it reports the record
number. The report also prints part of file for examination.

By default the report prints the first 70 columns of the first 25
records. The report prints the "|" at the end of each record of
70 or fewer characters and a ">" at the end of lines of record
length 71 and longer. Additional lines may be printed by using
the .B -n flag (see below).

```
.SH OPTIONS
  -h  Prints short help message.
```

-m Prints this man page.

-n The report includes the first 70 characters of the
    first 25 records automatically. Additional records may be
    included by using the -n option followed by a number.
    Cio will then print every nth record in the file as
    specified by the number following the -n flag. A
    number must be specified.

-q Large files may take a few minutes to process. The -q
    flag is the "quick" option. It produces a report with
    the first 25 records of the file, plus the first -n
    record (if specified) and reports record lengths based
    on its examination of the first n + 25 records only.

-l By default, cio assumes that a file being examine has
    a newline character delimiting each record. For those
    files that do not have newline characters but that do
    have fixed length records, the -l flag followed by a
    number may be used to specify the "logical record length."
    The number following the -l is the record length used
    by cio to examine the file. A number must be
    specified.

.SH EXAMPLES

    cio -h

Prints brief help message.

    cio -m

Prints this man page.

    cio < datafile

This reads "datafile" and sends report to stdout. The report
includes the first 70 characters of the first 25 records.

    cio < datafile > reportfile

As above, but writes report to "reportfile".

```
cat datafile | cio
```

Since cio reads from stdin, it can take the output of any pipe.

```
zcat compressed_datafile.Z | cio
```

As above, but reads data in "compressed_datafile.Z".

```
zcat compressed_datafile.Z | cio | more
```

Naturally, reports can be piped through a pager such as "more".

```
cio < datafile -n 500
```

This reads "datafile" and sends report to stdout. The report includes the first 70 characters of the first 25 records and every 500th record (e.g., records 500, 1000, 1500, etc.) in the file.

```
cio < datafile -q
```

This reads "datafile" in the "quick" mode. The report is based on an examination of only the first 25 records of "datafile." The first 70 characters of records 1-25 are printed in the report.

```
cio < datafile -q -n 500
```

This reads "datafile" in the "quick" mode. The report is based on an examination of only the first 525 records of "datafile." The first 70 characters of records 1-25 and record 500 are printed in the report.

```
cio < datafile -l 80 -n 500
```

"datafile" is assumed to be a datafile with no newline characters and a fixed record length ("logical record length") of 80 characters. The report includes the first 70 characters of the first 25 records and every 500th record in the file.

```
.SH ENVIRONMENT
No environment variables are used.
.SH FILES
None.
.SH AUTHOR
Jim Jacobs
.SH "SEE ALSO"

.SH DIAGNOSTICS

.SH BUGS
```

E Security

Breaking into computers has become quite chic these days. There have been movies about it (remember *Sneakers*?) and even the President's into it (the [ugh] Clipper Chip). UNIX security is at once very good and really terrible. It's good because, when you really know what you're doing, you can do a pretty fair job of locking people out. It's really terrible because there aren't that many people who know what they're doing. Here are my pointers.

FIRST LINE OF DEFENSE: PASSWORDS

Have you changed your password since your system administrator gave you your account? Does your account even *have* a password? (If you're feeling smug now—is your password anything obvious, like your name, your spouse's name, or anything like that? Is it a recognizable word at all?)

The best passwords are those that have both numbers and letters and are rather long—like eight characters (most UNIXes don't understand more than eight characters of uniqueness). This isn't so hard to do. `Born2BFree` is an okay password—it mixes uppercase and lowercase letters and has a number, and it's not a word. What could be better? Well, `783392278` is probably better, because it's a lot harder for somebody to figure out, and a *whole* lot less memorable.

See what I'm getting at here? Crackers (security breakers) know all the secrets of getting into systems—and most of what they know is that people are lazy. If you don't change your password once a month (at least), you're leaving a hole for a cracker.

Even the best password is useless if you let somebody know what it is, so don't! Never, ever tell anyone your password. Don't write it down anywhere—I don't care how bad your memory is. Memorize it along with your home phone number and the number of your local pizzeria. (Embarrassingly enough, I keep forgetting my home phone, but I remember my password.)

Here's a wizard's tip, from one "Vince Chen": Take a favorite phrase from a movie, a joke, or whatever, then take the first letter of each word and make them into a password. Sprinkle with random spaces and capital letters. Not undecipherable, but pretty hard to crack.

Your password is the first line of defense between your computer and the outside world. Make sure it's a strong one.

SECOND LINE OF DEFENSE: PERMISSIONS

If nobody can get into your computer except those that are supposed to, you've eliminated the need for all other forms of protection, right? I wouldn't be asking if the answer were, "Right." In fact, you can't rely on the other people on your system to be as assiduous as you are in keeping your passwords locked up. You can't even be sure that they aren't going to try something on their own. So it's important to set your permission bits so that people can't do what you don't want them to do.

UNIX bases its file access on the concept of users, groups, and everybody else. When you're given an account on a UNIX computer, you get a unique user ID and you're assigned to a group (or a few groups). For example, my user ID is `john`, and I'm in the group `users`. When you create a file, UNIX notes that you own it, and assigns permissions about who can access it.

When you type `ls -l`, you'll see, in the far left column, some kind of output—composed largely of hyphens, `r`'s, `x`'s, and `w`'s, that looks a bit like this:

`-rw-r--r--`

What you're looking at is the permissions on your file. They break down like this:

Type	User	Group	Other
-	rw-	r--	r--

The file type will most commonly be a dash (for a normal file), the letter `d` (for a directory), or `l` (for a link). But that's not too important to file permissions. Instead, the next three groups of three are. They tell you who has read (`r`), write (`w`), and execute (`x`) access to this file. Here, you, the user, have read and write access, but not execute access (notice that the space where the `x` would go has a dash in it). Other members of your group have read access, as does everyone else on your system.

You can set file permissions with the `chmod` command. In general, `chmod` works like this:

```
% chmod permissions file
```

The `file` part of that equation is pretty easy, but the `permissions` part is trickier. Permissions come in two flavors: numbers and letters. Both of them boil down to setting those r's, w's, and x's that we were just talking about, but neither is quite as easy as it could be. In order to set a file's permissions, you need to know two things: what permissions you want and who you want to give them to. Say you want to give yourself every kind of permission (`rwx`), but give everybody else none (`---`). There are two ways.

The first, with numbers, works like this. `chmod` thinks of each of those letters as a number: an `r` is worth 4, a `w` is worth 2, and an `x` is worth 1. You add together the numbers for the permissions you want. Since I want the owner of the file to have all permissions, I want 4+2+1, or 7, for the first of the three groups. Since I want no one else to have access to the file, I want 0 for the other two groups. To assign these permissions, I'd use a command like this one:

```
% chmod 700 file
```

This tells `chmod` to change the permissions on this file so that the owner has 7 (r+w+x), the group has 0, and the others have 0. Each number's position in that series of three numbers represents who you're setting permissions for: The first position is the owner of the file, the second is the group that the owner was in when s/he created the file, and the last is everybody else. See? Easy, once you get past the math.

I could just as easily give my group read permission, like this:

```
% chmod 740 file
```

You can also use letters to set permissions: `r` for read, `w` for write, and `x` for execute. You also use letters to represent who you're setting permissions for: u for the owner, g for the group, and o for everyone else. You then use +, –, and = to assign permissions. Let's take our first example again, where I wanted to assign myself all permissions, but none to anyone else. That would look like this:

```
% chmod u=rwx,g=,o= file
```

As you can see, it takes a little longer to set permissions using letters.

It's a good idea to keep most of your files to yourself by setting their permissions either to 600 or 700 (depending on whether you need to execute them). Rather than having to do this every time you create a file, you can set a default permission level with the `umask` command. Open your `.login` or `.profile` file, and add a command like this:

```
umask 077
```

`umask` works by taking permissions away from a default set that UNIX keeps. By default, UNIX has very lenient file permissions and grants everybody read and write access to your files. You use `umask` to *remove* permissions (numerically only) from the full set of permissions (777). So the `umask 077` command takes nothing away from the owner's permissions, but everything away from everybody else. Do it now.

The next thing to play with (security-wise) is what's called the `setgid` bit. First a little history. When you create a file, the group you're in may not own it. It depends on what kind of UNIX you're running. If you're running BSD UNIX, the file will be owned by whatever your primary group is (remember, you can be a member of multiple groups, but only one at a time). With a System V (pre–Release 4) UNIX, the file will be owned by the group that owns the directory it resides in.

With SVR4, you get the best of both worlds. Or, actually, you can choose. By typing

```
% chmod g+s mydir
```

you set the `setgid` bit, which means that System V rules will apply. If you type

```
% chmod g-s otherdir
```

you'll have BSD rules. Why do you care? You probably don't, but it's important to know what group is going to own the files you're creating, and being able to set the `setgid` bit as you wish is vital to that.

THIRD LINE OF DEFENSE: HIDING FILES

After you've set up a good password and corrected UNIX's rather lax permissions, you may need yet more protection. The next thing to try is hiding your files, using the forest-and-trees method. See, every tree looks like every tree in a forest, right? So make your files all look alike, then create a whole lot of them. Don't keep files with names like `Personal` or `Budget`, or `who-to-fire` lying around. The first thing a cracker will do after he's on your system is to look for files with really obvious names. Keep names somewhat cryptic, and then keep a lot of them.

LAST (AND LEAST) LINE OF DEFENSE: ENCRYPTION

If something absolutely, positively must be protected, you can encrypt it using the UNIX `crypt` command. `crypt` works by taking a filename and a password and encrypting the file using the password, like this:

```
% crypt filename
```

`crypt` has two drawbacks: First, if you forget your password, you'll never see what's in that file again; and second, `crypt` isn't the most secure encryption around. There's even a widely available program called the Crypt Breakers Workbench (`cbw`) that can break a `crypt`-encrypted file in a matter of minutes.

You can make `crypt` more secure by doing things such as compressing a file before you encrypt it or putting it into a `tar` archive with other files, compressing the archive, and then encrypting it; but eventually `cbw` will break it. Better not to bother: If it's really vital, store it on a floppy and carry the floppy with you at all times.

Index

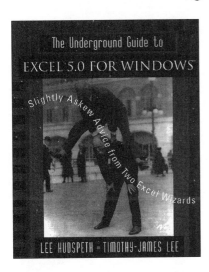
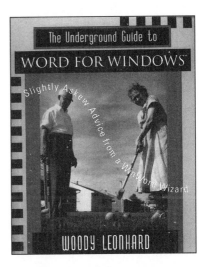